Working with Loss and Grief

Working with Loss and Grief

A New Model for Practitioners

Linda Machin

Los Angeles • London • New Delhi • Singapore • Washington DC

First published 2009

SAGE Publications Ltd
1 Oliver's Yard
55 City Road
London EC1Y 1SP

SAGE Publications Inc.
2455 Teller Road
Thousand Oaks, California 91320

SAGE Publications India Pvt Ltd
B 1/I 1 Mohan Cooperative Industrial Area
Mathura Road
New Delhi 110 044

SAGE Publications Asia-Pacific Pte Ltd
33 Pekin Street #02-01
Far East Square
Singapore 048763

Library of Congress Control Number: 2008924334

British Library Cataloguing in Publication data

A catalogue record for this book is available from
the British Library

1005621716

ISBN 978-1-4129-4667-4
ISBN 978-1-4129-4668-1 (pbk)

Typeset by C&M Digitals Pvt Ltd., Chennai, India
Printed in India at Replika Press Pvt. Ltd
Printed on paper from sustainable resources

DEDICATION

To all those grieving people who have been my teachers

Contents

List of Figures and Tables

Figures

Tables

Foreword

There is renewed interest in end-of-life care and bereavement at all levels in health care planning. This timely book responds to the need for well-informed decision making and effective practice. It describes a new model of grief, the Range of Response to Loss, which identifies themes emerging from both practice and research-based accounts of bereavement and seeks to understand the competing experiences of distress and a desire for control. The book describes the research and development process with engaging clarity, showing how resulting patterns are used to develop a new tool, the 'Adult Attitude to Grief' scale (AAG). The AAG is firmly placed within a coherent and comprehensive overview of past and current theories of the experience of grief and the historical background and social context to their development. Machin uses a wide variety of case studies to demonstrate how the validated scale is used in practice. Her work is underpinned by the belief that bereaved people can grow and develop through adversity, whilst helping to identify those who will need support if they are to do so. The book encourages a practice shift from the traditional focus on risk to a balanced appraisal of strengths as well as vulnerabilities. It offers a fascinating insight into research in practice and shows how listening closely to the narratives of the bereaved can lead to new ways of looking at loss. I commend it to everyone involved in the endeavour to understand and respond to the needs of those experiencing loss.

Barbara Monroe, CEO at St Christopher's Hospice

Acknowledgements

Over many years I have been privileged to work in research and in practice with a large number of bereaved people. They have contributed to my understanding of grief and been inspirational in encouraging my continued commitment to finding ways of optimising good care to all those who are burdened by loss. To all of these unnamed people and especially those whose stories have been told within this book, I give my thanks.

I am indebted to colleagues and co-researchers who have travelled the journey of exploration and writing with me, cooperating in practice studies, providing case material, engaging in thought-developing discussions, and offering critical comment on my work. They include Bernadette Bartlam, Bob Spall, Anne Burrows, Alan Gatland, Marilyn Relf, Nikki Archer, Anne Marie Lydon and others who along the way have given feedback on the practice use of the Adult Attitude to Grief scale. This volume also owes much to the conversations with many practitioners who have encouraged me in the development of my ideas.

Finally, I want to express my heartfelt gratitude to those closest to me who have endured the research and writing process with patience and persisting encouragement; to Gill for her sustaining friendship and support, to John, Peter and Richard for believing in me and the possibilities for my work, my thanks.

1

Introduction

There is something new to be chronicled every day. Grief is like a long valley, a winding valley where any bend may reveal a totally new landscape. As I've already noted, not every bend does. Sometimes the surprise is the opposite one; you are presented with exactly the same sort of country you thought you had left behind miles ago. That is when you wonder whether the valley isn't a circular trench. But it isn't. There are partial recurrences, but the sequence doesn't repeat. (Lewis, 1961: 47) (A Grief Observed by C.S. Lewis copyright © C.S. Lewis Pte. Ltd. 1961)

Lewis (1961) described in this word picture the often frighteningly unpredictable journey of grief. The metaphors he used provide a depth to his account of loss which go beyond the simple use of adjectives to describe his grief. His words – valley, landscape, trench – convey a sense of the vulnerability of the lone traveller making his way through exposed, unknown territory. His account of the valley as a circular trench conjures up images of the physical conditions endured by soldiers in the First World War and the emotional disorientation of the experience. The terrain was unfamiliar, winding and with bends and the traveller was having to interpret what the aspects of the unfolding journey meant – revisiting the same place, feeling lost but recognising progress etc. Metaphor is often used by grieving people (Spall, Read and Chantry, 2001) as a way of 'understanding and experiencing one kind of thing in terms of another' (Lakoff and Johnson, 1980: 5). It generates a richness of conceptual language which captures multiple layers of meaning. This book will use the metaphor of journey to describe and explore the experience of grief. It elaborates on the metaphor by conceptualising theory as a 'compass' and a new practice model as a 'map'. These are the tools needed by practitioners as they become fellow travellers on the grief journey with their clients/patients.

Individual accounts of grief are heard in everyday life, in counselling/therapy and are also found in much autobiographical literature, both that which focuses upon loss and that which weaves within a larger life story an experience of loss or bereavement. Personal stories provide a rich source of knowledge about grief, which is distinct from the research-based theoretical literature on loss and bereavement. The two contribute to different ways of understanding the nature of grief as an integral part of life experience. One provides an account of the highly individual nature of grief and the other explores and conceptualises the universality of grief (Rosenblatt, 1993). Stroebe, Stroebe and Hansson (1993) believe that it is necessary to develop a coherent theory to bring together these different ways of understanding and defining grief, in order for the universal and the individual to find a complementary place.

This book provides a new model and practice tool, which together propose a way of integrating broad perspectives on loss and individual variations within it. The notion of travelling with loss and mapping grief are introduced in this chapter through the following themes:

- The social context of loss and grief.
- The broad spectrum of life losses – the landscape of loss.
- The theoretical background to grief and therapy – establishing theoretical bearings.
- A new practice model for understanding grief and a tool for its implementation – a compass and a map.
- Therapeutic ways of working with the Range of Response to Loss model and the Adult Attitude to Grief scale – the territory of loss and the journey through grief.
- Practitioner perspectives – travelling with grief.

The social context of loss and grief

It is important to give brief consideration to the social context in which loss and grief occur within contemporary Western society. The experience of loss is influenced by the ways in which society perceives life and death issues and how it regulates grief. The expression of grief has changed considerably over the last century. The First World War transformed the overt mourning of the Victorian era to one in which expressions of grief were suppressed. The pain of loss was subsumed within the greater national imperative to express pride in the heroism of its young men and the need to sustain national morale and patriotism. Individual grief was often suspended because of the absence of a body. The stiff upper lip was a national response to the slaughter of a generation of men. Private grief was replaced by controlled public remembrance (Walter, 1999).

The need to 'leave the dead behind' was largely confirmed by the rising movements in psychology, particularly the psychodynamic school (Freud, 1957) which saw extended mourning as pathological (Walter, 1999). However, it has been in the evolving sphere of psychotherapy that attention to the 'continuing bond' with the dead (Klass, Silverman and Nickman, 1996) has been reasserted as desirable for the healthy adjustment to bereavement. With the proliferation of counselling and psychotherapy, loss is seen as a personal experience needing personal remedy, and emotion is seen as a component of grief as acceptably present in men as women. The redefining of grief is described by Walter (1999), as the 'clinical lore of bereavement experts'. This clinical lore has influenced a shift in perceptions about grief, and is powerfully exemplified in the change from soldiers at the beginning of the century being shot for cowardice, to intense medical treatment and social compassion being afforded to modern-day soldiers trau-matised by war. An understanding of the impact of traumatic loss has become widely integrated into the theory and practice of health and social care practitioners.

The change in how death and loss is seen has been accompanied by the rise in secu-larism and cultural diversity which has contributed to wide variations in expressions of public and private grief. Ritual may vary from traditional public rites to personally con-structed ceremony to mark death or other life-changing loss. In the spirit of the post-modern era what is individually meaningful has become more important than what can collectively be demonstrated. However, finding individual meaning may generate a per-sonal sense of ambiguity or ambivalence, as old certainties are swept into a tide of social change (Machin, 1998).

The interface between scientific/medical advances and life and death perspectives impact upon political judgements and private attitudes. Fast-changing ethical concerns shape the context in which contemporary life and death takes place:

- The possibilities for creating life – IVF, selecting embryos for their value, for example, one life to save another, cloning, etc.
- The possibilities for extending life – experimental life-saving surgery and medicine, trans-plant surgery (including stem cell transplants), hi-tech life-support machines, etc.
- The possibilities for ending life – abortion, switching off life-support machines, euthanasia, etc.

Dilemmas are produced when the state of knowledge outstrips the capacity to manage the social and legislative consequences of new life and death possibilities. For many people medical longevity is not met with adequate care provision and continued social inclusion but results in 'social death' (Mulkay, 1993).

Perceptions and understanding about life and death issues reflect the social climate in which they take place. Often the influence of contemporary psychological, social and ethical perspectives may be unconsciously or unreflectively absorbed into our thinking. If we are to understand the nature of loss experience(s) for those who seek support we need to recognise the centrality of these contextual factors.

The landscape of loss

Chapter 2 sets out the diverse situations in which loss might be experienced. Equating grief with death and bereavement often obscures the reality that multiple losses are experienced across the life cycle. Those most readily overlooked are the losses which come with developmental change – starting school, leaving school, moving house, retirement, etc., which may be so absorbed into the fabric of day-to-day life that the impact may hardly be noticed (Sugarman, 2001). However, some of these 'little' losses are rehearsals for more profound encounters with loss and provide a strengthening of the emotional and cognitive capacities for dealing with grief. The coping demands will be more forcefully tested when relationships or health are damaged or disintegrate, and where deeply held aspirations are thwarted, or unexpected or traumatic death occurs. Where the internal resources and external sources of support are inadequate for the meeting of loss, vulnerability will result (Folkman, 2001; Lazarus and Folkman, 1984). Recognising loss and the vulnerability it may produce is central to the agendas encountered in health and social care.

Within the broad range of loss experiences, the sensitive and expert involvement of practitioners is required at various stages in the grief journey (see Figure 1.1):

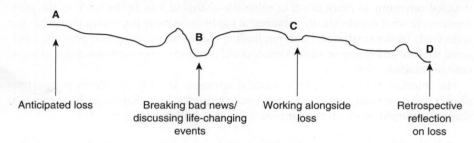

Figure 1.1   Practitioner involvement at various points in the loss journey

A – Practitioner engagement in anticipation of a loss, for example, supporting people making choices about placing a child for adoption, preparing for an abortion, pre-bereavement support, etc.

B – Breaking bad news or discussing emerging life-changing events/circumstances, such as imparting a medical diagnosis where there will be a poor outcome, emergency services informing people of serious accidents and deaths, etc.

C – Giving support during the process of loss, for example, support for people with a chronic disability who are physically/mentally deteriorating, providing palliative care for the dying, etc.

D – Retrospective support, for example, as the result of abuse, following the break up of a relationship, following a bereavement, etc.

A knowledge and skill base are essential for the challenges faced by practitioners in this demanding work.

The theoretical background to grief and therapy – establishing theoretical bearings

Theory provides a conceptual background for understanding loss as part of psychosocial development, for recognising the characteristics of grief, and for defining practice approaches for engagement with loss. The acquisition of psychosocial competence for dealing with life's losses is undertaken from birth. Erikson's account of life span development (1980), described in Chapter 2, explores the interface between the individual and his/her social world. He saw maturation as a sequential process in which there are biological and social challenges to be met, in order to move from the dependence of infancy to a fully functioning, autonomous adult. Erikson's theory has remained influential along with others such as Havinghurst (1972), Levinson et al. (1978), Reese and Smyer (1983), who have used a life-course perspective to understand human developmental social psychology.

Chapter 3 looks at how early experience of positive nurturing provides the psychological and social basis for the development of well-being and competence in coping with life changes and losses. Foremost among the theories which have made the link between psychosocial development and loss response, is Bowlby's Attachment Theory (1980). This theory has been foundational in the study of relationships, in defining the quality of human attachment, and in accounting for the consequent reactions to separation and loss. The work begun by Bowlby was taken up by his colleagues, who refined his concepts with further empirical evidence about the nature of styles of attachment (Ainsworth et al., 1978).

Contemporary theorists have moved the focus to adult attachment (Hazan and Shaver, 1987) and are particularly interested in how far early attachment styles are enduring traits, and how far they are properties of individuals or of relationships. Bartholomew (1990) and Bartholomew and Horowitz (1991) have developed a framework for categorising four adult attachment styles. These attachment styles are based on the Bowlbian concept of the 'internal working model', a model carried internally as a representation of what has been learned about the interaction between self and others. The four elements consist of secure, preoccupied, dismissing and fearful attachment, and are characterised by the varied combination of positive and negative self-view and other-view. The quality of adult attachments has significance for understanding the nature of lost and severed adult relationships.

Theories of psychosocial development and attachment form the background against which concepts of grief have developed. The characteristics of grief, particularly as they relate to bereavement, have emerged from Bowlby's work, along with other field-leading colleagues like Parkes (1996), who have contributed hugely to the literature on loss. Students of grief and bereavement are familiar with the defining symptoms associated with grief – denial, despair, guilt, anger, hopelessness, etc., which have been embedded within a structure for understanding the processes of grief. The stage and phase models of grief (Bowlby, 1980; Kubler-Ross, 1970; Parkes, 1996) have been very influential in shaping practice. Whilst the intention of these theorists was never to make grief formulaic or prescriptive (Parkes, 2001), the reality is that many practitioners have applied their work with disregard for the individuality of grief and its fluctuating timetable. The importance of this extensively researched elucidation of the nature of grief should not be overshadowed by its misapplication.

Classical grief theory based on Freudian concepts had been predicated on the belief that grief was a process of disengagement from the deceased, and that severing bonds was indicative of readiness to form new attachments. A gradual recognition that this perspective was an inaccurate reflection of the true nature of grief and unhelpful to practice eventually found recognition with the publication of the book *Continuing Bonds* (Klass, Silverman and Nickman, 1996). The sense of continuity both through memory and through a revised inner representation of the deceased (or person or thing which has been lost) becomes a process of reconciling the past with the present in order to move into the future. Many non-Western cultures demonstrate the significance of this continuity through their religious beliefs and rituals (Irish, Lundquist and Nelsen, 1993; Klass, 1999).

The notion that a satisfactory outcome in loss or bereavement depends fundamentally upon the emotional expression of grief was implied within the psychodynamic tradition and was a perspective carried into practice. This concept of 'grief work' was challenged by Wortman and Silver (1989) and by Stroebe (1992–93). A significant new theoretical perspective, the Dual Process Model of grief, emerged from the research, which sought to test the validity of the grief work hypotheses (Stroebe and Schut, 1999). Stroebe et al. proposed that adaptation to grief consists of a two dimensional process: loss orientation and restoration orientation. The former attends to the distress of grief and the latter focuses upon diversion from it and attention to ongoing life demands. Successful movement, oscillation, between these two grief modes is necessary for successful adaptation to loss. Giving theoretical recognition to the restoration aspect of grief alongside a focus on traditional grief work, not only addresses the multidimensional nature of grief but also makes visible the variable ways in which individuals may respond to it.

Taking a multidimensional view of grief also means that responses to loss which were previously regarded as pathological or abnormal, now fall within a spectrum of normality. Using culture as a lens for viewing grief also gives recognition to the ways in which symptoms and intensity of grief will be variably understood in different cultures and communities (Rosenblatt, 2001). The shift in perspective, which previously made clear distinctions between normal and pathological grief, should be fully understood and recognised as a way of embracing diversity. Nevertheless, persistent grief remains a clinically identifiable condition which may result from unresolved loss issues and/or an ongoing life grief, such as a long-term disability. Roos (2002) describes this as chronic sorrow. The new ways of defining and understanding 'problematic' grief have significant implications for practice in health and social care settings.

Having explored the background theories of grief, Chapter 3 examines those concepts which look at the process of adjustment to loss. Worden (2003) has influenced practitioners working with grief since his book *Grief Counselling and Grief Therapy* was first published in 1983. It has been revised in the light of new theoretical perspectives and in Chapter 3 the tasks of mourning are integrated within the conceptual frame of the Dual Process Model of grief and Continuing Bonds theory.

Theories of intervention (counselling/therapy) are explored in Chapter 4. Fundamental to all counselling/therapy is the creation of a safe base within which the client/patient can disclose his/her concerns and feel free to explore new ways of understanding their troubled situation. Attachment Theory identifies the conditions which promote security (Holmes, 1993), and a person-centred approach to counselling/therapy (Rogers 1961; 1980) provides the principles for the acceptance and valuing of people, which is crucial to engagement with individual grief.

Stories are the means of communicating the nature of distress felt by clients/patients. Angus, Levitt and Hardke (1999) suggest that the narrative heard in therapy consists of three elements – the external narrative, the internal narrative and the reflexive narrative. It is a structure which, when working with grief, identifies what has been lost and how (external narrative), its impact upon the teller (internal narrative) and the emerging therapeutic process of making sense of experience (reflexive narrative). The role of the practitioner is to facilitate the telling of the story of loss (construction), to assist in the exploration of the story (deconstruction), and to work towards the 'reconstruction' of the story which has a sustaining meaning for the client/patient (McLeod, 1997). This narrative approach will be used as the basis for exploring the case studies used in Chapters 7, 8 and 9.

A number of therapeutic approaches are pertinent to the process of reconstruction, that is, moving to an acceptance of reality and finding more satisfying ways of understanding the experience of loss. Recognising differences in grieving style (Martin and Doka, 2000; Nolen-Hoeksema and Larson, 1999) is an essential starting point when considering the most appropriate therapeutic focus. Schut et al. (1997) found that countering the usual (gender biased) grief response in therapy was beneficial, that is, men gained from emotion-orientated interventions, while women gained from problem-focused interventions. Consistent with this perspective, Martin and Doka (2000) propose a therapeutic objective in which intuitive grievers are helped to a cognitive and active approach to their loss while instrumental grievers are confronted by their feelings. They conclude that 'those with the widest range of adaptive strategies are best able to surmount crises' (Martin and Doka, 2000: 144).

Achieving a wide range of adaptive strategies is likely to begin with the exploration of significant relationships; relationships which may have been lost or damaged and relationships which are necessary, and may or may not be available, for the support of a client/patient. Attachment Theory can be helpful in suggesting the relationship factors which have produced individual security or insecurity. In looking more closely at the nature of communication within relationships, Transactional Analysis can provide a framework for identifying effective or destructive interactions (Berne, 1961; 1964; 1975). Care of grieving people needs to address the way in which clients/patients are thinking about the losses in their lives. This aspect is sometimes forgotten within the dominant grief-work perspective, which has traditionally attended more to feelings than thinking. Cognitive and cognitive/behavioural approaches to grief focus on mastering new situations and reappraising changed life situations (Beck, 1976; Ellis, 1962, 1989). The approach to meaning-making developed by Frankl (1959) is concerned with the transformation of perspectives, from tragedy to triumph, and is explored as part of the reflexive narrative which seeks to reconstruct a story which can be 'lived by and lived with' (McLeod, 1997: 86).

While Chapter 4 predominantly focuses upon counselling theory and therapeutic engagement with grief, the principles of person-centred sensitivity and careful attention to the story of loss, can also be applied by those people whose role is not primarily therapeutic.

A new practice model for understanding grief and a tool for its implementation – a compass and a map

Chapters 2, 3 and 4 form a background to the introduction of a new model for understanding and working with grief, described in Chapter 5. The model and the approach to practice which flow from it are described in Chapter 6 and constitute the central themes of the book.

Listening to accounts of loss, heard in counselling practice and in research, lead me to a greater understanding of the highly individual nature of grief but it also drew my attention to three broadly different loss reactions (Machin, 1980; 2001). This observable pattern was contained within three kinds of discourse:

1 A deeply distressed discourse where grief is experienced as **overwhelming**.
2 A balanced account of grief, where emotions are accepted and faced, and the practical consequences of loss approached with realism and a sense of agency – a **balanced/ resilient** reaction.
3 A discourse dominated by the need to suppress emotions and remain focused on ongo- ing life demands – a **controlled** reaction.

The categories of difference were conceptualised in the language heard in practice – 'I feel **overwhelmed**', 'I need to be back in **control**', 'I can (want to) feel able to **balance** all that's going on (as a result of the loss)'. These grief reactions were incorporated into a frame- work – the Range of Response to Loss model – which identified the socially constructed perspectives likely to produce the proposed categorical variations in loss responses. The model also suggested how these influential social constructs might lead to identifiably dif- ferent personal perceptions about loss as experienced by self and by others.

Exploring the validity of the notions proposed in the RRL model was undertaken in two ways. First, by looking for conceptual consistency with other theoretical propositions. The ideas did clearly resonate with other key theories, significantly with Attachment Theory (Ainsworth et al., 1978; Bowlby, 1980) and the contemporary Dual Process Model of grief (Stroebe and Schut, 1999). The categories in the RRL model equated well with descrip- tions of attachment style: overwhelmed with anxious/ambivalent attachment, controlled with avoidant attachment, and balanced/resilient with secure attachment. Similarly with the Dual Process Model of grief there were echoes between overwhelmed responses and loss orientation, controlled responses and restoration orientation, and balanced/resilient responses, represented by the capacity to oscillate between these two grieving modes.

Comparison with other theories provided some justification for the concepts in the RRL model but research was undertaken as a second form of validation. An attitude scale was devised to explore the grief perspectives of a sample of bereaved people seeking counselling support (Machin, 2001). The scale, the Adult Attitude to Grief scale, consists of nine self-report statements, which reflect three perspectives for each of the three categories in the model (see Appendix 1). Along with questions about past experiences of loss, the current bereavement, and a number of psychometric tests (Beck Depression Inventory, Beck et al., 1961; Impact of Events scale, Horowitz, Wilner and Alvarez 1979; and Leiden Detachment Scale, Cleiren 1991), the AAG scale was sta- tistically analysed. Factor analyses indicated that the AAG scale provided a good mea- sure of the three categories proposed in the RRL model. However, the 2001 study demonstrated that the differences could most appropriately be applied to understand- ing the complex blend of overwhelmed, controlled, balanced responses taking place within individuals, rather than as a simple account of categorical difference between people. This suggested that the AAG scale might be used within practice as a measure to access and gain understanding about the complexity of individual loss experiences and perspectives.

Further study to test this proposition supported the use of the AAG scale in practice settings (Machin, 2007a; Machin and Spall, 2004). The AAG scale was used effectively as a measure of assessment, as a tool for the exploration of the grief dynamic, as a cue for therapeutic dialogue and as a measure of change. Both clients and practitioners affirmed its face validity as a tool pertinent to the therapeutic focus on grief and as a measure readily integrated into the wider practice repertoire.

Chapter 6 explores in more detail the components of grief described in the RRL model. Overwhelmed and controlled reactions are seen as core elements of grief. They represent the emotional and cognitive tension prompted by an experience of loss. The capacity to manage this tension is reflected in the responses to the balanced/resilient items on the AAG scale. Agreement with the balanced/resilient items reflects the resourcefulness necessary to manage grief, and disagreement implies vulnerability. Vulnerability, therefore, represents a position at the opposite end of the coping spectrum to resilience. The intersection between the core grief states (overwhelmed and controlled) and the mediating factors (resilience and vulnerability) is viewed as a theoretical compass for understanding the grief dynamic (see Figure 1.2).

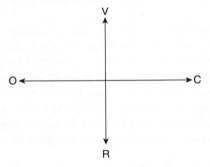

Figure 1.2 'Compass' showing the core grief responses and the mediating factors

In listening to the story of loss, the practitioner can begin to identify the detailed characteristics of their client's/patient's grief (O ⟷ C) and gauge the level of resilience or vulnerability (R ⟷ V) (see Figure 1.3). Distress alone is not a measure of vulnerability. It is important to distinguish between temporary overwhelming feelings (O/R) and distress which persists and is symptomatic of an inability to accept the loss and its consequences (O/V). Similarly, control may be used effectively to counter the powerlessness of grief (C/R) or it may be an anxious and ineffective struggle to master overwhelming distress (C/V). For the practitioner, the RRL model provides a structure for appraising the client's/patient's grief reaction, and gives a focus to the helping process by indicating the desired direction of change from vulnerability to resilience.

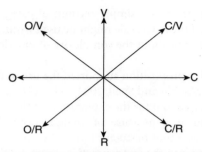

Figure 1.3 'Compass' showing additional bearings – overwhelmed and resilient/vulnerable; controlled and resilient/vulnerable

A second innovative area of practice is where the AAG scale is used as a specific clinical 'mapping' tool (Machin 2005/6/7). The quantative aspects of the scale and the qualitative themes which arise from it, form the first four steps of a six-step practice protocol. Client/patient responses to the nine items on the scale reveal the complex individual variability in grief and its change over time. The wider social context of a client's/patient's grief is explored in the fifth step, as a way of understanding the influences which shape grief perspectives and in order to appreciate the level of available support, or lack of it. Step six uses the individual grief 'map' to consider which therapeutic route should be taken to restore a sense of balance/resilience. This includes a cognitive approach to restoring a sense of agency, that is, encouraging the client to think and make decisions about ways in which they can be empowered to think and act outside the emotional distress generated by grief. Alternatively, for those people whose controlling instinct is proving ineffective in regulating their grief, a person-centred approach provides the possibility for the safe exploration of damaging early experience (a psychodynamic perspective) and cultivates opportunity for the development of trust and self-worth. Identifying painful emotions and thinking about new life perspectives (cognitive perspective) can be undertaken in a climate of acceptance.

Therapeutic ways of working with the RRL model and AAG scale – the territory of loss and the journey through grief

Chapters 7, 8 and 9 each provide detailed case examples (names and identifying features have been changed) to demonstrate the application of the RRL model and the AAG scale. Chapter 7 focuses on the essential characteristics of the grief story brought to counselling/therapy by looking at the external narrative – what happened, and the internal narrative – the impact on the narrator. In listening to the initial account of loss, the primary therapeutic approach is person-centred, in which the client/patient is heard, accepted and understood (Howe, 1993). This provides the climate in which the loss

Table 1.1   The dimensions of grief, narrative structure, therapeutic approach and narrative process in working with loss

Dimensions of grief (RRL model/AAG scale)	Narrative structure (Angus and Hardke, 1994)	Therapeutic approach	Narrative process (McLeod, 1997)
Overwhelmed/ controlled	External	Person-centred	Construction
	Internal	Psycho-dynamic	Deconstruction
Balanced/ resilient	Reflexive	Cognitive Meaning-making	Reconstruction
			Rehearsal

story can be developed ('construction') and sensitive exploration ('deconstruction') can take place. In Chapter 8, the focus is on the nurturing and promotion of resilience which occurs as client and counsellor explore the loss narrative through the reflexive process. Increasing the capacity to function with resilience is seen as the goal of therapy (Machin, 2007b). Chapter 9 examines more complex grief reactions and the vulnerability this produces. The limitations which this puts upon the practitioner needs to be recognised and more restricted therapeutic goals may have to be set. Table 1.1 shows how the dimensions of grief described in the RRL model are applied to the narrative structure, and suggests the range of therapeutic approaches which might be used to facilitate the process for achieving a more satisfying narrative outcome for the client/patient (McLeod, 1997).

Practitioner perspectives – travelling with grief

In focusing on loss, and providing a theoretical concept and a tool which can be taken into practice, this book attempts to make the process of engaging with grief one that can readily be undertaken by a wide range of practitioners. The roles in health and social care are variable but the demands of working with another's grief is potentially challenging at all practice levels. Openness to a client's/patient's emotional pain can be a reminder of personally experienced losses, or generate anxiety about what life might hold in the future. Achieving a balance between being the objective 'professional' and a subjective human being is central to providing useful and sensitive care to grieving people. This is only possible where the value put on those who seek care is matched by recognition of the need for practitioner support, and by putting in place strategies to sustain resourcefulness. Good collaborative team work embedded in supportive supervision is essential to the maintenance of good practice. A restoring balance of relationships and activities outside work are vital for practitioners to function with resilience.

Conclusion

Loss is not always recognised as central to the fabric of human experience. Theories of grief, therefore, have tended to focus on indisputable life losses – death, dying and bereavement. While the application of these theories to all other losses might not be appropriate (Sapey, 2002), they are broadly pertinent to an understanding of loss and change. Chapter 3 explores how theoretical perspectives on grief have evolved during the twentieth century. However, the growth in research-based knowledge has not been matched by methods for putting theory into practice. This book seeks to make a clear connection between theory and practice by providing a new practice-generated theory (Machin, 2005), conceptualised as the Range of Response to Loss model and a tool, the Adult Attitude to Grief scale, to operationalise the notions contained within the model.

The book provides practitioners with a way of looking at the nature of loss across the life cycle and identifying ways in which support might be given to those who are grieving. The valley of grief, spoken of by Lewis, is a route which can be undertaken with courage and optimism, when the innate ability for healing is recognised and the nurturing care of others is available. The role of practitioners in health and social care plays a crucial part in supporting travellers on this journey.

2

Exploring the Landscape of Loss

Literature and poetry, drama and film are full of themes of loss – lost love, defeat in war, separation from place and people, etc., and yet the scope of attention to the impact of loss within health and social care settings is often limited to that of death, dying and bereavement. It is central to an understanding of what it is to be human that the broader landscape of loss and the intrinsic grief responses to it are explored. This chapter will look at two dimensions of loss:

1   Developmental loss and change across the life course. The impact of some of these psychosocial events may pass almost unnoticed but nevertheless provide rehearsal for more emotionally significant losses.
2   Circumstantial loss and change across the life course. These losses are unpredictable and produce more profound and visible distress resulting from broken and damaged relationships, illness and disability, disappointment and untimely death. Such losses may be faced by individuals or, for example at times of war, disability and death are experienced across communities.

The cultural, social and economic context of loss will determine whether there are positive opportunities for support and the nurturing of resilience, or whether negative factors, such as poverty, prejudice or social alienation are likely to produce:

3   Invisible grief and undervalued people (a third dimension for discussion in this chapter).

Autobiographical accounts of loss are used in this chapter to illustrate the experience and the impact of the many forms of loss.

Developmental loss and change across the life course

A number of theories have been developed to account for the psychosocial changes which parallel biological maturation and decline over the life span (Erikson, 1980;

Havighurst, 1972; Newman and Newman, 1995). Implicit within these concepts is the notion of change, and the implication this has for the management of transitions across the life cycle. Erikson (1980) conceptualises the life course progression as consisting of eight developmental, psychosocial tasks or crises. The task at each stage, if not completed, will render the next developmental stage a more complex process. Erikson (1980) proposed the following stages:

- **Infancy** – was seen as a period when trust is developed. The child begins to discover through the quality of his/her caregivers how safe (or not) the world is. The spectrum of possibilities within this task consist of BASIC TRUST or BASIC MISTRUST.
- **Early childhood** – with increasing skills of mobility and social interaction the child becomes more able to make choices. However, lack of experience will result in some task failure, an inability to distinguish what is unsafe and a limited appreciation of what will bring approval from caregivers. This experimental phase of development is characterised by AUTONOMY versus SHAME AND DOUBT in which learning about self-control without loss of self-esteem is crucial.
- **Play age** – where a greater sense of autonomy emerges and the child has a more developed sense of self, a new challenge emerges as he/she can begin to imagine and rehearse for the kind of person they may become. Implicit in this concept of self is the development of conscience resulting in a tension between INITIATIVE and GUILT.
- **School age** – the formal process of learning brings into consciousness those processes already begun. It engages the growing child with the possibilities of mastery through knowledge and a sense of his/her own competence in engaging with the learning task. It is not without hazard and for many it may be a time of feeling inadequate or a failure. The two ends of the developmental spectrum are characterised as INDUSTRY versus INFERIORITY.
- **Adolescence** – defined as the time of intense physical change and the growth into physical maturity and is a period when a new sense of integrity is sought. The attributes of earlier stages have to be reintegrated into values and beliefs, which are personally as well as socially coherent. It can be a turbulent time when aspirations and the choice of role models can lead to new IDENTITY or ROLE CONFUSION.
- **Young adulthood** – while earlier developmental tasks have centred on the capacity of the child/young person to form a separate identity, at this stage there is a new challenge, that of sacrificing individuality for commitment to another person/people. At this stage there may be evidence of success in achieving a separate identity and a mature ability to enter intimate relationship(s) with others. However, such relationships may also demonstrate the need to subdue personal identity by engagement in an intimate, symbiotic relationship. If this task is unsuccessfully negotiated it may result in a love relationship made up of a dominant and a subordinate partner. It is a task of INTIMACY versus ISOLATION.
- **Maturity** – as the adult becomes a parent so the role of offering guidance to the next generation becomes one with societal importance too. Within work and leisure, creativity and altruism may also feature as ways in which the adult makes a contribution to a wider good. At this stage if the individual continues to be self-centred then personal growth is limited and the tension of GENERATIVITY versus STAGNATION is evident.
- **Old age** – the emergence of wisdom as the person is able to integrate an acceptance of the realities of experience from the past with contentment in the present. Where this does not occur there will be discomfort with life and the limited possibilities for change together with fear about death. EGO INTEGRITY versus DESPAIR and DISGUST mark this final life crisis described by Erikson (1980).

Erikson has had his critics who have variously modified the stages he proposed (Gould, 1978; Levinson et al., 1978) or have judged his assumption about the nature of society and the family as conformist (Buss, 1979). Nevertheless, his formulation remains one which provides an important structure for exploring the psychological and social challenges of development, and explains both the possibilities for success and more limited achievement. What is clear is that the journey from birth to death is punctuated by challenges which can cumulatively contribute to the development of personal and social resources and an increased capacity to face the risks encountered in dealing with life and its losses (Hendry and Kloep, 2002).

Central to the developmental process are relationships which shape experience in childhood and through the life course. Bowlby's theory of Attachment (1980) has provided significant understanding about the conditions which contribute to well-being and the successful management of separation and loss (see Chapter 3).

Figure 2.1 identifies key points across the life course where change brings an ambiguity between loss and gain. Within this ambiguity it may be difficult to recognise that some of these events prompt an emotional reaction which has any likeness to the grief felt in more obvious circumstances of loss, such as bereavement. At the least, temporary discomfort and disturbed feelings often accompany new experiences and the positive opportunities are tentatively weighed in the balance. Five-year-old James describes his first day at school (Machin and Holt, 1988: 8):

> When I left Mum I was very scared, I didn't want to leave Mum. Finding my way in the big building that I'd never been in before was very hard. I can remember the first morning when all the children cried. I felt sad myself as well as other children. But I was very excited to learn to read and write.

An apparent absence of distress is most likely where the process of change is a shared transition, and is seen as a normal part of growing up such as a peer group moving schools. Some changes may be welcomed, even though they are accompanied by a measure of apprehension and ambivalence, for example, leaving home, retirement, etc. The actor, Tom Courtenay, recalls his return to drama school after a Christmas holiday spent with his family and highlights the way in which change is a complex interpersonal experience:

> My departure for London after Christmas is stuck in my memory. ... Mother was so downcast by my imminent departure ... it [a play on TV] could not permeate the gloom Mother felt as I waited to leave for the strange drama school about which, having finally got to it, I seemed so uncertain and uncommunicative. (Courtenay, 2000: 120)

Social and cultural influences on change	LIFE COURSE Developmental change (and loss)	Circumstantial loss
Positive social and cultural context Political and economic advantage Social integration	**Birth** (location in family) ↓ **School** (independent social development) ↓ **Changing school** (transitions and change) ↓ **Leaving school** (making new life choices) ↓ **Forming significant relationships** (friendships) ↓ **Establishing permanent relationships** (marriage/partnership)	**Broken and damaged relationships** (separation, divorce, child/elder abuse etc) ← **Physical/mental, illness/disability** (acute or chronic incapacity) ←
Social and cultural deprivation Political and economic disadvantage (marginalisation) Social isolation (disenfranchisement)	↓ **Creating (or not) a 'family'** (birth of children) ↓ **Development of self** (career, occupation, beliefs, philosophies) ↓ **Retirement** (leaving the world of work, leisure, old age) ↓ **Death** (timely)	**Unfulfilled ambitions/ disappointment** (for example, childlessness) ← **Death** (sudden, traumatic, untimely) ←

Figure 2.1   Loss and the life course: the social and cultural factors which influence the experience of loss and the significant circumstantial losses which may occur

The ending of years of study and a return to her homeland brought a different kind of emotional ambivalence for Benazir Bhutto (1989: 98):

> I was sad at leaving Oxford and so many friends. But I was also excited about the prospects awaiting me in Pakistan.

In many of these normal and accepted circumstances of loss and change, a degree of emotional discomfort may arise with temporary feelings of vulnerability. Lorna Sage describes her marriage and pregnancy, neither occurring in the way she would have chosen:

> Our shotgun wedding took place on Boxing Day … that year we were the only customers. No one took any photographs, there was not a soul in sight …
>
> For the first time in our lives (on our wedding night, like a respectable couple) Vic and I shared a bed, and in the morning, after my father left for work, my mother brought us mugs of sweet tea and that settled the matter. Vic was one of the family. (Sage, 2000: 248–9)
>
> [...]
>
> I wanted my body back. I'd never until now thought of it as mine, really, now that it wasn't. Pregnant, I was in my own prison but you could tick off the days on a calendar; it wasn't a life sentence. (ibid.: 245)

The years of old age may bring a gradual decline in functioning or more sudden malfunctioning through a heart attack, stroke, etc. Where death occurs at the end of a long life there is often assumed to be a philosophical acceptance of it. However, for an older person acceptance of the inevitability of death may be countered by profound grief, for example, for a partner of 50 or 60 years.

> When you're a young soldier you can lose friends but when you're old you never quite get over losing anyone or anything. I think you know real loss when you're old. (Blythe, 1979: 168)

In another example, Fred, aged 76, gives a moving account of his growing acceptance of his wife's death (Machin and Holt, 1988: 32):

I had two dreams. In the first, I was in a busy crowded shopping street with my wife. For some minor reason we became separated. I saw her about fifty yards away and began to move in her direction. Then I realised I was not catching her up. I put on a spurt to do so. Without turning round she did the same. I found that, try as I would I could not come nearer to her. The dream faded but when I awoke I recalled it vividly. In the second I was seated with her in a familiar park one sunny afternoon. After a time she asked me to go to the shops to make some simple purchases. So I did. When I got back to the park I found the gates locked and I couldn't get in. I couldn't find a way of getting her out. From those dreams, I infer, that the loss I had sustained had penetrated to that part of my mind which emerged into consciousness in my dreams.

Preparation and choice as mitigating factors

In the process of developmental change two factors help to reduce the harsher impact of loss.

First, where there is an opportunity for PREPARATION the process of anticipation and rehearsal provide time to think about the impact of the event and the most appropriate responses to it (Fahlberg, 1994). Understanding about this need to prepare is in evidence, for example, in the availability of books for children about starting school, visiting the dentist, the arrival of a new baby, etc. This affords conversation and some adjustment to be made ahead of the event. It can be equally important for changes later in life. An inevitable move into residential care for an older person, for example, will be more readily accomplished if that person has had the opportunity to think about the physical, practical and emotional consequences of such a move. However, a reluctance to face loss sometimes means that people may be unwilling to prepare, for example, for either their own death or that of the people close to them.

A second factor, which cushions the impact of change, is where there is a possibility for CHOICE. A chosen change is calculated on the basis that it is in a person's best interest. For example, the losses which may be the consequence of marriage – moving house, living away from friends and family, etc. – are countered by a wider view that this is a positive change with many benefits. Similarly, there are many changes which may accompany a new job opportunity, and where this has been sought the advantages will have been thought to outweigh the disadvantages. Choice may not prevent the ambivalence seen in some of the autobiographical accounts included above, but it will reduce the sense of powerlessness which is a significant factor in triggering grief.

Attitudes towards loss and change across the life course

Wider social attitudes contribute to perspectives on loss and change. In infancy, reaching physical and psychological milestones signal welcome evidence of normal development. In adolescence, the nature of physical and emotional change marks the dawn of adulthood; a turbulent time but one heralding new freedoms. In societies where youth and beauty are synonymous, the decline in reproductive functioning in women and an overall slowing of physical capacity in both men and women is often viewed unfavourably. The beauty industry, cosmetic surgery and the general priorities in health care all suggest that in the West there is an attempt to limit both the appearance and the associated losses of ageing. In contrast, traditional societies see age and wisdom as synonymous and therefore revere older people.

Traditionally society has provided, through its elders and priests, mechanisms of support in the management of transitions. Ritual has played its part especially at times of birth, marriage and death but, increasingly, in more individualistic secular societies, it is the role of professionals who participate in these transitions to help facilitate good outcomes. Teachers may be engaged with transitions through the education system, health professionals may be the bringers of bad news and supporters at times of life-threatening illness, counsellors may be the new priests at the times of death and bereavement. Throughout the life course loss and change will bring challenge to the individual and to those who wish to support them.

Circumstantial loss and change across the life course

Unlike the experiences of developmental loss and change, which are common to everyone, circumstantial losses are not universal. Although considered as four discreet categories (see Figure 2.1), they are integrated into the life course and may be particularly difficult if they coincide with other life changes, such as moving schools and the separation of parents, birth of a child and redundancy, etc. Circumstantial losses are not simply private experiences but may be socially generated and confer wider community loss. For example, a country's decision to go to war will result in the death of soldiers and civilians, a council's unwillingness to provide ramps to public buildings add to the existing limitations of a disabled person, an inadequate benefits system will result in some individual poverty, etc.

Broken and damaged relationships

Relationships are fundamental to human experience. They are the context of nurture, and of learning about the world and about self. Relationships span psychological and social development and provide the foundation for potential vulnerability or resilience (Bowlby, 1980). The ending of relationships is part of normal life experience: the dispersal of friendships at the end of school life, the anguish of a lost love as a teenager, the emigration of loved relatives to Australia, the departure to university of children, etc. As with developmental losses, these may be woven into the fabric of life as hurtful but also strengthening experiences. However, for some people they will constitute damaging events, which influence the making and sustaining of future relationships.

Problematic relationships in childhood are particularly damaging. Mistrust, shame and guilt, the negative end of the developmental spectrum described by Erikson (1980), may consequently typify the responses of a child/young person who has experienced unsupported separation from parents, inconsistent parenting, physical violence, sexual abuse, etc. Fahlberg suggests that the consequences of multiple moves of young children in foster care means that they are 'particularly vulnerable to severe problems in the development of social emotions, carrying with it long-term implications for interpersonal relationships, conscience development and self-esteem' (1994: 138). The same could also be said of other early experiences of loss and change. The crucial role which relationships play in the healthy development (or not) and the social integration (or not) of individuals will determine much of the individual capacity to cope, as an adult, with relationship loss and other life losses (Gerhardt, 2004).

Traumatic relationship experiences include divorce and separation from a partner. It is not uncommon to hear people describe divorce as a bereavement. What is being identified is the pain of being severed from a relationship that has had meaning in the past, in spite of being ambiguous and distressing in the present, together with a (possible) sense of abandonment, betrayal, and anger. Further potential losses arise from the break-up of a significant relationship, for example, loss of home, of children, etc. – as well as the loss of a sense of self. Children whose parents divorce are caught within a situation where they are at the mercy of other peoples' choices, while forced into choices they would prefer not to make – for example, where to live, how to ration leisure time, how to manage their 'go between' relationship with their parents. The wider impact of relationship breakdown may also be seen where grandparents are refused access to grandchildren. Relationship breakdown is a common feature of contemporary Western society. It constitutes an important experience for individuals and wider social networks and contributes to identifiable trauma for many people. It is clear that grief is the likely response to these experiences and may be seen in children as verbal or physical aggression or turned inwards with an inability to play or speak. Adults may show a similarly variable reaction, between acted-out anger and silent withdrawal. These reactions echo the grief responses made in bereavement.

Kroll describes her work with Robert, an eight-year-old boy carrying his own anger, as well as that projected by his parents in the aftermath of their separation. Some of Robert's words reveal the venom and hurt he was feeling:

Me and mummy will kick him in the teeth', 'Send him a nappy as he's so full of shit', 'I'm confused, I'm in the middle' – he sobbed. (Kroll, 1994: 162)

In contrast, five-year-old Beatrice was a retreating child:

'I don't want to see you and I don't want to talk to you'.

Kroll recounts how Beatrice sat on her mother's lap with a blanket over her head.

> She regularly reappeared, then disappeared behind her protective cover, effectively reflecting the loss and reclamation of her father, and the life she had known when her parents were together … a game very reminiscent of the 'peep-boo' play of babies and toddlers who are coming to terms with separations and reunions and need to feel they have some control of the situation. (ibid.: 135–6)

It is clear that damaged relationships are likely to carry grieving consequences of a disturbing kind. However, this is especially evident in the case of child abuse and elder abuse, which are characterised by malevolence and violence, in a relationship where one person has power over another. Abuse may be characterised by sexual exploitation, physical violence, emotional humiliation; all demeaning experiences for the victim. The perpetrator robs the victim of essential freedoms and human rights, which result in significant and often life-changing losses. The abused child will lose innocence, mistrust other people and feel degraded. These losses are not easily placated. The damage is often perpetuated as the capacity to create and sustain good relationships is confounded by the person for whom good role models and good experience are absent.

Trevane (2005) describes how Shannon and her sister were abused by their father when they were children. Shannon describes the impact of this on her adult sister and her own (mistaken) sense of culpability.

> She suffers from depression and is on medication for it. Her marriage didn't work because she couldn't stand to be touched. She moved back in with me and became a virtual recluse, suffering from anxiety attacks, and cutting herself. A psychiatrist worked with her to overcome her demons, but she could not forget. Pappy ruined her life. She hasn't been able to move on, and she'll never have children of her own. She remembers the pain when he forced himself inside her, and the horror at the blood the first time. She still cries out in her sleep. If he wasn't dead, I'd kill him. But he's not the only one to blame. I should have noticed. I should have taken more care of her. (2005: 229)

Abused children often find themselves in abusive marriages which is a pattern continuing the cycle of violence and victimhood (Harvey, 2000). The abused may also become the abuser and again demonstrate a pattern in which early damaging relationships set in train an incapacity to relate to others through the regulation of emotion and behaviour, and appropriate responsiveness to others. It is important to recognise that the pattern of violence – abuse – violence is not inevitable (Sandford, 1990).

Elder abuse has received less public attention than child abuse but is now seen as a significant issue for many incapacitated and dependent older people (Pritchard, 1995).

A person's need for care at the end of their life may frustrate the economic and social lifestyle of younger family members. Care may demand competence and sensitivity, which is undeveloped in poorly trained and pressurised care staff, resulting in abuse of older people. Elder abuse often remains undetected but where it has been exposed it is seen to involve the humiliation and degradation that is also associated with abuse and violence against the person in younger age groups. It exploits vulnerability and adds to the other potential losses of old age – loss of independence, control, identity, freedom to choose, etc. (Thompson, 2002).

So far, damaged and broken relationships have been seen to fall within the private domain of interpersonal experience. However, loss also occurs in the social context and larger groups of people may be implicated in relationships which breakdown between communities. This may be witnessed as anti-social behaviour, inter-gang violence, or tension between ethnic and religious groups. In Western societies the postmodern trend to individualism, characterised by aggressive competitiveness and materialism, together with the disaffection of marginalised groups, plays a part in the loss of trust and antagonism between sub-groups of people.

Loss of trust and antagonism produce broken and damaged relationships as conflict occurs within the wider community. Contentious disputes about land usage, inner-city gang attacks and the wider context of war, for example, bring communities into conflict and harms or destroys relationships within them. Bell, a war correspondent, describes the personal anguish and confusion of individuals caught up in the Bosnian war which brought dislocation to community life and severed relationships between neighbours:

On this I offer a Bosnian example from the war between Muslims and Croats. At a time when it was raging most fiercely in September 1993, the front line shifted to the grounds of a mental hospital in the old spa town of Fojnica in central Bosnia. The Bosnian army held one side and the Bosnian Croat Defence Force the other. The hospital itself was in no man's land, its staff fled, and its demented patients were wandering about in both sides' line of fire as helpless as children, and yet it was notable that there was no operation, no international campaign on their behalf. I had wished to end my report with the thought that this was what the conflict had come to, and there could hardly be a crueller image of it than a madhouse in a war zone. I was told that the use of the word 'madhouse' was no longer admissible: there were people who might be offended by it. I tried to make my case. The issue was a small one, but it seemed to me to be symbolically quite important. (Bell, 1995: 225)

The personal cost of conflict in another war, the First World War, is described by Vera Brittain (1978), who experienced through the death of a brother, fiancé and friends, the destruction of a generation of young men. She expressed outrage at the impact of war upon individuals and the anguish of lost relationships:

> 'Public opinion has made it,' I remarked to Roland, 'a high and lofty virtue for us women to countenance the departure of such as these and you to regions where they will probably be slaughtered in a brutally degrading fashion in which we would never allow animals to be slaughtered … To the saner mind it seems more like a reason for shutting up half the nation in a criminal lunatic asylum!' (Brittain, 1978: 203)

Both Bell and Brittain address the cost of social conflict for individuals and their relationships. They poignantly articulate, through the metaphor of madness, the futility, helplessness and loss which is the consequence of war.

Illness and disability

Deficits in normal physical and mental functioning may be congenital or acquired. Illnesses and disabilities may be acute or chronic. Across this spectrum of incapacity are huge variations in types of disablement; it may totally incapacitate or temporarily inconvenience. The limitations, which come with all disorders, consist of two elements. First, the innate reduction in functioning, resulting from the disease or disability. Jean-Dominique Bauby describes 'locked-in syndrome', the major physical incapacity he suffered following a massive stroke:

> Paralysed from head to toe, the patient, his mind intact, is imprisoned inside his own body, but unable to speak or move. In my case, blinking my left eyelid is my only means of communication. … My weekly bath plunges me simultaneously into distress and happiness. The delectable moment when I sink into the tub is quickly followed by nostalgia for the protracted wallowings that were the joy of my previous life. Armed with a cup of tea or a Scotch, a good book or a pile of newspapers, I would soak for hours, manoeuvring the taps with my toes. Rarely do I feel my condition so cruelly as when I am recalling such pleasures. (Bauby, 2004: 12; 24–5)

Bauby's account of his illness highlights the impact of multiple physical losses, and the cognitive and emotional challenges to his capacity to cope.

However, a second dimension of loss is experienced through the handicap imposed by a society unwilling to accommodate the limitations of those with an illness or disability. Negative social perspectives and apathetic attitudes compound innate loss, by passively ignoring the needs or actively preventing sick or disabled people from participating fully in the life of the community. The restriction on movement and reduced opportunity to make choice is a loss imposed by society and its institutions, and constitutes disablism

Table 2.1   Perceptions of disability

How I see myself	
What I am told	**What I perceive**
You are – epileptic, paraplegic, etc.	I am my illness/disability
I can't bear your pain, appearance, etc.	I am not an OK person
Your carers know what is best for you	I have no choice/I have no control

(Sapey, 2002). Sapey cautions practitioners against applying psychological theories to people who have a disability and making assumptions based upon socially constructed notions of what it is to be 'normal'. Clearly many people who have a disability will not readily connect with the ideas of grief, in relation to their physical or mental incapacity. However, they may have a profound sense of oppression as a result of their exclusion from full participation in social life (Oliver and Sapey, 1999). Great strides have been made in ensuring equal access to educational and employment opportunity, and in providing access to buildings etc. but the legislative recognition of the rights of disabled people is not always matched by the actual opportunities available.

Listening to the impact of disability on the individual and the meanings attached to it, remains essential to understanding what it is like to have reduced physical or mental capabilities. However, it must not be forgotten that the identity of the person has already been powerfully shaped by external perceptions (see Table 2.1).

The construction of self, 'as others see me', is powerfully evident in the story of Alison Lapper (2005) who has been able to move beyond the disabled image of herself.

When I began my art degree I continued to attend life classes and produced a large number of paintings and drawing of the human form. My studio was covered in them. I didn't think anything of it. For me, it was simply what I was interested in doing at the time. Then, about halfway through my second term, one of the art tutors said, 'I think you paint all these pictures of beautiful people because you don't want to face how you look, and who you really are.' I was stunned. It felt like a personal attack and completely unfair. ...

After she left, I sat down and thought about it and realised it was true. I had never really looked deeply at who I was and maybe she had made me aware of something that was significant and important. Maybe.

I went off to the art library in a restless mood and began aimlessly flicking through books, using my nose and mouth to turn the pages. And then one particular book I was looking at fell open at the photograph of the Venus de Milo. It showed a white marble statue, in the ancient Greek style, of a woman with her arms missing. There was a flash of recognition – hey, that's me! That moment was the starting point of the journey I am still on today, looking at my own body and how I feel about myself, and how others feel about me. (Lapper, 2005: 185–6)

Lapper has gone on to be the inspiration for a statue in Trafalgar Square. She says of the sculpture of her pregnant, naked image:

> I think it makes the ultimate statement about disability: that it can be as beautiful and as valid a form of being as any other. (ibid.: 247)

Reaching this point demands a challenge to the socially limiting and negative concepts of disability.

Unfulfilled ambitions and disappointment

The postmodern perspective, which emphasises the primacy of the individual and the importance of autonomy and control, has led to an expectation that most personal ambitions can be realised. Scientific advances in the field of medicine and technology, economic wealth, and social stability all contribute to the assumption, in the West, that a long, healthy and happy life is universally possible. In this climate it is not easy for people to openly acknowledge those aspirations which have been thwarted and which contradict the expectation of a life free of disappointment. It is difficult to admit to what might appear as failure. Unfulfilled ambition may be carried as private loss over a long period of time. Morley (1996) calls it 'grieving for what has never been'. Feelings of grief may only emerge when the vulnerability of another loss provides an opportunity to disclose the emotional cost of an earlier profound disappointment. For example, a highly successful, single, career woman who reveals during a protracted illness the deep disappointment of never having been married or having a family.

Childlessness represents a significant example of human disappointment (Read, 1995). The wish to have children is a biological desire, and a recognised social aspiration for most people. However, in contemporary Western society, making decisions about the timing of parenthood, and even the desirability of having children, is a lifestyle choice. The choice brings dilemmas, and postponed parenthood and fertility problems have become a new phenomenon to challenge the pervasive assumptions about being in control of life. In these circumstances it is not surprising that considerable medical research and resources go into assisted conception and giving people continued reproductive choice. The initial disappointment of being unable to conceive and the ongoing anxiety of pursuing fertility treatment is a physically demanding and an emotionally stressful experience. Read (1995) gives a case example which illustrates some of the personal and interpersonal pain within this situation.

Zoe was having counselling help as a result of fertility problems. She gives an account of a telephone conversation with a friend, who was thinking of having an abortion.

'I have to say it seems a little bit unfair, I've been trying for three and a half years and you didn't even want this, and now you've got pregnant.' She said 'Well, I think the problem with you is you're too thin', and just started to say, 'It's your diet or something', and I just went mad, I just said 'fuck off' and it just came, I was just so angry with her.

[...]

I think I thought it would start to get easier (adjusting to the problems of infertility and to treatment), but it just doesn't. I know it's probably such a short time compared with other people, but it seems such a long time, I would have thought that it would have started to get easier. I just feel that I need to cry and cry and cry, I seem to cry really easily. (Read, 1995: 24–5)

Therapy has become a way of addressing life's grief but Craib (1994) and Walter (1996) are critical of some of the underlying assumptions which have grown with this sort of help seeking. They see that sometimes counselling/therapy becomes a way of heightening false expectations rather than assisting in adjustment to some of the inevitabilities of life's disappointments and losses. They believe it is unhelpful to perceive of the things which jeopardise well-being, as antithetical to the innate nature of human experience. On the contrary, part of what it is to be human is to confront the limitations of experience. It is in the mastery of hurt and disappointment that people find new depth to their own potential to be human.

Unlike the examples considered so far, personal disappointment is of a different order when the thwarting of ambitions is generated by social, political and economic conditions, which disadvantage certain groups and communities. Experiences of poverty and social marginalisation, based on sexism, racism, sexual orientation, etc., generate loss and a deep sense of powerlessness. The consequent emotional and behavioural reactions echo the grief reactions seen in response to other losses, although they may not be described as such. Apathy, underachieving and anti-social behaviour, for instance, may arise from being denied a recognised place in society. Apathy and anger are both known to be symptomatic of grief and they represent a behavioural spectrum at one end of which people are unable to respond to their circumstances and demonstrate helplessness. At the other end of the spectrum the anger and frustrations (about perceived injustice) generate an energy which is likely to be expressed in behaviour that is confrontational and/or aggressive. Maya Angelou, a successful and prolific writer, is a black woman who has known discrimination and extreme poverty. She describes in her autobiography the resignation to the hardship of servitude in her early years:

Looking through the years, I marvel that Saturday was my favorite day in the week. What pleasures could have been squeezed between the fan fold of unending tasks? Children's talent to endure stems from their ignorance of alternatives. (Angelou, 1984: 109)

Angelou describes how communities look to role models to contradict the wider misperceptions about their human worth but that hopefulness can easily be reversed into identification with the oppressors racist attitudes.

> If Joe [Louis] lost [his boxing fight] we were back in slavery and beyond help. It would all be true, the accusation that we were lower types of human beings. Only a little higher than the apes. True that we were stupid and ugly and lazy and dirty and, unlucky and worst of all, that God Himself hated us and ordained us to be hewers of wood and drawers of water, forever and ever, world without end. (ibid.: 131)

But Angelou's spirit was not quelled by her experience and she rose in rebellion against racism.

> From disappointment, I gradually ascended the emotional ladder to haughty indignation, and finally to that state of stubbornness where the mind is locked like the jaws of an enraged bulldog. (ibid.: 258)

This sequence of actions and reactions lies behind many sorts of political and social unrest. It is the consequence of the struggle to reconcile the powerlessness of loss with the desire for control. It was seen in the suffragettes' bid for voting rights in the 1920s, the race riots of America in the 1960s, the miners' strikes of the 1980s and many other visible challenges to the economic and political power base of a country or society. Underlying all of these is the thwarting of individual and collective potential, breeding deep-seated disaffection with systems, and a sense of unfulfilled ambitions.

Traumatic and untimely death

With medical advances extending the possibility for a long and healthy life, the occurrence of traumatic or untimely death is especially disturbing. Sudden and violent deaths at any age, and the deaths of children and young people, are profoundly distressing, individually and socially. The news is dominated by such deaths and demonstrates the hazards of much human activity, the arbitrariness of accidents, the malevolence and cruelty of people to each other and the overall fragility of human life. Deaths which people think should not have happened are an affront to the control they believed they should have over their destiny. Blame and retribution become typical ways in which people react to the powerlessness of such assaults on their invincibility. Traumatic and untimely death produces highly visible grief. Mourning may unite individuals and communities, where the predictability of the day-to-day routine is suddenly turned upside down.

A father (Thompson, 2006) describes the ordinariness of a day that was turned to tragedy when a train killed his 13-year-old daughter and her friend. There was no footbridge at the station and they were crossing the track to reach the platform for the train to Cambridge.

> At around 6.30 in the morning on 3 December 2005 I walked quietly into my daughter's bedroom. She was asleep, curled up on her side, her face towards the wall. ... I leant forward to kiss her on the forehead and as I did so she rolled over on to her back. ... 'Bye-bye, sweetheart. Be careful in Cambridge. Take care crossing the road and don't speak to strangers.' 'Love you daddy,' she said.
> [...]
> In attempting to catch the 10.42 Cambridge-bound train, Charlie and her friend Livvy had been struck by the southbound Stansted Express. According to the police, both girls died instantly.
> [...]
> I find it difficult to write about what happened that day. Eight months on, we are still trapped in the surreal nightmare that descended upon us that fateful morning. (Thompson, 2006: vii; viii; ix)

Thompsons' description of the personal trauma which resulted from this tragic accident is echoed in the experience of Joan Didion following the sudden death of her husband. In her book she confronted the devastation and powerlessness of her situation and attempts to make sense of the sudden severing of a long and happy marriage.

> Life changes fast. Life changes in an instant. You sit down to dinner and life as you know it ends.
> [...]
> Nor can we know ahead of the fact (and here lies the heart of the difference between grief as we imagine it and grief as it is) the unending absence that follows, the void, the very opposite of meaning, the relentless succession of moments during which we will confront the experience of meaninglessness itself.
> [...]
> ... when we mourn our losses we also mourn, for better or for worse, ourselves. As we were. As we are no longer. As we will one day not be at all. (Didion, 2005: 3; 189; 198)

Untimely death is a feature of war and conflict too.

> Roland's death, Edwards's departure and Geoffrey's readiness to take up once more a life which he knew must break him physically and mentally in a very short time, all increased my certainty that however long the War might last, I could not return to Somerville [college, Oxford] while those whom I loved best had sacrificed and were sacrificing everything that they cared for in the world. (Brittain, 1978: 259)

In these circumstances personal, national and international relationships are dislocated, and personal grief obscured by notions of valour and bravery; qualities extolled by nations to appease loss of life.

Invisible grief

The grief produced by the losses already described is variably visible and acknowledged. The connection between loss and grief in bereavement is the most clearly understood. To a lesser degree, the inherent emotional pain associated with divorce and disability is recognised. In contrast, individuals and communities marginalised and oppressed are not so readily seen as grieving for either personal or socially induced losses, such as unemployment, poverty, etc. Doka (2001) applies the term disenfranchised grief to those situations and categories of people where grief is unacknowledged and invisible. He argues that prejudice, the consequence of ignorance and fear, and judgmental perspectives create a climate in which some situations do not command the attention or the understanding of policy makers, practitioners and fellow citizens. Categories of disenfranchised grief, include:

- People in socially 'unacceptable' relationships, for example, gay lovers may not have their experience of loss, through separation or death, acknowledged.
- People engaging in socially 'unacceptable' behaviour, such as alcohol abuse, drug-taking, etc. may face loss of health, loss of relationships, loss of life. People may be judged harshly with little compassion or understanding.
- People experiencing 'stigmatised' losses, for example, suicide may invite misunderstanding and blame.
- People in 'minority' groups, such as ethnic or religious minorities, may not be integrated into communities with consequent misunderstanding about how their needs might be the same or different from the mainstream population.
- People who are socially 'vulnerable', for example, young, old, disabled people are often voiceless. Their grief may go unrecognised among their other care needs.
- People whose losses are usually not defined in terms of grief, for example, childless couples, the unemployed, prisoners, etc. may command no understanding about the impact of their losses.

Some people may have their grief ignored or misunderstood for several of these reasons. This may be particularly evident for older people who, in Western society especially, do not carry the same economic value as younger people, have restricted income, may suffer the chronic onset of illness and experience multiple bereavement (Thompson, 2002).

While disenfranchisement may largely arise from the values and perspectives within society, these views may be echoed or reinforced within the care system, which fails to address the grief of many of its clients/patients/service users. Theories of grief predominantly focus on bereavement and have developed within a medical model of practice, shaped by concepts of disease and treatment (Averill and Nunley, 1993). Within this medical perspective, grief has been defined in terms of 'risk', that is, identifying those people and/or categories of experience most likely to need professional help (Parkes and Weiss, 1983; Rando, 1992–93). As a result, sources of help have tended to emphasise some categories of bereavement and loss as more significant than others, for example, widows have commanded more attention than widowers, grieving parents rather than people with a learning disability, etc. This has been a very effective way of addressing majority need, using empirical evidence to anticipate difficult grief reactions and to target care resources. In addition to clinical merit, it also has the important benefit of being cost efficient (another way in which the meeting of need is socially defined). Against the advantages of focusing on 'risk' is the danger, for those people who fall outside a broad 'at risk' category, that they are likely to have their need unrecognised.

Traditional 'talking therapies' have depended to a large extent upon the capacity of the grieving person to articulate their needs and have an intellectual capacity to process their thoughts and feelings. In the absence of cognitive competence, psychiatric services have tended to treat people with medication rather than counselling/therapy. This professional perspective makes bereavement and loss care inaccessible for many people. However, the situation is changing and new approaches are being developed, for example, to provide therapeutic support to people with a learning disability (Read, 2007). These approaches, while clear about the nature of communication difficulties, are developing innovative ways of engaging with previously excluded client groups. An expanded repertoire of artwork, play therapy, storytelling, etc. is transforming the possibility of providing support in response to loss.

The social and professional challenge to make invisible grief visible

In the absence of social and professional recognition, it has fallen to individual grieving people to draw attention to their own particular loss and grief experience. For many of these people neither social support nor professional help has been available to meet their needs. The growing movement of self-help groups has resulted from people seeking self-empowerment in their loss. Groups such as the Gay Bereavement Project, Jewish Bereavement Counselling Service, Childline (a phone line for abused children), women's refuges, etc. are providing individual support and making public statements about overlooked losses.

Many of these self-help projects have established an identity for their members, provided support in situations where none is available, and made known their needs to the wider community. The search for charitable funding often makes small specialist projects visible, although their success may still depend on the appeal of their cause: for example, the tendency for children to command more support than older people or people with mental health problems.

Listening to the voice of disenfranchised mourners has made professionals increasingly alert to their needs. Through sensitive attunement to individual client/patient needs and greater attention in research to previously unrecognised loss, marginalised groups are finding an increasing place in the repertoire of services to bereaved and other grieving people. One such group is bereaved children whose profile of need has been raised considerably in the sphere of professional care (Christ, 2005; Munroe and Krause, 2005; Stokes, 2007). Children's needs were often subsumed within family dynamics where adults, such as a bereaved spouse or parent, were seen to have a greater legitimacy in making use of support services. Children now receive more support in their own right.

In contrast to the broadening of the social and professional recognition given to children's grief, those living with or bereaved by HIV/AIDs have received less sustained support. The emergence of the AIDs epidemic, while receiving increased professional and media attention, struggles to gain the support of many who regard it as a disease associated with gay sex and drug use, in spite of the evidence that it is a growing disease in the heterosexual community. Establishing this condition as one which demands universal understanding and compassion is clearly running counter to persisting social prejudice. In this situation, professionals and those in positions of power, such as celebrities, have a key role in challenging myth and ignorance.

Professionals are often in the privileged position of listening to and giving support to people who are outside the effective support of social networks. However, practitioners are products of their own culture too and need to be aware of the way in which they bring their own prejudice to their work. Such awareness needs to be raised in training and in supervision, with the goal of confronting and addressing social prejudice from an informed point of view. Practitioners have the responsibility of making the voices of people, whose grief has been hidden, more widely heard and understood. It requires attention to how people perceive and deal differently with loss, by giving them an opportunity to articulate their own grief experience. The challenge for professionals is to think more broadly about loss as central to life experience.

Conclusion

In this chapter the diverse landscape of loss has been examined. The psychosocial developments occurring across the life course incur changes, which can precipitate losses as well as gains (Erikson, 1980). These losses may carry little emotional distress, or they may provide a transitory encounter with grief and rehearsal for the more profoundly disturbing losses of relationships, health, aspiration and life. Parkes (1993) describes the attributes of the more profoundly disturbing life-changing events:

- The loss or change takes place over a relatively short period of time with little or no opportunity for preparation;
- The implications of the loss or change are lasting rather than transient;
- There is a need to revise one's assumptions about the world in a major way.

Loss is not just an individual experience. Political and economic disadvantage, conflict and prejudice, have a collective impact upon communities. This may produce responses such as apathy or anger, which are less recognisable as grief, compared with

```
Visible grief, for example:
    Bereavement
    Divorce

Obscured grief, for example:
    Developmental loss such as changing schools
    Childlessness
    Disability

Invisible grief, for example:
    Losses of childhood and old age
    Loss of cultural identity
    Poverty
```

Figure 2.2   The visibility and invisibility of grief

the visible and obvious anguish of bereavement (see Figure 2.2). For professionals, the challenge is to appreciate fully the significance of the wide spectrum of loss in the lives of their clients/patients and to raise the profile of unseen grief.

While the structure for looking at loss, set out in this chapter, provides a base from which to understand the experiences which prompt grief, it is important not to assume there is a universal response to it. The theories of grief and the individual manifestations of it will be considered in the following chapters.

3

Establishing Theoretical Bearings

In this chapter three areas of theory will be used as reference points (bearings) to guide practitioners in establishing a knowledge base for their clinical work with grieving people.

What determines the shape of grief?

- Lifespan development
- The nature of human attachment
- Predisposing factors – vulnerability and resilience
- Culture

What is grief like?

- The symptoms of grief
- Processes of grief
- Complicated grief

Managing grief – a personal journey

- The tasks of adjustment
- Coping
- Making sense of experience

Theories of human development provide a starting point for considering what determines reactions to loss. Nurturing conditions will result in psychological well-being and social competence, and loss is likely to be met with resilience. Conversely, when formative relationships and experiences of the wider social world have been negative there is a greater likelihood of loss prompting vulnerability. Culture as the context of human development plays a significant part in how attitudes to loss are integrated into the

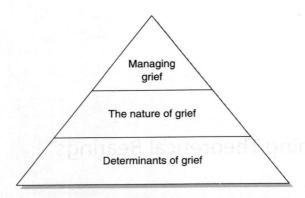

Figure 3.1   Antecedents, experience and tasks of managing grief

beliefs and perceptions of grieving people. A second area of theoretical reflection is upon the nature and characteristics of grief, and its complicating factors. The theories, which most significantly address the issue of loss, are those which focus primarily on bereavement, but their relevance to other loss experiences will be noted. A third theoretical element considers the process prompted by loss, in which grieving people revise their life perspectives and reappraise their own sense of self. Figure 3.1 shows the hierarchy of interconnections between these three theoretical perspectives.

What determines the shape of grief?

In this section four theoretical perspectives will be considered as factors which contribute to how grief is experienced. Firstly, key theories of psychosocial development provide basic concepts about the evolving structure of personality. Secondly, Attachment Theory, which has been central to understanding the nature of separation and loss, will look at relationships as the context of human security or insecurity. Thirdly, consideration will be given to how acquired emotional and social competence, in dealing with life losses, will be evident in a spectrum of responses from resilience to vulnerability. The wider cultural context of experience will be seen as a fourth determinant of the shape of grief.

Lifespan development

There are various theories which describe psychosocial development. Freud's theory (1957) of psychosexual development proposed concepts which have been foundational in the study of personality. The structure of personality proposed by Freud consists of:

- the id – the unconscious and instinctual dimension
- the ego – the conscious and rational dimension
- the superego – the dimension of conscience.

He linked the emergence of these dimensions to the oral, anal and genital phases, which mark the early biological/sexual development of the child. While Freud has had his critics (Fraley and Shaver, 1999) his ideas, which formed the psychodynamic school of thinking, have been highly influential in the evolving concepts of human development.

Piaget's theory (1969) of cognitive development has also contributed to insights into human development. His account of a person's evolving thinking processes has been used extensively within education training and teaching. The stages he identifies are:

- learning through activity and engagement with objects and the environment
- the development of language and the consequent emergence of symbolic thought
- the development of logic and an ability to classify objects and solve problems
- the emergence of abstract thinking and an ability to explore problems hypothetically.

The theories of both Freud and Piaget focus on child development but their concepts have also been used to illuminate how the foundational characteristics of personality and cognitive development influence responses and behaviour in adults.

Some theories like that of Erikson (1980), described in the last chapter, provide a lifespan account of human maturation in a sequential or stage form. While influenced by Freud, Erikson was concerned with the social rather than the psychosexual aspects of development, and on the conscious rather than the unconscious. Erikson saw psychological well-being related to the successful management of crises, for example, basic trust versus basic mistrust, autonomy versus shame and doubt, initiative versus guilt, industry versus inferiority, identity versus role confusion, generativity versus stagnation, ego integrity versus despair and disgust. These 'crises' represent developmental tensions and contribute to the acquisition of psychological and social competence. His framework has been criticised for being too rigidly structured but he believed that 'crises' can be revisited if not accomplished satisfactorily in the original developmental sequence. The theory has also been challenged for assuming that social institutions and society itself afford a benign background for healthy psychological development (Buss, 1979). Such challenges to theory help to secure refinements which make the concepts more robust (Sugarman, 2001). Havinghurst (1972) and his concept of development tasks, Levinson et al. (1978) and their concept of change and consolidation, and Holmes and Rahe (1967), and Reese and Smyer's (1983) notions of life events, have all contributed to a significant literature on lifespan development. Rogers (1961; 1980) provides in his therapeutic legacy a way of understanding the development of self. He conceives of it as a self-actualising tendency, in which there is an innate striving, and capacity, to move towards achieving full personal potential. This movement is dependent upon relationships, both those in normal human encounter as well as those within therapy, to provide the conditions necessary for increasing openness to experience, a focus on living in the moment and a capacity to feel confidence in self. While there are common threads in the classification of human development, their variable theoretical analysis of the elements which make up key milestones and processes in the life course provide a rich reference point for understanding the factors which influence response to loss (Hendry and Kloep, 2002; Sugarman, 2001). The concept of life story as development (McAdams, 1997) will be explored more fully, as a theoretical connection with therapy, in the next chapter.

This brief account of developmental theories provides the conceptual structures upon which the complexities of individual relationships, attitudes and response to life losses, and cultural perspectives will be added.

The nature of human attachment

The quality of early relationships contributes crucially to the way in which human beings develop. Bowlby (1980; 1984), while following in the psychodynamic tradition, focused on relationships and developed a theory of attachment, which represented a 'new psychological paradigm' (Holmes, 1993: 66). This 'new paradigm' looked not only at the formation of attachment bonds in infancy but at the impact of this bond when significant relationships are subject to separation or loss.

Bowlby believed that 'observations of how a very young child behaves towards his mother, both in her presence and especially in her absence, can contribute greatly towards our understanding of personality development' (1984: 3). Bowlby's concept of attachment makes the connection between the individual and his/her social world and has been highly influential not only in the field of child psychology but for subsequent research, theory and practice in the study of grief and bereavement.

Bowlby and his fellow researchers began to identify the patterns of attachment through empirical study, looking at the way mothers and their children relate to each other (Ainsworth et al., 1978). Fundamental to the development of the theory was the notion of the 'secure base', the climate within which attachment could most readily flourish.

> A young child's experience of an encouraging, supportive and co-operative mother, and a little later father, gives him a sense of worth, a belief in the helpfulness of others, and a favourable model on which to build future relationships. Furthermore, by enabling him to explore his environment with confidence and to deal with it effectively, such experience promotes his sense of competence ... not only do these early patterns of thought, feelings and behaviour persist, but personality becomes increasingly structured to operate in moderately controlled and resilient ways, and increasingly capable of continuing despite adverse circumstances. (Bowlby, 1984: 378)

From birth the human infant will assimilate qualities of help and harm within his/her immediate environment. With increasing maturity that environment can be behaviourally manipulated by the infant to maximise the availability of nurturing and minimise the occurrence of alienation from care.

Bowlby's colleagues, Ainsworth et al. (1978), examined the nature of the relationship between mothers and their infants and identified patterns within their interaction. Their work contributed significantly to the development of Attachment Theory as a basis for understanding the structure of personality, in general, and as a response to separation/loss, in particular. They undertook an experiment in which the conditions of separation were simulated in a 'strange situation'. This was a standardised laboratory procedure devised in 1964 to explore, through a longitudinal study, the infant/mother relationship during the first year of life. It consisted of a seven-stage protocol:

1   The mother and infant were left in a strange room (that is, one unknown to the child) with toys.
2   The mother and infant were joined by a female stranger.
3   The mother left the infant with the stranger.
4   The mother returned and the stranger left.
5   The mother left the child alone.
6   The stranger returned to the room.
7   The mother returned to the room.

Ainsworth observed different responses to the 'strange situation' which lead to the classification of different attachment styles. In group A (avoidant attachment), the child avoids contact with the mother when reunited with her, and seems more interested in objects than people. In group B (secure attachment), the child is distressed by the mother's disappearance but is readily comforted by her when she returns. The child is then able to continue exploring the environment. In group C (ambivalent attachment), children react strongly to separation but are not easily comforted upon reunion. They may show either anger or passivity and fail to engage in exploratory behaviour. A fourth pattern, group D, was later identified by Main (1991) as disorganised–disorientated, where children react in a confused and disorientated way on reunion with their mother.

The characteristics, which define the opposite positions of secure and insecure attachment, were used to define the equivalent loss response as normal and pathological. The securely attached child (group B) is seen as one who is more able to tolerate uncertainty, is more sociable and more able to control emotions. While the insecurely attached child (groups A, C and D) shows anxiety in the face of uncertainty, is less able to relate to others and manages emotions less effectively, either by over-controlling them or under-controlling them. The pattern of reaction to separation (or its threat) is established, reinforced and/or modified as the child develops and grows, but in common with psychodynamic theory the initial experience of attachment is seen by its earliest proponents as foundational to the development and structure of personality and loss response.

Bowlby's theory has been the base for considerable research and conceptual advances in relation to adult attachment. 'In the last decade, no single area of research in personality/social psychology has attracted more interest than the application of attachment theory to the study of adult relationships' (Simpson and Rholes, 1998: 3). However, some authors, such as Birtchnell (1997), contend that Attachment Theory is essentially child-centred and not readily adaptable to adult relationships. Clearly, adult attachment is fundamentally different in that it is based on care-giving and sexuality that is reciprocal, unlike the care-giving and -receiving of carer and child.

Central to this new dimension of research has been two questions. How far does the attachment style of infancy persist beyond childhood (Hazan and Shaver, 1987) and to what extent are attachment styles properties of individuals or of relationships (Feeney, 2000)? These questions address the issues of attachment, as either an enduring trait which is located within the individual or as susceptible to modification within diverse and changing adult relationships. The development of the study of adult attachment, while maintaining its conceptual roots within classic theory, has focused upon the nature of close relationships in adulthood and upon the consequences of loss (Kirkpatrick and Hazan 1994; Rholes, Simpson and Stevens, 1998; Umberson and Terling, 1997). Shaver and Hazan (1988) observed strong parallels between attachment style in infancy and adult romantic love. They used the 'love styles' of Lee (1988) and linked them to attachment styles. Secure attachment was seen to be associated with passionate love (eros) and selfless love (agape); avoidant attachment was associated with game-playing love (ludus); and ambivalent attachment was associated with possessive and dependent love (mania). Bartholomew (1990; Bartholomew and Horowitz, 1991) who made a significant breakthrough in the work on adult attachment developed these ideas further. Using the Bowlbian concept of the 'internal working model', that is, an inner representation of self and others, a four-category classification of attachment was proposed based upon two dimensions, self-view and other-view, on a positive–negative continuum (see Figure 3.2).

MODEL OF SELF

		positive	negative
MODEL OF OTHER	**positive**	**Secure** Comfortable with intimacy and autonomy	**Preoccupied** Ambivalent and overly dependent
	negative	**Dismissing** Denial of attachment	**Fearful** Fear of attachment, avoidant and socially avoidant

Figure 3.2   Bartholomew's four-category classification of adult attachment style (1990)

According to Parkes (1991), the findings of his studies on attachment indicated that the patterns of attachment formed in childhood influence the bonds of adult life and that these, in turn, effect the pattern of bereavement in distinctive and logically comprehensive ways. More contemporary writing suggests that strong empirical evidence does not exist to predict that security in childhood is correlated with adult security (Thompson, 2000). This is a continuing debate which is central to the ongoing research in the field of attachment theory.

However, what is clear is that relationships, their meanings and consequences for self-perception are key to the nature of grief responses.

Predisposing factors – vulnerability and resilience

What can be seen from the theories of lifespan development, and from Attachment Theory are the potential hazards in negotiating the acquisition of psychological and social competence and well-being. Where there is a failure in achieving competence and well-being, the capacity to deal with loss and change (stressful events) is likely to be seriously compromised. While it is very clear that some life experiences are stressful (Holmes and Rahe, (1967) identified a list of 43 life events likely to cause stress), it is equally clear that a stressful event does not produce the same reaction in everyone. Stress is activated by an external event, which demands personal reappraisal and adjustment to changed circumstances. The coping process which follows 'begins with a person and his or her belief, values, goals, and resources for coping, and an event or condition that signals a change or threatened change in the status of a valued goal. The person appraises the personal significance of the event or condition (primary appraisal) and his or her options for coping (secondary appraisal)' (Folkman, 2001: 565). A limited capacity to manage this process will reveal some measure of vulnerability, while personal resourcefulness is likely to activate resilience.

Figure 3.3 shows the interface between psychological aspects, positive and negative, and the absence or presence of social resources – stress factors, which contribute to

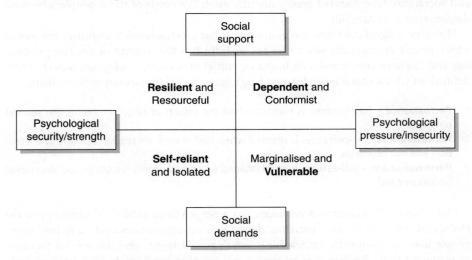

Figure 3.3   The balance of stressful events – psychological and social resources and limitations

potential resilience or vulnerability. A degree of vulnerability (isolation) may result from a situation where social demands exist in spite of psychological strength, or where there is adequate social support but some psychological pressure or insecurity (dependence).

Bowlby and his colleagues have already provided a template for the quality of relationships (attachment styles) which produces vulnerability in the face of loss and change. Parkes reports that there is 'clear evidence of negative parental influences' (2001: 39) in bereaved adults referred for psychiatric treatment. Some were people who lacked trust in themselves, had been anxious/ambivalent children and had conflicting relationships as adults. Others lacked trust in people and were seen to have been avoidant children for whom closeness in relationships was a problem. Parkes sees those people who were deemed to have been disorganised as children, that is, showing some of the characteristics of both anxious and avoidant attachment responses, as the most deeply unhappy, trusting neither themselves nor others.

Seligman (1992) suggests that negative perceptions about self and the world one inhabits can result in 'learned helplessness'. He identifies three factors which characterise explanations people may attribute to bad events, and which produce learned helplessness.

1   **Permanence** – a pessimistic belief that bad events are always going to affect life.
2   **Pervasiveness** – a disappointment, failure or set back in one area of life is used to confirm a belief in helplessness in many situations.
3   **Personalisation** – loss of self-esteem results from blaming oneself when things go wrong.

Vulnerability is generated by perspectives which undermine the capacity to meet life contingencies with equilibrium, and by circumstances which make excess demands upon personal resourcefulness. Understandably, practitioners in many fields of health and social care have focused predominantly upon the needs of those people who have demonstrated vulnerability.

However, a significant new theoretical focus has emerged which identifies the way in which people do meet life adversities successfully. It is the concept of positive psychology and has been concerned with human qualities of resilience. Seligman uses the three definitions which characterise learned helplessness to explore its opposite, resilience.

1   **Permanence** – helplessness is resisted when the effects of negative events are seen as temporary.
2   **Pervasiveness** – helplessness is resisted when bad events are seen as specific to a situation and not universal.
3   **Personalisation** – self-esteem is not damaged when bad events are attributed to external factors not self.

One source of literature on resilience has emerged from studies of survivors of the Holocaust. In spite of such extreme, dehumanising experiences and suffering, many people have survived with remarkable psychological integrity and this has led theorists to recognise that, 'Resilience is an innate self-righting mechanism that assists people in redirecting their lives onto an adaptive path following disadvantageous or stressful circumstances' (Greene, 2002: 4). Three common elements characterise resilience (Machin, 2007b):

1   **Personal resourcefulness** – involving qualities of flexibility, courage and perseverance.
2   **A positive life perspective** – in which there is optimism, hope, a capacity to make sense of experience and motivation in setting personal goals.
3   **Social embeddedness** – in which support is available and there is the personal capacity to access it.

The psychological and social resources available to cope with stressful life events and the perspectives towards those events are highly influential in shaping whether the grieving process will be met with resilience or vulnerability.

Culture

Cultural traditions and perspectives lead to diverse attitudes to life and death experiences, and to the meanings attributed to them; they are socially constructed (Kastenbaum, 1993). Traditions may be based on particular religious beliefs, or none. Attitudes may be shaped by whether life risk and death are familiar and everyday realities, or whether mortality is held at a distance by medical science and affluence.

The management of social change through social ritual provides a bridge between the individual and the culture of which he/she is a member. Death ritual for Van Gennep (1909) serves as a rite of passage and fulfils three objectives: psychologically, ritual gives a framework in which grief can be expressed; philosophically, it affords a base from which to make sense of experience; and socially, it provides for shared experience and the re-integration of the mourner. The decline in traditional ritual in the West, robs many people of meaningful opportunities to give social expression to their grief but it has also resulted in people devising their own forms of ritual to give meaning to their loss.

Culture is the context in which loss is experienced (Vachon and Styllianos, 1988). Family systems and social support networks determine the nature of what has been lost through the death of another but also the nature and extent of available support (Gelcer, 1983; Jordan, 1992). Culture, therefore, is a powerful component in determining the experience of grief.

Summary

In this section factors which determine the likely shape of grief have been explored. Lifespan development and attachment relationships provide the background against which resources and perspectives to deal with difficult life events will produce a propensity for learned helplessness or a capacity for resilience. Culture provides a context in which these factors operate and a further dimension in which experiences of loss needs to be understood.

What is grief like?

Having explored the factors which help to determine likely grief reactions, this section will look at the nature of responses to significant life losses. Bereavement is one of the most profound types of loss and has been central to the literature on grief. However, many of the elements of grief will be evident in other losses. Marris was writing at the time of many of the early theorists but as a sociologist looked not only at bereavement but at the impact of other losses such as slum clearance. He formulated the idea of the 'conservative impulse', a process in which people resist change, and noted that 'The impulse to preserve the thread of continuity is thus a crucial instinct of survival. But its characteristic expression is more anxiously intuitive than conscious or deliberate' (1974: 17). Parkes made a comparative study of bereavement and the loss of a limb (1996) and has also co-edited a book reviewing the impact of other losses (Parkes and Markus, 1998). It is important for practitioners to be able to make the link between theories of bereavement and other life losses.

The symptoms of grief

Grief is a multifaceted response to loss. There are physical, emotional, cognitive, behavioural and social reactions, which have been identified as typifying normal grief (Stroebe et al., 2001).

- Physical – loss of appetite, sleep disturbances, loss of energy, somatic complaints, increase in illness and disease, etc.
- Emotional – despair, anxiety, guilt, anger, depression, sense of loneliness, etc.
- Cognitive – preoccupation with thoughts of the deceased, self-reproach, hopelessness, difficulty in concentration, etc.
- Behavioural – crying, tiredness, agitation, increased alcohol (medication, drug) consumption, etc
- Social – withdrawal, changes in relationships, etc

It is important to note that these symptoms have been identified within Western research and practice. Variations will occur within other cultures.

Processes of grief

Integral to his study of attachment, Bowlby's work contributed significantly to the development of grief theory. An important focus within his work, *Loss: Sadness and*

Depression (1980), related to mourning the death of a close relationship. The earlier observation of children's reactions to their mother's absence was developed into a systematic account of the 'phases of mourning'. Bowlby described the phases as follows:

Phase of numbing that may be punctuated with intense distress.
Phase of yearning and searching for the lost person.
Phase of disorganisation and despair.
Phase of greater or lesser reorganisation

Bowlby (1980) makes it clear that the duration and sequence of these phases is very individual. It is interesting that he used the term 'oscillation' to describe the likely movement backwards and forwards between the phases, anticipating a key concept within one of the contemporary theories of grief, the Dual Process Model (Stroebe and Schut, 1999), which is discussed later. Parkes worked with Bowlby at the Tavistock Institute and his studies in bereavement (1996) provided data in support of the phases of grief – 'Bowlby and I published a descriptive classification of the phases of grief (Bowlby and Parkes, 1970). This classification has given rise to a great deal of controversy and spawned a number of alternative classifications. The sequence was never intended to be more than a rough guide, and it was recognised from the start that people would move back and forth through the sequence rather than following a fixed passage' (Parkes, 2001: 29–30).

A similar systematic account of grief was proposed by Kubler-Ross (1970) in respect of terminally ill patients and arose from listening to patients tell their end-of-life stories. Her stage model, consists of:

Stage one – denial and isolation.
Stage two – anger.
Stage three – bargaining.
Stage four – depression.
Stage five – acceptance.

The work of Kubler-Ross has received a lot of attention, both for the model she developed and also due to the fact that, in uncovering the grief experienced by terminally ill people, she promoted a new openness to talking with the dying. This has powerfully influenced of the study of grief and the therapeutic responses made to it. As with the Bowlby/Parkes model, there has been criticism of the rigidity of the stages conceptualised by Kubler-Ross. The arguments of rebuttal are the same in her case as for Bowlby and Parkes; the stages were never intended as a linear timetable. In spite of the contemporary criticisms of these models, the identification of the symptoms of grief and the articulation of a dynamic process following loss, have provided a significant conceptual background against which theoretical and research developments have taken place.

The foundational theories and models owed their perspective to the psychodynamic school of thinking. The emphasis upon intense, introverted, emotion-focused activity and the notion of recovery was predicated upon undertaking 'grief work' (Freud, 1957). It asserted that the process of detachment frees the bereaved person to rediscover their full psychological resourcefulness. It is a view that has been reinforced by the medical concept of grief (Averill and Nunley 1993) in which grief, like illness, is seen as a process requiring recovery. The traditional concept of 'grief work' as an emotional pathway to 'getting over' a loss was challenged by Wortman and Silver (1989), who pointed to a lack of empirical evidence to support this view.

Further research followed, and cross-cultural evidence emerging from Stroebe's (1992–93) work suggested that inhibited or repressive coping styles did not result in a breakdown in physical or mental health in those societies which practice limited mourning periods. The research of Bonanno et al. reaches the same conclusion that 'avoiding unpleasant emotion might not be such a bad thing' (1995: 975). This has important implications for practitioners who have based their therapeutic approach on traditional assumptions about the need to confront emotion and foster its expression.

In contrast, other traditions continue to focus on the deceased, rituals reinforce an ongoing connectedness to the person who has died (Rosenblatt, 1993), and the process of detachment implicit in grief work does not occur. Practitioners over the years have also observed situations in which persisting focus on the deceased has occurred but where, by any other measure of mental health, the bereaved person would not be deemed to be responding pathologically to their loss (Rosenblatt, 1996). The empirical evidence which challenges the notion of detachment asserts that the 'Continuing Bond' is more than a revisiting of memories but is a fuller integration of the person of the deceased and the meanings held in the relationship with them (Klass, Silverman and Nickman, 1996). This is a perspective which has long been incorporated within many cultures and is characteristic of feminine styles of grieving (Stroebe et al., 1996).

Contemporary thinking, in challenging the dominance of the notion of grief work, seeks to embrace wider elements of grief, and more diverse expressions of it, recognising that cognitive, social and cultural dimensions have a place in the lexicon of reactions to loss. The challenge has resulted in a new and influential contemporary concept of grief, the Dual Process Model, developed by Stroebe and Schut (1999). The model gives equal recognition to the process of cognitive and social adaptation to loss, restoration orientation, as to rumination on painful emotions, loss orientation. Diversion from feelings, which had previously been seen as avoidance and/or pathological, is now embraced within a broader definition of grief and viewed as part of the mechanism of adjustment. Stroebe and Schut see the movement between loss orientation and restoration orientation, in their Dual Process Model, as one of oscillation; a balancing of psychological and social realities by grieving people (see Figure 3.4).

A comparable theoretical formulation can be seen in the work of Horowitz et al. (1979) who saw painful life events impacting upon the individual either through intrusive thought and affect (loss orientated) or by avoidant responses (restoration orientated). Similarly, Martin and Doka (2000) describe two types of reaction to loss: that of intuitive grievers whose focus is primarily on painful feelings (loss orientated), and that of instrumental grievers who channel energy into activity (restoration orientated). These characteristics form a spectrum of grief reactions with a blended variation – 'reflecting the greater symmetry between the cognitive and affective responses of the individual' (Martin and Doka, 2000: 32), which is comparable to the notion of oscillation.

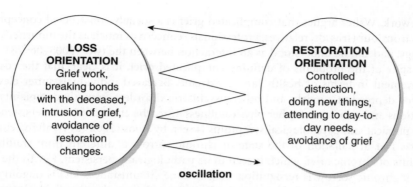

Figure 3.4   The Dual Process Model of grief (Stroebe and Schut, 1999)

A significant conceptual shift has taken place, in which the theoretical dominance of grief work formulated within the psychodynamic tradition, has given way to understanding grief from the position of new empirical and cross-cultural evidence. This new perspective provides a way of recognising individual responses to loss as part of a spectrum of styles rather than a polarity between healthy and unhealthy, normal and abnormal.

Complicated grief

The classification of complicated/pathological grief was linked, in the psychodynamic tradition, to the grieving manifestations of insecure attachment. Evidence of excessive intensity or duration of grief, or too little intensity or duration in loss response, were linked to anxious attachment or avoidant attachment styles, respectively. Contemporary research is revising the previous categorisation of absent or delayed grief as pathological, seeing them instead as variable styles of coping which for many people is an effective way of adjusting to loss (Bonanno et al., 1995). As greater recognition is given to the complex phenomenon of interconnecting elements – affect, cognition, coping, etc., as part of normal grief, definitions of problematic/complicated grief have become elusive. The complexity of disentangling and defining complicated grief has been evident in its absence from any official diagnostic manuals or as a defined clinical syndrome. However, debate continues about whether complicated grief is a psychiatric disorder and whether it warrants classification as a separate condition from traumatic grief (Prigerson and Jacobs, 2001; Stroebe and Schut, 2005–06). The symptoms often used to describe pathological grief overlap with other conditions such as depression, anxiety and Post Traumatic Stress Disorder. Middleton et al. concluded that 'In many instances it may be more valid to view grief as a risk factor for such disorders than to view such disorders as manifestations of pathological grief' (Middleton et al., 1993: 59).

Stroebe et al. (2001) suggest that pathological/complicated grief should be culturally defined. This allows for diversity and deviation to be seen as relative rather than absolute, and definitions of complicated grief conceptualised within a culture-specific framework. Walter argues that complicated grief is a socially constructed concept and arises from 'our (friends, relatives, professionals) concern as much as the mourner's psychology, and can be understood as an interaction between the two' (2005–06: 78)

In spite of the problems of defining complicated grief, it is clear 'that the costs of bereavement in terms of health can be extreme. Bereaved individuals suffer elevated risks of depression, anxiety and other psychiatric disorders, somatic complaints and infections and a variety of other physical illness' (Stroebe et al., 2001: 8). Persistence of these physical and psychological symptoms is seen by Roos (2002) as typifying chronic sorrow. Her articulation of the state of chronic sorrow is different from traditional accounts of chronic grief, which is seen to be pathologically persistent. Key to the concept of chronic sorrow is recognition that in some circumstances loss is ongoing and there is no prospect of resolution or healing. Roos defines these as living losses, for example, bringing up a child with a severe disability, giving up a child for adoption, having a chronic and deteriorating illness, a person presumed dead but where there is no body, a missing person, living with abuse, etc. It is clear from these examples, that many of the losses described in Chapter 2 are likely to incur chronic sorrow and this is especially the case for categories of disenfranchised grief. A significant characteristic of chronic sorrow is the role of fantasy; 'of what could have been or what should have been. Activation of the fantasy intensifies painful emotions, as the disparity between the fantasy and current living reality can be cruel and wounding' (Roos, 2002: 27). Anger may be an especially dominant reaction while the 'revision of the assumptive world' (Parkes, 1993) is a task likely to produce continuing anguish and disappointment.

The increased incidence of morbidity and mortality in grieving people suggests that more important than defining pathological or abnormal grief is the identification of those factors which increase risk of a poor outcome. Two key factors contribute to potential risk. Firstly, the predisposing vulnerability/resourcefulness of the grieving person, and, secondly, the nature of the external circumstances, which have resulted in the loss. The first of these factors is created by life events and personality, which have developed either to give resilience and effective coping mechanisms in the face of experience of loss, or not. The second dimension of risk is created by the nature of the actual bereavement or loss experience (Sanders, 1993). When the two elements are juxtaposed the factors of stress (Folkman, 2001; Lazarus and Folkman, 1984) will test the strength/weakness of the person's resource base.

Sanders (1993) has identified a number of factors which she sees as contributing to risk:

- **Sudden unexpected deaths**, including suicide, murder, catastrophic circumstances and stigmatised deaths, such as AIDS etc. Other losses might include sudden onset of illness, separation, etc.
- **Ambivalence and dependency** in a relationship where anger or self-reproach contribute to unfinished business and where a dependent partner is left, there is an increased likelihood of anxiety and a general inability to cope, for example, in bereavement, divorce, etc.
- **Parental bereavement,** the devastation of losing a child produces varied grief reactions in mothers and fathers which may make mutual support problematic.
- **Health before bereavement/loss** – for example, mental or physical health problems that pre-date a loss or bereavement are likely to add to the stress of managing grief.

- **Concurrent crises** which compound the stress produced by bereavement may arise from multiple bereavement, or other losses such as unemployment, divorce, financial problems, health problems, etc.
- **Perceived lack of social support**, as well as actual inadequate social support, contribute to loneliness and a reduced capacity to adapt to the loss.
- **Age and gender** – while the sudden death of a husband produced a greater negative effect in younger women, being older resulted in an initial lower intensity of grief but in the longer term was a further debilitating factor in ageing. The gender differences in reaction to spousal bereavement point to greater evident distress in widows but men may suffer from a greater inability to access the social support that they need, leading to isolation.
- **Reduced material resources** compound the vulnerability arising from loss and may lead to poor adjustment and increased health problems.

The study of risk factors has been taken forward by an appraisal of current research in this area (Stroebe and Schut, 2001) and by a proposition that an integrative risk-factor framework should be developed rather than specific factors considered in isolation (Stroebe et al., 2006). Stroebe et al. argue that such a framework 'builds on a generic cognitive stress, appraisal and coping model (Lazarus and Folkman, 1984) and a compatible bereavement-specific stress model, namely the Dual Process Model of coping (Stroebe and Schut, 1999)' (Stroebe et al., 2006: 2443). Within the framework, five key components constitute a pathway through grief:

A: the nature of the stressor – for example, loss stresses such as predictability or unexpectedness of a loss, the quality of lost relationship etc. together with secondary restoration stresses such as, adjustment to changes in everyday life.

B: interpersonal resources – the demands and resources at a social and cultural level.

C: intrapersonal resources – the quality of attachment, personality, relative optimism/pessimism, etc.

D: appraisal and coping processes – coping is understood as 'constantly changing cognitive and behavioural efforts to manage specific external and/or internal demands that are appraised as taxing or exceeding the resources of the person' (Lazarus and Folkman, 1984: 14). 'Oscillation is considered a fundamental regulatory process of adaptation (too exclusive a focus on either loss- or restoration-oriented stressors will not lead to healthy adaptation to loss)' (Stroebe et al., 2006: 2447).

E: outcomes – all the preceding factors (A–D) impact upon outcome.

This framework provides the basis for future research and has links to the concepts and methods of assessment proposed in this publication (see Chapter 6).

Summary

In this section, evolving theories of grief and contemporary thinking about loss and bereavement have been considered. The movement to recognise diversity in response to loss has emerged from wider culturally based definitions of grief. Consequently, previous accounts of loss response, which were regarded as pathological, have been embraced within a wider concept of normality. Nevertheless, complications in grief do occur but they need to be understood in terms of complex interconnecting personal, social and coping risk factors. Current theorists (Stroebe et al., 2006) are arguing for an integrated approach to appraising risk in which the mediating factors are taken into account alongside the loss or bereavement, which has prompted the stress. This represents an area for more research and one in which practitioners may have a role as they explore the most effective ways of assessing heightened vulnerability in grieving people and identifying those most in need of support.

Managing grief – a personal journey

Having looked at the predisposing factors which influence how grief is experienced, and at the characteristics of grief itself, it is important to look at the personal journey through grief. For practitioners, 'What needs to be examined … is the content of the cognitive activity in coping with loss. What positive and negative meanings, reappraisals, and attributions underlie the ability to regulate grieving and make progress through ones grief?' (Streobe and Schut, 1999: 220). This lies at the heart of adjustment, coping and meaning-making.

The tasks of adjustment

In the influential book, *Grief Counseling and Grief Therapy*, Worden (2003) identified the tasks necessary for grieving people to complete, whether or not therapeutic help is offered. It implies that people are actively engaging with the grieving process rather than passively submitting to it. The tasks have evident links with other theoretical models of grief, particularly the Dual Process Model (Stroebe and Schut, 1999), and the concept of Continuing Bonds (Klass, Silverman and Nickman, 1996). Figure 3.5 demonstrates the points of connectedness between these theories, which allows the mourning tasks to be seen in their dynamic form rather than as a linear process.

The four tasks of mourning (Worden 2003) describe the grief journey:

1   The sense of disbelief which accompanies the initial impact of loss has to be overcome if the grieving person is to adjust to the consequences of the loss. In some circumstances it may be difficult to accept the reality of the loss. In the case of the absence of a dead body, grief may be suspended for years in the hope that the person may return. Difficulty in accepting the reality of a loss is especially problematic in non-bereavement losses such as divorce, where perhaps for the deserted partner there may be unrealistic hopes of reconciliation. Worden asserts that, 'You cannot handle the emotional impact of a loss until you first come to terms with the fact that the loss has happened' (2003: 27). Stroebe and Schut (2001) suggest that the task needs to include acceptance of the changed world after a loss as well as the loss itself. Attig (1996) sees this as an active process of 'relearning the world' in which personal reference points have been changed by the loss of someone or something of significance.

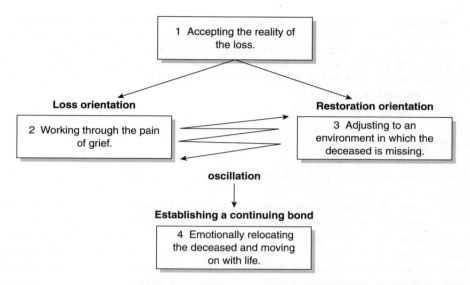

Figure 3.5   Integrating the theories of the tasks of mourning (Worden, 2003) with the concepts of grief in the Dual Process Model of grief (Stroebe and Schut, 1999) and the notion of Continuing Bonds (Klass, Silverman and Nickman, 1996)

2   When the anaesthetic qualities of numbness and disbelief begin to subside, the full force of grief will be felt in the despair, guilt and anger, etc., which follow. Working through the pain of grief is a process, which echoes the imperative of grief work. For many people the powerfulness of their emotions in an otherwise powerless situation is a distressing element of grief, which has to be processed. It is a loss-orientated focus (Stroebe and Schut, 1999). Anger and guilt may have to be articulated in order for them to be dissipated. However, as discussed earlier, the need to focus on distress, in order to satisfactorily manage grief, is contended by Bonanno (2001). In some circumstances very painful experiences which are too difficult to process, for example, surviving the Holocaust, some forms of abuse, etc., can be negotiated and managed by suspending emotional engagement.

3   Adjusting to an environment in which the deceased (or lost person or object) is missing is a third task and equates with restoration orientation in the Dual Process Model of grief (Stroebe and Schut, 1999). This task demands attention to the practical aspects of day-to-day living in which new skills may have to be acquired, and new roles, directions and goals established. These elements of adjustment are not merely compensations for what or who has been lost but are revisions in the sense of self following a major loss. The feeling of personal disorientation may be considerable when a significant person has died or deserted a relationship, or a person is faced with a life-changing disability. This task, although focused upon practical issues, calls for considerable emotional as well as personal adjustment and is indicative of the need to move between loss and restoration orientation.

4   With the emergence of a new emphasis in adjustment to loss, based on the concept of Continuing Bonds, the task of emotionally relocating the deceased (or lost person, object, etc.) as part of the process of moving on with life, is seen differently from that of leaving the deceased behind. It is about finding a new location within the thoughts, memory and

meaning of the grieving person, which serve to integrate the past with the present in a way that is emotionally and cognitively satisfying to them. It is also a task in which new roles, identities and relationships have to be fully reintegrated into life. Essentially, it is not a return to how life was before the bereavement, as changes brought about by the loss cannot be reversed, but it is 'negotiating a meaningful life without the deceased' (Wortman and Silver, 2001: 421).

Coping

The way in which people undertake these tasks is very individual. It will relate to their acquired coping styles, and their attitudes to difficult life events, whether bereavement or some other major life loss. According to Lazarus and Folkman (1984) and Folkman (2001), these pre-existing coping mechanisms and perspectives will become operational in the face of stress and be used to appraise the nature of the threat or challenge. If the threat is perceived as harmful, problem focused (restoration orientation) and emotion focused (loss orientation), coping strategies will be variably used to manage the shifting reality and consequences of the stress/loss (Stroebe et al., 2006).

Evidence has emerged of the role that positive emotion plays in sustaining the coping process during the period of adjustment to loss and change, and of it leading to a positive outcome (Bonanno, 2001; Folkman, 2001). Positive emotions are seen to afford some relief and diversion from the distress of dealing with an ongoing stressful situation. Respite comes with perceiving, even in everyday events, something positive. Positive affect/emotion results in a capacity to redefine and focus on positive meaning within life-changing and stressful events. Folkman found that when people adopted a problem-focused coping approach, such as engagement with practical caregiving, it gave a greater sense of control in circumstances where a person might otherwise feel out of control. The research of Bonanno and Keltner (1997) also concluded that minimising negative emotion facilitates clearer problem-focused coping, which more readily invites the support of other people. The significance of this link between a positive perspective and a positive outcome will be picked up in the next chapter looking at therapeutic engagement with loss and bereavement.

Making sense of experience

For grieving people, making sense of experience is coping with the emotional, physical, social, spiritual and intellectual consequences of loss by transforming the chaos into a newly meaningful order. In some societies, the collective meaning derived from religion or philosophy provides the individual with personal meaning, which is shared through ritual and a supportive sense of community. Where society has become fractured into diverse belief systems the journey of grief is more isolated, and the struggle for meaning has to be undertaken individually. What is clear is that significant life losses evoke spiritual awareness and yearning for meanings which transcend everyday explanations (Martin and

Doka, 2000). In searching for these explanations religion is concerned with particular beliefs about the nature of life, the meaning of suffering, humans in relation to god(s), and the practices which accompany these doctrines. These beliefs may provide comforting continuity with the past and scriptural guidance provides answers to fundamental questions of life and death. Conversely, a loss experience may challenge previously held beliefs and create a crisis in faith. Unlike religion, spiritually is not centred upon systematised dogmas or practices but is focused on the essence of life and its meaning, which could be regarded as seeking the apex of self-actualisation (Maslow, 1987).

The personal journey demands a revision of the inner representation of those views of life which had previously provided a predictable notion of the world and one's place in it, but which no longer fit the changed circumstances brought about by loss. The framework for understanding these concepts of acquired personal meaning, has been variably described by Bowlby (1980), as an 'internal working model', by Parkes (1996) as the 'assumptive world' and by Marris (1974) as the 'structures of meaning'. They describe, in slightly different ways, the cognitive mechanisms which are operationalised in response to loss. Martin and Doka suggest that 'the reconstruction of meaning in the face of loss may become one of the most critical aspects of the grieving experience. ... Loss can create an intense spiritual crisis that challenges all of an individual's core beliefs, necessitating re-evaluation, if not a reformation' (2000: 19). Central to the process of re-evaluation is the recovery of a sense of coherence, which may become visible through the changing narrative account of loss (Dallos, 2006). Antonovsky (1988) suggests that a sense of coherence develops across the lifespan, and where it exists there is a capacity to recover balance in the face of disturbing experience. He identifies three elements which make up coherence:

1 **Comprehensibility** – where cognitive sense is made of experience by arriving at a perspective which has order, consistency, structure and clarity.
2 **Manageability** – where both personal resources and social support are adequate for the demands being made within a (loss) situation.
3 **Meaningfulness** – where cognitive and emotional processes are used to discover meaning in an experience (of loss).

Ways of achieving meaningfulness are developed in Meaning Reconstruction Theory (Neimeyer and Anderson, 2002); a complex and demanding process which lies at the heart of the grieving agenda. This theory argues that it is necessary to conserve as much as possible of the meaningful life view, from before the loss. Alongside this, it is necessary to construct new meanings and a new sense of self (revise the internal working models, assumptive world and structures of meaning) which fit more appropriately with the changes that have taken place. Reconciling old and new meaning is itself a task of reconstruction. Joseph and Linley see this as 'adversarial growth' (2005: 125) in which growth can occur when revised assumptions, which come from the tension between old perspectives and new circumstances, result in the world and self being seen in a positive way – 'finding a silver lining of existential benefit in the dark cloud of bereavement' (Neimeyer and Anderson, 2002: 61). A revised identity comes gradually as latent resources and experiments with new roles and ways of being take shape.

Summary

The challenge to adjust, cope and find meaning in loss is the often lonely journey demanded of grieving individuals. These may be tasks which are undertaken with therapeutic support. Chapter 4 explores meaning-centred psychotherapy (Frankl, 1959) and the concepts of positive psychology, which has emphasised the growthful potential for resilience. This theme will also be the focus of Chapter 8.

Conclusion

In this chapter, theory has been used to help understand how human development and variable experiences across the life course determine responses to loss. Psychodynamic theory has been foundational in the study of loss, separation and bereavement and within that tradition Attachment Theory has continued to make a central contribution to what is known about human love and loss (Parkes, 2006). Contemporary ideas have challenged the dominant focus on the psychological component of grief work and have broadened the perspectives on loss to include an appreciation of the diversity of cognitive, social and cultural variations. Theory also addresses the individual processes of managing grief. The tasks of mourning and stress theory examine frameworks for travelling the journey of loss. The personal process of managing grief is one of coping, adjusting and meaning-making. All of these elements are visible in the stories people tell of their grief and loss. How practitioners can listen to and engage with those stories will be explored in the following chapters.

4

Establishing Therapeutic Bearings

This chapter explores therapeutic ways of working with grieving people. It will also consider the role of practitioners whose professional activities bring them into contact with grieving people but whose work does not carry a psychotherapeutic function, for example, doctors, nurses and generalist social workers, etc.

The last chapter addressed in detail the significance of Attachment Theory in defining the link between relationships and the development of security in the formative years, and in adult bonds. Recognising the power of secure relationships to act as a catalyst for positive experience and the successful management of change, the primary consideration for practitioners is to replicate that security in the context of their care-giving.

The humanistic approach to counselling, developed by Rogers (1961, 1980), suggests the principles on which such security might be established. In this facilitative therapeutic climate, personal stories of loss can be told and the impact of grief revealed in a shared client–counsellor journey. Attention to stories and narrative has developed as a particular focus for engaging with the concerns brought to counselling (McLeod, 1997). The narrative perspective will be used in this chapter to provide a structure for listening to accounts of loss and grief. A range of therapeutic approaches will be integrated within the narrative structure, and the concept of positive therapy will also be used to examine the ways in which resilience can be nurtured. Writing, music and art will be examined as techniques to facilitate clients in the telling of their story. These issues are examined through the following four themes:

1   The therapeutic starting point –

- Using Attachment Theory to understand the nature of a secure therapeutic base.
- A person-centred way of being with the client.
- A practical example – ways to provide a secure base when giving 'bad news' or undertaking discussions about life-changing events/situations.

2   The therapeutic process –

- The narrative structure of the story of loss.
- Working with the narrative process.

3 Integrating other therapeutic perspectives within the narrative structure –

- Personal history.
- Relationships and communications.
- Thinking/acting/believing.
- Meaning-making.
- Some ways of working for non-therapists.

4 Tools to aid storytelling –

- Writing.
- Music.
- Art.

The therapeutic starting point

Using Attachment Theory to understand the nature of a secure therapeutic base

In *A Secure Base: Clinical Applications of Attachment Theory* (1988), Bowlby sees the natural human tendency as being directed towards healing. The therapist is called upon not to be an expert, but to provide the conditions in which self-healing can take place. A secure base provides safety and the opportunity for supportive appraisal of what is troubling to the client. The client is enabled to explore the painful realities and subjective experiences of loss and grief, in a way that is most conducive to strengthening and growth (Holmes, 1993). Based on Attachment Theory there are three elements which make up the secure base in therapy:

1 Attunement – a quality of engagement that nurtures a positive sense of self in the client.
2 Autobiographical competence – the therapist engages with the client and his/her story to achieve a more coherent narrative.
3 Affective processing – the ventilation and exploration of feelings associated with loss.

A person-centred way of being with the client

The characteristics of a secure base, associated with Attachment Theory, fit well with the humanistic approach of Rogers (1961, 1980). Both of these theories, one emanating from the psychodyanmic tradition and the other from a contemporary humanistic one, recognise how the self-view is shaped in the context of relationships. The person, in the person-centred approach to therapy, is seeking self-actualisation (attainment of full human potential) and to be valued by other people. Rogers proposes the core conditions necessary for facilitating this process:

- Unconditional positive regard
- Empathy
- Congruence.

The first of these, unconditional positive regard, is a description of the counsellor's attitude towards the client. It is an attitude which is valuing of human beings in general and is demonstrated within particular therapeutic relationships by a consistent acceptance and warmth towards the client. This quality will not deviate even when the behaviour and perspectives of the client are inappropriate, aggressive, manipulative or self-defeating. Clearly, some of these behaviours and responses will be challenging to the practitioner who has constantly to be able to distinguish between unacceptable actions and the innate worth of the client. The ground for safety and growth can be considerable when a damaged and hurting client can feel the consistency of this acceptance.

Empathy is a process in which the counsellor suspends his/her own way of perceiving reality in order to engage, at a deep level, with the client's perceptions and way of experiencing the world (Mearns and Thorne, 1988). In entering the client's frame of reference, the counsellor's insight into his/her emotional and cognitive experience can begin to grow. Empathy is more than the capacity to understand the client's perspectives but is the ability to communicate that deep level of understanding in the reflections made to the client. Counsellors seek to acquire skills in making empathic responses but 'the responses themselves are not empathy, but they are the products of the shared journey which is empathy' (Mearns and Thorne, 1988: 40). Empathy combined with unconditional positive regard is a way of being with the client and facilitating his/her journey to the discovery of fuller potential.

The third of Rogers' core conditions is congruence, which comes from the counsellor possessing a high level of self-awareness, and a capacity to be transparent in their relationship with the client. It is a state of genuineness, in which what the counsellor says and does accurately reflects his/her feelings and thoughts. This capacity for authenticity is often intuitively recognised by clients, especially children, who will readily realise when a counsellor/therapist or carer is incongruent or not genuine. Revealing the inner feelings and awareness of the counsellor to the client is not an indiscriminate sharing of self, but is offered in response to the client's experience, is relevant to the concerns of the client and is proffered when the counsellor's feelings are persistent and striking (Mearns and Thorne, 1988).

An understanding of the qualities which contribute to secure attachment, and those defined as core therapeutic conditions, provide a central base from which to offer support to people who are dealing with loss and bereavement. Whatever the role of the practitioner, counsellor, social worker, nurse, etc., these characteristic attitudes towards people and their situations, and the way of being with them will nurture potentially powerful opportunities for promotion of well-being. There are also practical implications in health and social care settings. The reality of working with loss and bereavement often means that the practitioner is not helping a person retrospectively to process a loss but is travelling the journey of loss with them. That journey may include breaking bad news or planning action following bad news, such as a life-threatening diagnosis being given, a child being taken into care, etc. How those events are handled will contribute to whether the long-term outcome, for the client or patient, is a straightforward or problematic one.

A practical example – ways to provide a secure base when giving bad news or undertaking discussions about life-changing events/situations

A six-step protocol devised by Buckman (1992) addresses the ways in which a secure base can be created in imparting bad news and can be usefully employed in other situations where life-changing events are being discussed.

- **Getting started**: Breaking bad news should not be seen as an incidental part of a wider working brief but as a task demanding particular personal sensitivity and practice skill. The qualities needed to provide a 'secure base' are fundamental to engagement with people who are facing life-changing events. Personal and communication skills take time to acquire and should be firmly on the agenda of health and social care workers whose clients/patients are in situations likely to result in profound loss and change. Generating a sense of 'safety' is a prerequisite for all other considerations about the practicalities of breaking bad news. It is important to get the physical context right in terms of privacy and reasonable physical comfort. Normal courtesies should be extended to the client(s) and a check made on the state of the person receiving the news, such as distressed, hostile, distracted, etc. The information giving (sharing) should be undertaken in an unhurried manner.
- **Finding out what the client/patient already knows**: What does the client/patient already know or deduce from events that have already taken place? Adjust the communication to fit the person's readiness to hear and to their own style of communication: their vocabulary, articulacy, etc.
- **Finding out how much the client/patient wants to know**: Understanding that people may not always be able to assimilate bad news on a single occasion and that a sense of denial may temporarily protect them, especially where the circumstances of the loss are traumatic. Where preparation is possible, imparting bad news may be an extended process. Where it is not, recognition of how much detail can be taken in by the client/patient is all part of the need for sensitivity in the practitioner.
- **Sharing the information**: It is important to give information simply and in small chunks, checking frequently that the client/patient understands what they have been told. Clarification and repeating information help to reinforce what it may be difficult for the person to hear. Allowing for questions helps the client to integrate the new information into their concerns, for working out the implications of the bad news in their life situation.
- **Responding to the client/patient feelings**: Identifying and acknowledging the client/patient's reaction will contribute to a positive process of imparting bad news. Initial feelings may include shock, fear, anxiety, anger, relief, etc.
- **Planning and follow-through**: By looking at what is fixed and what can be changed, an understanding of the implications of the bad news can be addressed. Strategies for coping and sources of support need to be identified.

This protocol, although moving ahead into elements of action, provides an example of how to ensure a sensitive starting point when working with and offering support to people in situations of loss and grief.

The therapeutic process

The narrative structure of the story of loss

'If you want to know me, then you must know my story, for my story defines who I am. If I want to know *myself*, to gain insight into the meanings of my own life, then I, too, must come to know my own story' (McAdams, 1997: 11). McAdams suggests that narrative structures begin in childhood and in the progression to adulthood accumulate increased sophistication, starting from a basic optimism or pessimism in tone which is linked to security of attachment, and moving to increasingly complex themes, character, ideologies and narrative evaluation. The developments of these narrative structures are culturally embedded and form a bridge between the individual and his/her cultural context (White and Epston, 1990). The evidence for this may be much more obvious in societies where there is an oral tradition and people grow up with shared stories, and clear social space is made for the telling of those stories. However, even with the diversity of multicultural Western experience, there is a familiarity with the enduring fairy stories of childhood, the classical legends of Greece and Rome and the stories contained within religious tradition. They all seek in one way or another to convey a 'truth' or 'moral' or 'meaning', which is integrated to provide a conscious sense of coherence. 'Story represents the basic means by which people organise and communicate the meaning of events and experiences' (McLeod, 1997: x). It is the object of therapy to rediscover a coherence which has been lost within a disruptive and disturbing story of loss and change: 'negative experiences in themselves do not invariably lead to problems. Being able to form a coherent story about negative events can contribute to the possibility of being able to transcend them' (Dallos, 2006: 115).

Angus and Hardke (1994) have described the narrative processes as consisting of three elements, the external narrative, the internal narrative and the reflexive narrative.

1 External narrative

The external narrative is often the starting point of a story – what happened, when and how. In therapy, the external narrative provides an account of the events and circumstances which define the experience brought by the client. Worden (2003) saw the exploration of the facts of a loss as an initial task of mourning: through telling their story of bereavement, divorce, illness, etc., a person becomes more able to accept and 'actualise' it. Talking about all the circumstances surrounding death, for example, helps to counter the sense of unreality ('may be this awful thing hasn't happened'), which initially cannot be fully emotionally and mentally absorbed. The external narrative within the story begins to activate the cognitive and emotional processing of the loss. The manner in which the story is told will provide some preliminary indication of how grief is being experienced. A confused and convoluted story may indicate that the client is feeling overwhelmed by events. A minimal account of loss may suggest that the client is not fully engaged with the loss experience and wishes to stay within controlled boundaries. A coherent story, which provides a clear and comprehensible account of loss, is indicative of resilience and is interpreted in the Adult Attachment Interview (Main, 1991) as evidence of a secure attachment style.

2 Internal narrative

The internal narrative is concerned with the impact of events upon the teller. The subjective account of experience reveals the emotional and cognitive reactions to what has been lost. The emotional component has traditionally been the central ground of much grief counselling – 'grief work'. Attention to feelings has been regarded as paramount, and without it the grieving person was thought to be rendered vulnerable through denial or other defence mechanisms which prevent the grief from being processed. Worden (2003) saw this as a task in which the pain of grief needs to be worked through and for the practitioner attention is given to facilitating the identification and expression of feelings. Counselling has countered a prevailing Western tendency to undervalue feelings, by considering the interior processes as crucial to a satisfactory outcome for grief. However, in common with some of the newer perspectives described in the last chapter (Bonanno et al., 1995), Angus and Hardke found in their research (1994) that where there had been a higher percentage of attention paid to the internal narrative there was a poor therapeutic outcome, whereas a good outcome was associated with a broader therapeutic focus.

In listening to personal accounts of grief, counsellors begin to understand something of the attitudes and life perspectives which shape the impact of a bereavement or loss experience. Grief may be seen as engulfing and the account of loss lack coherence, while the narrator may assume the role of victim. This clearly demonstrates a highly distressed state and the story may include words like 'overwhelmed' or 'despairing', and metaphors be used which convey a similar overpowering state, such as 'being in a black hole', 'at the end of my tether', etc. In contrast, clients who value stoicism may embellish their story very little with accounts of their own grief, but rather focus on the need to be brave. Where a client can give a balanced account of their loss, showing a capacity to face the emotional implications of grief but equally able to be in touch with their own resources, the counsellor/therapist will see evidence of resilience. In Chapters 5 and 6 a new model and tool for exploring these contrasting responses will be introduced.

3 Reflexive narrative

The reflexive narrative process is concerned with gaining a new perspective on a loss event and making sense of experience (Angus and Hardke, 1994). This element is central to the goal of therapy and involves, 'the reflexive analysis of the related experiences and circumstances of "what happened" such that a new understanding or story is formed which either supports or challenges the implicit beliefs about self and others that underscore the dominant narrative' (Angus and Hardke, 1994: 192). The client brings together the external and internal narrative themes and in the context of therapy explores and reconstructs a narrative, which attempts to make sense of experience and bring new meaning to the encounter with loss. Worden's tasks of mourning all carry with them a reflexive element, whether that is consciously processing feelings or making social adjustments to change. However, the final task – 'emotionally relocating the deceased and moving on with life' – suggests that adaptation to the consequence of loss has been achieved and that overall sense has been made of the experience of loss. This is a process of 're-learning the world' (Attig, 1996) and a journey towards a new self. The management of the changed reality of the world is at the heart of bereavement stories (Rosenblatt, 1996).

Table 4.1 Linking the Dual Process Model of grief and the tasks of mourning with the narrative process

Dual Process Model of grief (Stroebe and Schut, 1999)	Tasks of mourning (Worden, 2003)	Narrative process (Angus and Hardke, 1994)
Loss event	1 To accept the reality of the loss	External narrative – the story of 'what happened' helps confirm the reality the of loss
Loss orientation – focus on the painful emotions of loss	2 To work through the pain of grief	Internal narrative – telling the story of the impact of the loss helps address the emotional consequences of it
Restoration orientation – focus on the social consequences of loss and the process of day-to-day living	3 To adjust to an environment in which the deceased (lost person, object) is missing	Reflexive narrative – the story is a way of integrating the loss into changed life circumstances and making sense of the loss experience
Oscillation – capacity to move between feeling, thinking and doing	4 Emotionally relocating the deceased (lost person, object) and moving on with life	

Table 4.1 shows how grief and the tasks of mourning can be combined with the narrative process to provide an integrated theoretical approach to working with grief. As was made clear in earlier chapters, when theoretical models were described, apparent simplicity and linear sequence should not be interpreted in a rigid way but seen as the strands which make up the much more complex fabric of experience. The narrative process is complex, but recognising the components within it can facilitate a clearer understanding of how the telling of the story might be facilitated and how therapeutic advantage be made of natural reflexive mechanisms.

Table 4.2   The counsellor/therapist has a task which matches that of the client

The narrative – client tasks	The narrative – counsellor tasks
Telling	Construction
Deconstructing	Deconstruction
Adopting	Reconstruction
Proclaiming	Rehearsal

Working with the narrative process – facilitating adjustment and making sense of experience

McLeod (1997) identifies a four-stage therapeutic process with complementary tasks for the client and the counsellor (see Table 4.2)

Working with the narrative process is a joint enterprise (Dallos, 2006). The client begins by **telling** their story, and the counsellor/therapist needs to be sensitive and receptive to the story process and facilitate its **construction**. The story will bring together the external, internal and reflexive narrative, often in a mixed or cyclical way. For example, Anna tells her story – 'My father died last year' [external narrative]. 'It shouldn't have happened to such a good man' [reflexive narrative]. 'I am trying to clear out his house' [external narrative]. 'I'm finding it very hard to cope – I can't stop crying' [internal narrative]. In the telling process the practitioner assists in the construction of the narrative by encouraging the development of the story:

> Tell me about (your loss) [external narrative].
> Tell me what you are feeling and thinking about (your loss) [internal narrative].
> What does this experience of loss mean to you? [reflexive narrative].

As the initial story is told the elements which are troubling or unsatisfactory will emerge, for example, Anna had said 'I'm finding it hard to cope'. The evidence is in her tears and the fact that she can't understand why this should have happened to such a good man. As the discomfort with the presenting story is confronted, perhaps because of its lack of congruence and consistency, the client will show a readiness to consider constructing a new and more satisfactory narrative. Clients will vary in the timing and indications of willingness to begin processing the narrative they have brought and it is the therapist's task to be able to recognise the client's capacity to engage in change (Greenberg, Rice and Elliot, 1993). In the example of the bereaved daughter used earlier, it is perhaps her account of 'trying to clear out his house' which metaphorically mirrored her readiness to address the 'sorting out' of her loss experience. The task for the client, with the help of the counsellor/therapist, is a process of **deconstruction**, in which the unsatisfactory elements of the story can be identified.

Adopting and reconstruction are the client and therapist's respective quests to find a different version of the story which can be 'lived by and live with' (Mcleod, 1997: 86). Weiss (1988) suggests that there are three adaptive tasks involved in the severing process of loss: cognitive acceptance, emotional acceptance and identity change. Collectively these adjustments demand attainment of another goal, that of making sense of what has happened to change the previously predictable order of the world. The narrative process can be used to facilitate this journey. The chaos and disturbance of loss has to be transformed into order and a sense of comprehensibility, manageability, meaningfulness achieved (Antonovsky, 1988). Attitudinal reconstruction at the micro level might involve inviting the client to think of other ways of telling their story. For example, in the process of reconstruction for Anna – 'It shouldn't have happened to such a good man' might be changed to, 'How fortunate I've been to have such a good man for a father for so many years of my life'. Or the therapist might offer an alternative version for the client to think about. Even in the limited example of the bereaved daughter, it is possible to see how painful feelings of grief (crying) result in a cognitive perspective ('I'm finding it hard to cope'), and combine with a denial of the realities of mortality ('It shouldn't have happened to such a good man'). They provide multiple dimensions – emotional, cognitive, existential – within which to explore alternative narratives. The methods of working in these dimensions will make use of a range of approaches and tools. These will be considered later in the chapter.

Arriving at what seems like a satisfactory alternative narrative can be explored and **rehearsed** within a therapeutic session, as a prelude to sharing (**proclaiming**) the revised version of events and experiences in the wider social context of the client's world, for example, Anna – 'My father died last year' [external narrative]. 'How fortunate I've been to have such a good man for a father for so many years of my life' [reflexive narrative]. 'I've been clearing out his house' [external narrative]. 'It's a painful task but one that brings me close to him' [internal narrative]. 'It's a job I must do and I realise that I have the strength to do it' [reflexive narrative].

Practitioners in health and social care, as well as those with a direct counselling role, will hear stories of loss from their patients and clients. The opportunities for working at any depth with these stories may be limited by the scope and remit of being a nurse, social worker, etc. (although a specialist palliative social worker may be an exception). However, that caring role will be enhanced where stories of loss, recounted in fear and anxiety, can be heard and accepted with the sensitivity which facilitates the courageous development of new perspectives.

Integrating other therapeutic perspectives within the narrative structure

The approach to working with grief has so far suggested a structure within which the components of loss experience can be heard through the stories people tell. In this section a range of therapeutic approaches will be considered as ways of encouraging the telling of the story, as ways of understanding it and as methods of responding to it.

Personal history

Is often the starting point for therapeutic engagement. It may constitute background to the story, which the client has to tell, or it may be the therapist who prompts accounts of early life experience in order to give context to current grief. Psychodynamic theory is concerned with the relationship between childhood experience and the development of emotional problems. From this perspective, the theory most pertinent to working with grief is Attachment Theory. As seen in the previous chapter, the links between early relationships and the security/insecurity generated by them is crucial to the way in which separation and loss will be experienced (Bowlby, 1980; Parkes, 2006). The view of self and others, acquired through attachment experience, will be reinforced or contradicted in the wider messages of community and culture, which also shape personal history. Dissonance between personally and socially constructed views of the world produces cognitive conflict, which is often the catalyst for seeking help. For example, 'I still can't get over my husband's death but everyone is telling me I should be feeling better by now'.

Relationships and communications

Current relationships and communications within them give context to a loss experience. The quality of relationships and interactions is variable – generally supportive, socially demanding, emotionally undermining, etc. Dallos (2006) makes theoretical links in the conceptual development of Attachment Narrative Therapy between meaning-making processes in families and attachment patterns by addressing patterns of interpersonal communications revealed through narrative. A theory, which has the benefit of using everyday language to describe psychological structures and interpersonal functioning, is Transactional Analysis. Berne (1961; 1964; 1975) proposed a model of 'ego states' which have an equivalent in Freudian theory; parent (super ego), adult (ego), child (id). The ego states represent the dynamic elements of personality and their different levels of functioning:

- Parent – a state which resembles those of parental figures and may be controlling, critical, nurturing or rescuing.
- Adult – a state which is objective, can organise, solve problems, make decisions, listen, observe and reason.
- Child – a state which resembles early ways of functioning and may be free, conforming or rebelling.

Berne refers to relationships as transactions and an understanding of the nature of the communication, between the ego states, as transactional analysis. While a description of the full range of transactions is not possible here, some examples demonstrate how complexities within relationships may arise when people are grieving or processing a loss. The following examples show different communication styles and how they might operate in a simple exchange about seeking help (see Figures 4.1, 4.2 and 4.3).

Figure 4.1 represents a straightforward communication of information sharing, uncomplicated by other emotional agendas.

Figure 4.2 represents a communication in which a question is seen as interference and the reply indicates this by adopting a 'rebellious' child response to the perceived 'critical parent'.

Figure 4.3 represents an apparently straightforward question and answer from the adult state but hides an underlying criticism (from the critical parent) and underlying anxious

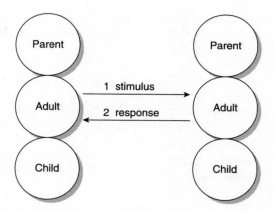

Figure 4.1   A complementary transaction

1   'When are you going to see the counsellor?'
2   'I've arranged to go next Wednesday.'

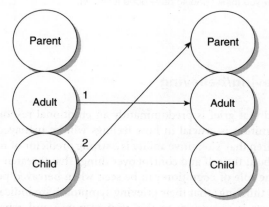

Figure 4.2   A crossed transaction

1   'When are you going to see the counsellor?'
2   'What's it got to do with you?'

response (from the conforming child). Ulterior communications are often conveyed through the manner in which words are spoken, body language and social atmosphere.

These examples demonstrate both the visible and the unspoken (ulterior) nature of communications and the positive or negative contribution they make to communications within relationships. Disentangling problematic relationships, by exploring the lines of communication, can contribute to establishing more effective relationships and social support networks. This, as an element of the therapeutic process, may be especially important where relationships lie at the heart of a loss – marital separation, child abuse, community conflict, etc.

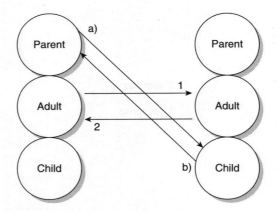

Figure 4.3   A ulterior transaction

1   (spoken)'When are you going to see the counsellor?'
     (Ulterior) a) 'It's about time you sorted yourself out.'
2   (spoken) 'Next week.'
     (ulterior) b) 'I know you think I should have done it sooner.'

Thinking/behaving/believing

It is often assumed that grief is predominantly an emotional response to loss but the part played by cognition is crucial in how feelings will be managed and understood. Stokes says of children that 'Cognitive ability is a strong predictor of resilience … In particular, thoughts about the self and control over things that threaten self-safety are crucial' (2007: 40). The role of cognition can be seen when bereaved people report a fear (arising from their thinking) that their grieving symptoms are indications that they are going mad. The fear is secondary to the grief response and represents a cognitive appraisal that their feelings are in some way abnormal. Ellis (1962; 1989) saw this 'crooked thinking' as arising from misconceptions which may be part of a wider range of irrational beliefs. Beck (1976) described these as cognitive distortions in which people might draw over generalised conclusions from limited evidence, for example, 'that counsellor didn't help – all counsellors are a waste of time'. Describing reality in polarised terms, for example, a widow saying, 'My husband was the most wonderful man in the world, whereas I was the most terrible wife', or personalising events by ascribing personal culpability, are also examples of cognitive distortion and learned helplessness (Seligman, 1992). Vulnerability resulting from experiences of loss is likely to activate previous distortions in thinking or generate new misconceptions. When looking at the therapeutic use of narrative earlier in the chapter, a central component was that of assisting in the reconstruction of stories and their meaning. Some of the techniques which might be employed to assist in that reconstruction, using a cognitive/behavioural approach, are identified by McLeod (2003: 138–9):

- Challenging irrational beliefs by bringing them to the attention of the client and exploring them.
- Reframing a faulty perspective by changing the concepts used to describe a situation, for example, regarding a problem as a challenge.
- Exploring different statements about self in role play, for example, 'I'm not the sort of person who (is liked, can take social risks etc.)' changed to – 'I am the kind of person who (has likeable [specified] qualities, can have a go at [specified tasks])'.
- Testing out new statements about self in real situations, for example, by going into feared situations which would ordinarily have been avoided.
- Quantifying feelings of anxiety, fear, anger, etc. on a scale of 0 to 10.
- Learning to stop an obsessive or anxious thought taking over by using thought stopping 'tricks', such as consciously giving attention to something trivial like today's shopping list.
- Learning relaxation when confronted, in therapy, with reminders of fearful situations.
- Assertiveness skills training.
- Practising new behaviours and cognitive strategies between counselling sessions.

This approach can usefully be integrated into a wide-ranging therapeutic repertoire.

Meaning-making

Maslow (1987), a key contributor to the development of humanistic psychology, believed that a positive perspective should be adopted in order to help discover full human potential and new aspirations. Emphasising the capacity for growth and renewal, positive psychology has emerged as an important contemporary perspective (Seligman, 1999). Positive psychology believes that the focus of therapeutic endeavour should be upon what it is that makes life worth living, enjoyable and meaningful; enrichment not just remedy. This demands a change in approach to therapy and a change in assumptions about its role and about the needs of the people it serves. This perspective is based on the belief in the 'self-actualising' or 'self-realising' tendency of human beings.

As Joseph and Linley state:

'The fully functioning person is someone who is accepting of themselves; values all aspects of themselves – their strengths and their weaknesses; is able to live fully in the present; experiences life as a process; finds purpose and meaning in life; desires authenticity in themselves, others, and societal organisations; values deep trust in relationships; is compassionate toward others, and able to receive compassion from others; and is acceptant that change is necessary and inevitable' (2006: 129–30).

This description of what it is to be fully human also reflects qualities of resilience, described in the last chapter as: personal resourcefulness, a positive life perspective and social embeddedness (Machin, 2007b).

Logo Therapy, developed by Frankl (1959), a Holocaust survivor, embraces the concepts of positive psychology as the basis for therapy and the promotion of resilience as a desired outcome. He defined Logo Therapy as a 'meaning-centred psychotherapy', in which the client is confronted with and reoriented towards the meaning of his/her life, a primary motivational force in human beings. Frankl saw that people's inner tensions arise from existential distress and the therapeutic process is to open the client to what he 'longs for in the depth of his being' (1959: 108). Frankl suggests three components make up meaning in life:

1   Creativity – striving to produce something, setting a personal goal or a cause to follow.
2   Experiential – focusing experience on truth and beauty but most of all found through love.
3   Attitudinal – a capacity to turn tragedy into triumph, transforming human predicament into achievement.

Helping a client explore these larger themes of meaning facilitates a move towards the reconstruction of a more satisfying and coherent narrative. While not denying the real distresses prompted by loss, this is an area in which all practitioners can give recognition to patient/client's striving for a positive perspective (Cutcliffe, 2004).

Arriving at a satisfactory sense of meaning is also the territory of religion and spirituality (Martin and Doka, 2000). It is particularly pertinent to experiences of loss and bereavement, that people are searching for explanations about situations which appear not to make any sense – they are beyond human comprehension. It is at this level that the search takes people outside their ordinary ways of knowing and understanding and becomes an existential quest for answers. As with so many other aspects of practitioner engagement with loss and grief, it represents an area of 'unknowing' that can be uncomfortably challenging. While clergymen/women have a particular pastoral role in this dimension, it is not theirs alone; clients/patients do not package their concerns and reflections into tidy profession-specific boxes. It calls for an awareness of ways in which stories of loss and grief, which often contain hints of searching and discovery in relation to meaning, are revealed in many of the contexts in which care is given (Stanworth, 2003). Listening to accounts of belief and faith, which grieving people are having to translate into their own life/death situation, needs time and space. This may be an overtly religious task but for many people who do not espouse clear religious convictions, the process of exploring existential uncertainty is equally real and poignant. Shared silence and stillness allows the client/patient to be in touch with their feelings and give expression to them. It also 'allows the client to get in touch with the hope that they have' (Cutcliffe, 2004: 87). Spall and Callis (1997: 115) pose a number of questions to aid the assessment of spiritual need:

- What is the client/patient's current source of strength?
- In the past, perhaps at times of particular distress, has the client/patient found special help?
- How well is the client/patient making sense of his or her illness/suffering? How well are family members making sense of it?
- Does the client/patient have important concerns/things he or she is thinking about?

Behind these questions there needs to be an awareness about the extent to which pre-existing beliefs/attitudes are currently helpful and the extent to which they create emotional and/or cognitive discomfort.

Canda and Furman (1999) believe that spirituality lies at the heart of helping and is expressed through the empathy, care, compassion and practice wisdom which motivates action. Additionally, the readiness and openness of the practitioner to hear, receive and travel alongside the quest for meaning can provide a glimpse of the transcendence reached by their client/patient which is itself a spiritual experience for the carer.

Summary

Research points to the benefits of countering the dominant grief orientation of a client/patient by focusing on alternative adaptive strategies, for example emotion-orientated interventions for those people who are predominantly focused on thinking/acting; problem-focus for those people who are primarily emotion orientated (Martin and Doka, 2000; Schut et al., 1997). A range of psychotherapeutic approaches are necessary to provide a repertoire capable of adjusting to the individual therapeutic needs of the client/patient. The psychodynamic perspective addresses issues of personal history, especially in respect of attachment relationships. Transactional Analysis provides a conceptual framework for examining relationships and their functioning, a crucial dimension in working with loss. The narrative process sees cognitive reconstruction as an essential part of arriving at a more satisfactory and coherent story (of loss). Cognitive behavioural approaches to therapy provide very clear protocols for appraising existing thinking, behaving and believing and revising faulty perceptions. Existential anxiety and the quest for meaning in the face of loss may be manifest as acute vulnerability in clients/patients, but a focus on the discovery or rediscovery of meaning has the potential to open new opportunities for growth and the development of resilience.

Some ways of working for non-therapists

Much of the discussion in this chapter has focused upon therapeutic ways of working with grief. However, other practitioners can integrate some of this knowledge and these approaches into their engagement with grieving clients.

- The story of loss can be heard and attended to within the wider brief of working with clients, for example, while giving a patient an injection; while accompanying a child to an access meeting with a parent, etc.
- Using knowledge of grief theories to recognise the impact of loss upon the client.
- Small tasks and goals for addressing loss can be integrated into other working engagement with clients, for example, lingering to talk with a widow about the photograph of her deceased husband; encouraging a fearful child, with a disability, to try new but manageable goals, etc.

- Without denying the pain of grief, helping a client/patient to recognise the ways in which he/she has coped well.
- Plan for a 'good' ending to the working engagement with a client, so that vulnerable clients do not have further experiences of loss to deal with. Review what has been achieved and help them look for positive possibilities in the future.
- Keep loss and grief on the agenda of the professional team and help colleagues have a clearer sense of how loss is impacting on their patients/clients.
- For all practitioners, therapists or not, listening to other peoples' pain is difficult. Supervision is essential for good practice.

Tools to aid storytelling

While larger theories can provide the concepts and the approaches to working with grief, a number of additional tools can usefully be employed to achieve the telling of the grief story.

The extract from the work of Lewis (1961), quoted in the introduction to Chapter 1, demonstrated how the depth and precise nature of grief can be more powerfully expressed through metaphor than through the simple use of adjectives. Tompkins, Sullivan and Lawley (2005) see metaphor as a fruitful dimension of exploration with clients. Within the narrative process, metaphor can be a mini-narrative which enables the client to capture some of the complex emotions and confusing thoughts in concrete, communicable forms. Sometimes people make use of metaphorical expressions which have become commonly used ways of describing grief, such as 'I feel as if I'm sitting under a black cloud,' 'I'm in a dark pit,' 'I'm on an emotional roller coaster', etc. These metaphors are readily understood but can sometimes be overlooked because of their familiarity. However, they still provide word pictures which practitioners can use as a focus to enter more deeply into the experience of their patient/client (Spall, Read and Chantry, 2001). Grieving people create new metaphors too and this is something for practitioners to listen for as it can lead to the development of greater empathy. Lewis contrasts his own grief with that of the suffering of his wife before her death:

> Grief is like a bomber circling round and dropping its bombs each time the circle brings it overhead; physical pain is like the steady barrage on a trench in World War One, hours of it with no let-up for a moment. (1961: 34)

In addition to aiding clarity, metaphor can also be used by clients, as in Rob's story (Chapters 7 and 9), to avoid or disguise the reality of their loss.

Much great writing is about loss and grief, whether in the form of fiction, autobiography, philosophical writing or poetry. Introducing grieving people to some of this literature can provide them with stories and experiences which resonate with their own, bringing new insight, a sense of not being alone and comfort. *All in the End is Harvest* (Whitaker 1984) is an anthology of such writing and takes its title from a poem, Eurydice, by Edith Sitwell:

> Love is not changed by death,
> And nothing is lost and all in the end is harvest.

This, in common with much other writing, powerfully suggests the journey of grief is not without hope. However, the therapeutic use of literature, bibliotherapy, needs to be undertaken with awareness of both the contents of suggested material and the perspectives of the grieving person, in order not to introduce an unhelpful or dissonant perspective (Martin and Doka, 2000).

While reading what others have written can be informative and provide solace, writing itself is a therapy. Many published and unpublished poems, journals and reflections attest to the benefits of exposing one's pain to paper and in the process finding new perspectives and meaning. Pennebaker, Zech and Rime have undertaken considerable research into the power of disclosure to address traumatic experience. On the subject of writing as a form of dealing with pain, they report:

> Even though a large number of participants report crying or being deeply upset by the experience, the overwhelming majority report that the writing experience was valuable and meaningful in their lives. (2001: 530)

A particular way of using writing therapeutically was devised by Progoff. It was conceived as an exercise to be carried out within a workshop where people were provided with prompts to their writing. The power of private writing but within a group context was seen to be derived from drawing strength 'from the presence of others without infringing on the privacy of the individual' (1975: 49). In the intensive journal process, Progoff explains the writing in metaphorical terms; the writer enters the well of his existence and begins to connect with and draw from the underground stream. The journal process consists of two dimensions.

1   The written log –

- Period log – an exploration of the people, relationships, feelings, etc. which make up the current period of life.
- Daily log – an interior reflection on external events for today.
- Dream log – a record of dreams or snatches of dreams.
- Twilight-imagery log – accounts of images which emerge when in the state between waking or sleeping or when day-dreaming.
- Stepping-stones log – an account of how 'I arrived at where I am now' based on the free surfacing of memories and not a careful editing of personal history.
- Life history log – an ordering of significant events and memories.
- Dialogue log – a dialogue with a person, events, circumstances, etc. as a way of finding meaning within confused or problematic relationships and experiences.

2   Feedback –

- Through reading what has been written and then writing more there is an increasing focus on the inner movements and processing of experience.

(The logs are comparable with the external and internal narrative, and the dialogue process and feedback system is comparable with the reflexive narrative described by Angus and Hardke 1994).

Progoff suggests that there are three natural divisions within the intensive journal process:

1   The life/time dimension, which reflects a person's life history. Both chronology and sub-
    jective experience are explored in the life history log, stepping-stones log, period log.
2   The depth dimension deals with unconscious levels of the psyche, and elements of cre-
    ativity and spirituality – dream log, twilight-imagery log.
3   The dialogue dimension which deals with the world of inner communication; the meeting
    place of ourselves in relation to other people, experience and objects through a dialogue
    with persons, dialogue with the body, dialogue with events, situations and circumstances.

The journal process is not an academic exercise but one in which free-flowing thoughts and feelings are committed to paper. Although conceived as a workshop exercise, it can be a very creative way to encourage individual clients to engage in private self-reflection. The practitioner needs to explain the journal structure and provide prompts to the progressive unfolding of 'self' on paper. The starting point for all of these journal processes is the stepping-stones log made up of a flowing of memories of significant moments leading to the present. This allows the client/patient to become more in tune with themselves and their own experience, as they write, read through and write more about what stirs inside as they 'connect and draw on the underground stream'. When the dialogue is with a person, it is necessary to begin by doing a stepping-stones log for that person, as a way of engaging deeply with them, and the things, so far as known, which shape(d) their lives. Chapter 8 will look at an example of using this form of journal with a bereaved client.

The presence of the counsellor/therapist may provide the same power of unobtrusive companionship as found in the intensive journal workshop. It also allows for the processing of material, without the necessary disclosure of its content. The dialogue dimension is particularly valuable as it provides a structure for an inner discourse in which distressed feelings, confusing thoughts and unfinished business can be expressed and put in to some sort of coherent order. For someone who is sick or disabled, a dialogue with the body might be helpful by addressing the body as if a separate entity. Externalising a problem by objectifying and sometimes personifying it, is a way of increasing the ease with which it can be described, spoken to, talked about, etc. (Dallos, 2006). For someone dealing with separation or bereavement, a dialogue with the person on whom the grief is focused can help deal with unresolved issues.

Bright asserts that the work of the grief therapist is aided through music:

> What music does is to lift the lid off emotions which are already there, it helps to create an atmosphere of trust and openness which permits freedom of conversation, the giving of information and enhanced insights. (1996: 5)

In addition to liberating grief and facilitating its expression, music can have innate therapeutic benefits by providing a different experiential mode of self-discovery. In a similar way, Read (2007) found that audiotapes were useful in enabling people with a learning disability to tell their stories and reveal their emotions.

Sometimes words do not exist to describe what grief is like. Children especially may lack the vocabulary to describe what has happened or what they are feeling about their loss. Children's own drawing or other trigger pictures, designed to prompt reflections on what has been lost (Heegaard, 1988; Machin, 1993), can be used to aid the insight of the grieving person and enable him/her to feel that they have communicated effectively with their therapist. Sitting alongside a child as he/she draws a picture of their loss, reveals to the counsellor/therapist the factors which are significant or troubling and which require therapeutic focus. Drawing provides a tangible medium through which to tell the loss story, as he/she verbally elaborates on the content of the picture. In a study by Schut et al. (1996) looking at the outcome of work with bereaved people who had complicated grief reactions, combining art therapy with psychotherapy was seen to be significantly more effective than using traditional psychotherapy alone. Art as therapy is employed in many hospices where people are addressing their own mortality. Bertman (1991) has developed some innovative programmes in the United States for using images and art in palliative care. She says, 'the arts cannot stay the flight of the birds of sorrow but they can help us to better appreciate and endure them' (1991: 88). All practitioners, not just therapists, can consider everyday ways in which images, perhaps photographs, and pictures can help to enter the grieving story of clients and patients.

Conclusion

Effective therapy depends on a relationship in which the client is valued and finds the courage to embark on a journey of self-discovery from a safe base. A person-centred approach (Rogers, 1961; 1980) defines clearly the values and qualities of engagement with a client, which will best facilitate the deeper exploration of grief. Accounts of attachment history (Bowlby, 1980) and the nature of current relationships (Berne, 1961; 1964; 1975) provide the psychosocial background against which reactions to loss can be understood. A cognitive-behavioural focus (Beck, 1976; Ellis, 1989) addresses the challenge to revise thoughts and actions, in the face of new life circumstances. The process of reviewing life assumptions (Marris, 1974; Parkes, 1993) will lead to the central task of therapy which is that of 'retrieval of meaning' (McLeod, 1997: 112). Overall, this is a process in which the client and the counsellor will work collaboratively to reconstruct a new narrative, made up of stories that can be 'lived by and live with' (McLeod, 1997: 86).

5

A New Model for Understanding Grief – a Compass and Map

For the practitioner working with loss and bereavement the extensive literature on grief produces a dilemma: 'two contradictory perspectives recur in psychology and the social sciences. One perspective holds that humans are basically the same. The other holds that there are enormous differences among people' (Rosenblatt, 1993: 110). The contradiction has until recently not been a real one for practitioners, as the perspectives which have most readily been integrated into the practice repertoire are those which simplify theories of universality, mainly focused upon psychology. The stages/phases/models of grief (Bowlby, 1980; Kubler-Ross, 1970; Parkes, 1996) and the structured approach to counselling (Worden, 2003) have contributed to a simplified approach to teaching and learning about grief. Like all simplification its merit is that it makes complex ideas more accessible and the practitioner more confident in working with grief. This simplification has led to distortion and misunderstanding about the significant and rich knowledge base contributed by these theorists and researchers, and a culture of care that perpetuates many misconceptions about the wide variations in individual experiences of grief.

Within the postmodern climate of theory-making, fuller attention is now being given to human diversity while attempting to find a conceptual frame that identifies common patterns and themes within grief (Bonanno and Kaltman, 1999; Stroebe et al., 1996). Stroebe, Stroebe and Hansson (1993) argue for an attempt to integrate varied perspectives into a coherent theory of grief and bereavement. For the practitioner this means finding theories within which diversity is not sacrificed for simplicity, nor theoretical concepts deemed too complex for clinical application.

In my own work, I have been exploring ways of bringing together the general and the particular and have developed a theoretical approach to grief pertinent to practice. This chapter will explore these ideas, looking in detail at:

- **The Range of Response to Loss model** – a new way of conceptualising general patterns in grief.
- **The Adult Attitude to Grief scale** – a tool to test the validity of the concepts contained in the RRL model.
- The Adult Attitude to Grief scale, as a tool for identifying the complexities of individual grief – **a process of mapping grief** in practice.

The Range of Response to Loss model – a new way of conceptualising general patterns in grief

A pattern for understanding difference in loss response emerged from detailed personal accounts of bereavement in research interviews (Machin, 1980) and from my counselling practice. While attending to the highly individual nature of grief and its personal impact there appeared to be evidence of three broadly different reactions to bereavement. These reactions were manifest in clients' loss stories as:

- **Overwhelmed** – a state of being deeply sunk into the distress of grief.
- **Balanced/resilient*** – a capacity to face the emotional, social and practical consequences of loss with equilibrium.
- **Controlled** – a dominant need to manage emotions and retain a primary focus upon ongoing life demands.

* When the RRL model was originally conceived, the second category was described as balanced. This reflected the capacity to hold both powerful feelings and the desire to retain control in a comfortable relationship. As the ideas for this model have developed, the balanced characteristics clearly also reflect the qualities of resilience upon which so much current thinking is being focused. Greater use will, therefore, be made of the term resilience although reference to the capacity for balance will be alluded to at some points in the text.

These three, broad grief reactions were incorporated into a framework and conceptualised as the Range of Response to Loss (RRL) model of grief. In developing the model it was important to look for the factors which might predispose to the dominance of one grief reaction rather than another. A number of theories suggest the connection between the responses to loss and previous relationships and life experience. Attachment Theory (Bowlby, 1980) clearly provides a way of understanding how early relationship patterns shape the responses made when separation, or its threat, are encountered (see Chapter 3). The wider cultural context also provides perspectives, which influence beliefs and behaviours in response to life events such as loss and bereavement. Social and cultural beliefs are transmitted through ritual, observed attitudes and behaviours of other people, media influences, etc. and these affect concepts about loss and change, and its management. This constitutes socially received wisdom (Epstein, 1990). The social constructionist view is that cultural 'wisdom' is not understood in the same way across history and in all communities, but is negotiated through the interactions which occur between people within specific times and places (Burr, 1995). How these constructs become internalised will depend upon the rigidity of the script and the person's own experience of relationships, life events and loss (Bowlby, 1980). In some circumstances constructs (beliefs) are reinforced by experience and produce a cycle of self-fulfilling prophecy (Snyder, 1984), while in others experience might serve to contradict the received wisdom and create an opportunity for a revision in beliefs (for example, the experiential system (Epstein, 1990); revision of assumptive world (Parkes, 1993); and relearning the world (Attig, 1996)). Assumptions are made when what has been learned from others is combined with personal experience to either reinforce or promote revision in a person's belief about the nature of grief. The nature of loss experience will be significantly effected by the degree of threat to well-being and how far the stress of the situation, such as bereavement, can be met with adequate personal resourcefulness (Folkman, 2001; Lazarus and Folkman, 1984).

A response to loss, therefore, is based on an acquired view of the world; 'my' place within it and 'my' capacity to handle loss, change and transition. Placed within a social constructionist perspective, the patterns of variability in response to loss, described in the RRL model, might be expressed in the ways shown in Table 5.1.

Table 5.1   The Range of Response to Loss model interpreted from a social constructionist perspective

Social constructs	The Range of Response to Loss		
	1	2	3
Perspectives on loss	An experience of loss is likely to be **Overwhelming**	An experience of loss can be met with **Resilience**	An experience of loss can be **Controlled**
Identification with loss perspective	'I cannot deal with loss and change'.	'I can face loss and change'.	'I can control the consequences of loss and change'.
Personal narrative account of loss	'This loss has taken over my life'.	'Although it is difficult, I know that I have the strength, and other people's support, to help me through this loss'.	'If I divert form this loss I can manage perfectly well'.
Response to other people's loss	'I have suffered much more than you have'.	'I recognise your pain and hope that, like me, you will find the support you need'.	'Don't trouble me with your loss. You need to get on with life, as I have'.

The view of self, in relation to challenging life events, will prompt a varied response to other people's loss. If a person is overwhelmed by loss, he/she is likely to find it difficult to look beyond his/her own distress to acknowledge the pain of others. Conversely, if a person believes that a response to loss should be controlled, they are likely to urge upon others that same control. For people who have felt able to cope effectively with loss (that is, neither completely overwhelmed by their own feelings nor constrained to control what cannot be changed), there is likely to be a greater capacity to empathise with others and share their pain. These different styles of response may be very evident in families or where group work with grieving people is undertaken (Zaider and Kissane, 2007). It can lead to misunderstanding and tension as people confront each other with dissimilar styles of coping (Stylianos and Vachon, 1993). This may be especially true in the family context where both before and after the death of a family member, tension is generated as different people respond to the situation in different ways and relationships have different meanings.

The Range of Response to Loss model provides a schema for differentiating grief reactions and a framework for understanding the processes which contribute to those differences.

Parallels between the Range of Response to Loss model and other theories of grief

The RRL model arose directly from listening to grieving people speak about their experience of loss. In developing the model further, the aim was not to compete with existing theory but to use the words and constructs encountered in practice situations as a way of reflecting clients/patients' lived experience of loss, and in a way which would resonate with practitioners' experience. Nevertheless, exploring the validity of these concepts was undertaken by examining their fit with other theories (see Table 5.2).

Table 5.2   Conceptual comparisons between the RRL model and other key models of grief

RRL model (Machin, 2001)	Overwhelmed	Resilient	Controlled
Attachment Theory (Ainsworth et al., 1978)	Anxious/ambivalent	Secure	Avoidant
Stress theory (Horowitz, 1997)	Intrusion	←	Avoidance
Dual Process Model (Stroebe and Schut, 1999)	Loss Orientation	——————→ oscillation	Restoration Orientation
Personality related (Martin and Doka, 2002)	Intuitive grief – emotional coping	Blended grief – emotional and cognitive coping	Instrumental grief – cognitive coping

What became clear at an early stage in developing the RRL model was the connection between attachment style (Ainsworth et al., 1978; Bowlby, 1980) and the three categories of response to loss.

- Overwhelmed loss response and anxious/ambivalent attachment.
- Balanced/resilient loss response and secure attachment.
- Controlled loss response and avoidant attachment.

Contemporary literature and research (Bartholomew and Shaver, 1998; Mikulincer and Florian, 1998; Simpson and Rholes, 1998) has taken concepts of 'attachment' further. Mikulincer and Florian (1998) looked at the emotional and cognitive reactions to stressful events and observed three patterns. The first was associated with anxious/ambivalent responses where people see stressful events as threatening, irreversible and uncontrollable. The second was associated with people who gave evidence of being securely attached, and who were resilient in the face of adversity and whose constructive attitude towards life is a buffer against psychological distress. Thirdly, people who showed avoidant responses dealt with stressful events by restricting their acknowledgement of distress and by being compulsively self-reliant. The RRL framework shows consistency with these concepts.

The RRL categories also match the theory developed by Horowitz, Wilner and Alvarez (1979) which looked at the nature of intrusion and avoidance as features of experience in bereavement and traumatic loss. Intrusion clearly demonstrates a position where the loss is dominant in the feeling and thinking of the person (overwhelmed) and avoidance shows an inclination to divert from the loss (controlled).

The theoretical fit between the RRL framework and the Dual Process Model of grief (Stroebe, 1992–93; Stroebe and Schut, 1999) is striking. The Dual Process Model provides theoretical justification to extend the concept of grief response to include social adaptation as well as focus upon resolving painful emotions; a radical move from earlier psychodynamic theories of grief work. While Stroebe and Schut (2001) see oscillation between these two positions as indicative of a natural/normal response, they also recognise that some people will have a bias towards one or other end of the spectrum. The three identified points in the RRL model match the structure within the Dual Process Model (see also Chapter 3):

- An overwhelmed response equates with the loss orientation dimension.
- A controlled response equates with the restoration dimension.
- A balanced/resilient response equates with a capacity to oscillate between the other two dimensions.

More recently, biases in grief have been explored by Martin and Doka (2000). While they see different coping styles as related to gender they are clear that these differences are not determined by gender. The pattern which they describe consists of intuitive grief which is largely expressed emotionally (overwhelmed) and is a typically female mode of expression, and instrumental grief which is expressed physically and cognitively (controlled) and is associated with a male mode of expression. A third type is represented by the blending of the intuitive and instrumental styles of grieving (balanced/resilient). The parallel between this account of grief and that outlined in the RRL model is clear.

The Adult Attitude to Grief scale – a tool to test the validity of the concepts contained in the RRL model

While parallels could be seen between the RRL model and other theories, it was necessary to look further into the nature of this pattern of grief reactions and to validate the distinctions proposed between the three categories in the model – overwhelmed, balanced/resilient, controlled. Validation of the notions contained in the RRL framework was undertaken by looking more closely at attitudinal perspectives on loss and grief. The narratives that people use to describe life events reveal their attitudes towards experience. Attitudes, therefore, reveal to the listener the way in which acquired perspectives and experience combine to produce a life view and a base for reaction to new situations. A scale using attitudes was developed to help elicit differing perspectives on bereavement and the manner in which individuals cope with it.

I devised a self-report attitudinal scale, the **Adult Attitude to Grief scale**, as a central tool in the process of validating the RRL framework. The (AAG) scale needed to embrace a life view and a self view, which would characterise the three elements contained in the RRL framework (see Appendix 1 and Figure 5.1) The attitudes needed to be framed in a way which would allow the event of loss, and the emotions and behavioural response to it, to be meaningfully understood and owned by the respondent. The nine statements, which make up the measure, were designed to capture the three defining points in the RRL framework. Respondents were asked to rate their attitudinal perspective on a five-point Likert scale, in a range from strongly agree to strongly disagree.

2 For me, it is difficult to switch off thoughts about the person I have lost.
5 I feel that I will always carry the pain of grief with me.
7 I believe that nothing will ever be the same after an important loss. (NB: changed in 2007)

The 'overwhelmed' items in the scale (numbered as they appear on the scale).
These elements carry notions of grief as being stressful, irreversible and uncontrollable (Mikulincer and Florian, 1998).

1 I feel able to face the pain which comes with loss.
3 I feel very aware of my inner strength when faced with grief.
9 It may not always feel like it but I do come through the experience of grief.

The 'resilient' items in the scale.
These elements carry notions of the capacity to face grief with courage, resourcefulness and optimism (Greene, 2002; Seligman, 1998).

4 I believe that I must be brave in the face of loss.
6 For me, it is important to keep my grief under control.
8 I think its best just to get on with life after a loss.

The 'controlled' items in the scale.
These elements carry the notion of a restricted acknowledgement of distress and a need to be self-reliant in loss (Mikulincer and Florian, 1998).

Figure 5.1   The Adult Attitude to Grief scale grouped (and numbered) in the three sub-scales – overwhelmed (2, 5, 7), resilient/balanced (1, 3, 9) and controlled (4, 6, 8)

A study into the Range of Response to Loss model using the Adult Attitude to Grief scale as a validating tool (2001)

The study was undertaken in a service for the bereaved in North Staffordshire, Bereavement Care. During a 12-month period, all new clients to Bereavement Care were invited to participate in the study. A letter was sent to clients after their first counselling session with a request for them to take part in the research. It was to involve two interviews, six months apart. Practical information was given about the conduct of the interviews and written consent obtained.

Method

Participants

At the first interview 94 people participated (78 females and 16 males) – a reflection of the gender make up of most counselling services. At the second interview, there were 64 participants (52 female and 12 male). There was a broad span of ages (see Table 5.3). The nature of the relationship to the deceased was that of spouse/partner, child, parent and other losses including friends and more distant relationships. Non-participants included those people who were counselled during the period of the research and were invited to participate, but who either declined or could not be contacted after their first and only counselling session (65 females and 18 males).

Table 5.3   Participants in 2001 study by age group and relationship to the deceased

Relationship to the deceased	Age group (18–35)		Age group (36–55)		Age group (56+)		Total	
	No.	%	No.	%	No.	%	No.	%
Spouse/partner	3	8.6	10	28.6	22	62.9	35	37.2
Child	16	45.7	19	54.3			35	37.2
Parent	7	58.3	4	33.3	1	8.3	12	12.7
Other	2	16.6	6	50.0	4	33.3	12	12.7

Interview schedule

Alongside the AAG scale a profile of participants' attachment history (Parkes, 1991) and attachment styles (Bartholomew, 1990) was obtained, together with accounts of childhood and adult experiences of loss and change, and the emotional and social characteristics of the current bereavement. In addition, three psychometric tests were used to examine evidence of depression (Beck et al., 1961), the management of distress (Horowitz, Wilner and Alvarez, 1979) and continued connectedness to the deceased (Cleiren, 1991).

Results

Factor analysis of the Adult Attitude to Grief items confirmed the validity of the three groups of three statements, associated with the categories in the RRL framework. The proposed characteristics of grief associated with the overwhelmed, balanced/resilient, and controlled categories were examined against the Beck Depression Inventory, the Impact of Events scale, and the Leiden Detachment scale, together with measures defining social need and support in bereavement (Cleiren, 1991). Correlation and regressions provided statistical evidence of a link between the presence of symptoms of grief, especially the inability to detach from the deceased and the overwhelmed category. The Leiden Detachment scale measures continued anxious connectedness to the deceased rather than the satisfactory emergence of a Continuing Bond. Conversely, the balanced/resilient category was characterised by negative correlation with the distress symptoms of grief, especially when the Impact of Events (IES) and the Detachment scale were analysed as an interactive variable. Analysis of the items in the controlled sub-scale showed there was an association between this category and increase in age and consistency over the two test times.

Statistical analyses of the AAG scale alongside measures of bereavement distress provided evidence of the qualities of difference identified in the RRL model. The strength of the association between the attitudinal statements and their conceptual categories was greater at the second interview. This may indicate that at a time of heightened distress (that is, shortly after requesting counselling help) the levels of ambiguity and transitional chaos were greater. Contradictions and wide variations in response to grief were noted by Bowlby (1980) and Lund, Caserta and Dimond (1993). With the passage of time, greater coherence in self-reported attitudes may reflect increased cognitive management of distress (Brammer, 1992) as the subjective feelings of 'agency' permits a return to structure within the narrative accounts (Burr, 1995) of loss.

Discussion

In the 2001 study, analysis of the AAG scale data across the whole sample provided clear evidence to justify the three categories proposed in the RRL model. However, what also became clear was that individual respondents could not be fitted unequivocally into a single category of loss response but rather showed a much more complex picture of grief. There were highly individual blends and biases across the overwhelmed, resilient and controlled categories. What emerged from the study, therefore, was that the attitudes contained within the AAG scale provided a structure within which the experience, beliefs and responses to bereavement could allow for the very individual story of loss to be told.

Taken together the conceptually linked Range of Response to Loss model and the Adult Attitude to Grief scale were able to identify both the more broadly based reactions to grief and the individual variations within it (Machin, 2001). The research data was used to extrapolate a number of case studies, as a way of finding out more about the nature of individual variability. This approach is urged by Hansson, Carpenter and

Fairchild (1993) as a counter to the use of mean values as a way of generalising findings across a population, and beyond.

Two examples of case studies are given here in order to illustrate the ways in which the responses to the AAG scale provided a picture of the complex and shifting grief dynamics occurring during bereavement. They were undertaken by looking at all nine items in the scale alongside other demographic details and psychometric data.

Case Study 5.1

Background details: Diane was aged 37 and had sought counselling help following the death of her husband Graham. He had died from a heart attack seven months earlier. As she was growing up, the dominant messages for Diane had been about her resourcefulness, and she was urged to be independent. She had not suffered any separation or serious illness in her childhood. The current untimely bereavement was very difficult for Diane.

Exploring the responses and the grief profile

In looking at the responses to the nine items on the AAG scale (see Figure 5.2), a changing profile of grief could be observed. It was clear at both interview times that, in varying degrees, all the categories in the RRL model featured in Diane's grief. While at the first interview the overwhelmed items dominated, there was some agreement with the resilient items (1 and 9) and with one of the controlled items (4). In managing the overwhelming pain, Diane's responses showed that she was having to be brave (4) in order to deal with her feelings (1). In these responses Diane was demonstrating some of the emotional tension in coping with the conflicting feelings, thoughts and actions at the time of bereavement. Consistent with the messages of her childhood, she was able to be optimistic about coming through the experience of grief (9).

Six months later, at the second interview, resilience dominated. There was a greater sense particularly of inner resourcefulness (3). While the sense that the painful reality of the loss would persist (5), other elements on the overwhelmed sub-scale had lessened (2) or, in the case of intrusive thoughts and feelings, no longer applied (1). Being brave no longer applied (4) and keeping grief under control (6) was also not a concern for Diane. Nevertheless, she felt that it was important to get on with her life (8).

The picture emerging from the responses to the AAG scale was confirmed by other tests in the study. Diane's score on the Impact of Events scale, measuring intrusion and avoidance, showed a bias towards intrusion at both interviews, but her overall score declined considerably from 23 to 8. Similarly, the Leiden Detachment scale (maximum score 21), exploring a continued sense of anxious connectedness to the deceased, moved from scoring 12 at the first interview to 4 at the second interview. This was exemplified when Diane indicated at the first interview a 'great longing' for Graham, while at the second interview her need of him reduced to 'sometimes talking to him'. A measure of the changed but continuing bond (Klass, Silverman and Nickman, 1996).

Appended comments by the interviewer reported that although Graham's untimely death produced an immediate overwhelmed reaction, Diane's own life views and the presence of social support enabled her to connect with her own resilience by the time of the second interview. In the intervening period, she had three counselling sessions.

AAG scale
Scoring (Strongly agree/agree/neither agree nor disagree/disagree/strongly disagree)

| +2 | +1 | 0 | −1 | −2 |

Adult Attitude to Grief scale – sub-scale **Overwhelmed**	First interview		Second interview	
	Scores	Summary	Scores	Summary
2 For me, it is difficult to switch off thoughts about the person I have lost.	+1		−1	
5 I feel that I will always carry the pain of grief with me.	+2	+5	+1	Mix across the range +1 and −1
7 I believe that nothing will ever be the same after an important loss. NB changed 2007	+2		0	

Adult Attitude to Grief scale – sub-scale **Resilient**	First interview		Second interview	
	Scores	Summary	Scores	Summary
1 I feel able to face the pain which comes with loss.	+1		+2	
3 I feel very aware of my inner strength when faced with grief.	0	+2	+2	+5
9 It may not always feel like it but I do come through the experience of grief.	+1		+1	

Adult Attitude to Grief scale – sub-scale **Controlled**	First interview		Second interview	
	Scores	Summary	Scores	Summary
4 I believe that I must be brave in the face of loss.	+1		−1	
6 For me, it is important to keep my grief under control.	0	+1	−1	Mix across the range +1 and −2
8 I think it's best just to get on with life after a loss.	0		+1	

Figure 5.2   Diane's responses to the (AAG) scale at the two interview times
(NB At the second interview the summary (aggregated total) of the
sub-scales showed a mix of agreement and disagreement in both the
overwhelmed and the controlled dimensions. It is important that this mix
is shown rather than numerically using the plus and minus to cancel each
other out.)

Case Study 5.2

Background details: Eric was 62 when his wife Joan died. She had been ill for a long time but died of a heart attack. He requested counselling support nine months after Joan's death. Strong messages of his childhood were: 'Nobody likes a cry baby' and 'You've got what it takes to handle difficult situations'. Eric had no experience of separation or illness as a child.

Exploring the responses and the grief profile

At the first interview, Eric showed a strong bias towards the overwhelmed items in the scale. He also agreed with two items (6 and 8) on the controlled sub-scale. Clearly some of these perspectives demonstrate the tension between having difficulty in switching off thoughts about the person who has died (2) and keeping grief under control (6). The combination of tension and Eric's disagreement with all the items on the resilience sub-scale, suggest a high level of distress (see Figure 5.3).

At the second interview there was a marked change to strong disagreement with two of the overwhelmed statements, although continued agreement with item 7, and agreement with all of the controlled statements. While these responses suggest that Eric had moved beyond the high distress of the first interview it was important to look more closely at the implications of all his responses to the scale. The mechanisms by which Eric was managing his grief were fragile. His capacity to face the pain of his loss (1) and his sense of his inner strength (3) were absent. This being so, Eric was having to be brave (4) in order to deal with the grief.

The supporting evidence for this interpretation of deep but hidden grief was in the scores on the Impact of Events scale and the Leiden Detachment scale, both of which increased from the first interview (IES, first interview = 15, second interview = 20; Leiden Detachment scale, first interview = 15, second interview = 20).

This picture of bereavement is consistent with what may often be seen in counselling; someone who is superficially coping but who has an inner struggle with processing the pain of grief. This is especially the case when there is a strongly held personal belief in the need to appear strong and there is limited social support for addressing emotional needs. At both interviews Eric indicated that there were insufficient opportunities to freely express his thoughts and feelings about Joan to other people. This no doubt compounded his need to conceal the ongoing degree of distress. Eric had received 10 counselling sessions between the two interviews and the counselling support was ongoing. However, he said that he had not been able to look at his feelings about Joan. The researcher's account of interviewing Eric was that he could be matter-of-fact about many of the questions but found discussing his current bereavement difficult because of the pain it evoked. This is consistent with his responses to the AAG scale in which his own incapacity to manage the deeper level of his distress was evident.

AAG scale

Scoring (Strongly agree/agree/neither agree nor disagree/disagree/strongly disagree)

| | +2 | +1 | 0 | −1 | −2 |

Adult Attitude to Grief scale – sub-scale **Overwhelmed**	First interview		Second interview	
	Scores	Summary	Scores	Summary
2 For me, it is difficult to switch off thoughts about the person I have lost.	+2		−2	
5 I feel that I will always carry the pain of grief with me.	+1	+5	−2	Mix of +1 and −4
7 I believe that nothing will ever be the same after an important loss. NB changed 2007	+2		+1	

Adult Attitude to Grief scale – sub-scale **Resilient**	First interview		Second interview	
	Scores	Summary	Scores	Summary
1 I feel able to face the pain which comes with loss.	−2		−2	
3 I feel very aware of my inner strength when faced with grief.	−2	−5	−2	Mix of +1 and −4
9 It may not always feel like it but I do come through the experience of grief.	−1		+1	

Adult Attitude to Grief scale – sub-scale **Controlled**	First interview		Second interview	
	Scores	Summary	Scores	Summary
4 I believe that I must be brave in the face of loss.	−1		+1	
6 For me, it is important to keep my grief under control.	+1	Mix of +2 and −1	+1	+3
8 I think it's best just to get on with life after a loss.	+1		+1	

Figure 5.3   Eric's responses to the (AAG) scale at the two interview times
(NB At both interviews the summary (aggregated total) of some the sub-scales showed a mix of agreement and disagreement. It is important that this mix is shown rather than numerically using the plus and minus to cancel each other out.)

Summary of case studies

In both of these case studies, the responses to the AAG scale provided a picture of grief which was made up of variable elements from all three categories in the RRL model of grief. Overwhelming, resilient and controlling aspects (or their absence) provided a profile of Diane and Eric's grief. The scale gave a revised picture of the contours of their grief at the second interview. For Diane, the change demonstrated movement in which her increased resilience enabled her to manage the competing forces of feelings of grief and control mechanisms. The change in Eric was more complex. There was an appearance of some resolution of his distress but when examined alongside an absence of two aspects of resilience, a continued and more difficult quality of grief was occurring. In both of these case studies the resilient elements on the scale were of central significance. It is the individual's capacity to process their grief, not just manage (control) it, which is strongly indicative of the level of distress. The case studies came from research data but the implications for how the scale might function within the context of practice is explored in two further pieces of research.

The Adult Attitude to Grief scale, as a tool for identifying the complexities of individual grief – a process of mapping grief in practice

What emerged from the 2001 (Machin) study was validation of the notions of loss conceptualised in the RRL framework but more importantly, for practitioners, the AAG scale provided insight into the diverse grief reactions taking place within individual bereaved people. Repeat use of the AAG scale was also able to show changes in perspective taking place over time. This suggested that the AAG scale might have a useful function within clinical practice.

Two studies were undertaken to explore this proposition more fully. The first of these studies (Machin and Spall, 2004) was conducted within a psychology service specialising in the care of older patients. The second was carried out within a voluntary sector community service offering bereavement and loss counselling to older clients (Machin, 2007a). The research set out to examine how far the responses to the nine items on the AAG scale would provide pertinent information about clients' grief, facilitate the telling of the individual story of loss and provide the clinician with useful indicators to guide the therapeutic process. In the second study the counsellors' experience of using the scale was explored more fully through a questionnaire. The studies were embedded within practice using a cyclical process, action research (Reason, 1988), in which the AAG scale was systematically reviewed and revised during its clinical use. Consideration was given to this new way of working with loss and integrated into therapeutic reflection and supervision. Implicit in the process was commitment to the maintenance of good, ethical practice including discussion with the clients about the use of the scale in therapy and informed consent for participation in the study (Bond, 1993).

Revisions and changes resulting from the studies into the practice use of the AAG scale

In the 2004 study, reflection on practice use of the AAG scale suggested that some new elements be introduced:

- The scale was modified to be used with losses other than bereavement, for example, 'For me, it is difficult to switch off thoughts about [my illness, loss of home, etc.] (see Appendix 2).
- General themes, suggested by the nine items on the AAG scale, were developed as cues for more detailed therapeutic exploration:

Overwhelmed themes –
2 The intrusion of thoughts about the person who has died (lost etc.) which may be either unwelcome or chosen.
5 The persistence of grief – an incapacity to see beyond the pain.
7 A sense that important things have changed and meaning has been lost.

Resilient themes –
1 The ability to confront the loss and the pain which goes with it.
3 A sense of personal resourcefulness, including a capacity to access and use social support.
9 A positive outlook which is optimistic about the future.

Controlled themes –
4 Valuing courage and fortitude.
6 The desire to keep emotions in check.
8 The need (for oneself or for the sake of others) to divert from the loss and focus on the future.

In the 2007 study changes from the earlier study were integrated, and some further revisions suggested. Two items on the scale were adjusted. Item 9 was changed from 'It may not always feel like it but I do come through the experience of grief' to 'It may not always feel like it but I do believe I will come through this experience of grief'. This modification gave recognition to the possibility of hopefulness even if the respondent had no previous experience on which to base their optimism.

Through use with a number of clients it became clear that item 7 did not clearly convey the nature of the shift in life perspective resulting from a significant bereavement. The element of change which was most significant to clients was connected to the revision in the meaning of life after a momentous loss. This was more adequately reflected in the change of item 7 to 'Life has less meaning for me after this loss'. The modification, although introduced in the middle of the study, increased the face validity of the measure as it conveyed a more appropriate notion of what it means to be overwhelmed.

Client/patient and counsellor experience of using the scale

In the 2004 and 2007 studies insight and affirmation about the scale and its efficacy came from looking in detail at the work with clients and from therapist/counsellor observations.

Practitioners considered the circumstances in which the AAG scale would be appropriate to their practice. It was clear in both studies that where a client was very distressed its use might be unhelpful or counterproductive. Nevertheless, in some situations the therapist made the judgement that the distress might be relieved, given an opportunity for a client to reflect on the experience of grief in a more systematic way. The case of Connie (2004 study) provides a clear example of this.

Connie was seen because she had suffered a number of losses. She had become estranged from her son, had been excluded from a day centre and had chronic health problems. The therapist seeing Connie was uncertain about whether to use the AAG scale as she was able to give an unprompted, though agitated and distressed, free-flowing account of her losses. However, when the scale was used it provided some structure to her narrative. In using the themes associated with the attitudinal statements, Connie became much calmer in describing and reflecting upon her situation. The structure gave her some control in an otherwise confusing and overwhelming experience of loss.

Autonomy for the practitioner, in deciding the timing and use of the scale, is an important way of giving full recognition to the professional judgement of counsellors, and counters the view that use of the scale is formulaic and prescriptive.

The initial impact of the scale was quite dramatic for some clients: 'It stopped me in my tracks'; 'The feedback [looking at the scores in response to the scale] was very shocking. I didn't realise how low I was' (two client reactions, 2007). These comments, along with feedback from other respondents, suggest that the scale is readily understood and interpreted by clients themselves, and is not a mysterious tool of assessment, understood only by the professional. It affirms the value of a self-report questionnaire. Comments from the counsellors (2007) confirms the value of learning directly from the client how grief is being experienced. One noted that, 'it [the scale] allows the components of grief to be assessed and so provides insight', whilst another observed that, 'The door had been opened and I had been invited in'. In different ways, these practitioners were experiencing the scale as a means of clarifying the nature of their clients' grief and also providing a therapeutic entrée into it. The range of the items on the scale was also seen by the counsellors as a means of 'helping to normalise clients' grief', without being 'rigid or intrusive' (2007).

Working therapeutically demands that the self-awareness of the client and that the understanding of the therapist/counsellor are extended. The AAG scale was a useful tool in achieving this.

John (2004 study) was dealing with three significant losses – the death of his mother, separation from his wife and a stroke. In responding to the items on the AAG scale in a different way for each of these losses, he was able to distinguish the variable impact they were having on him. The therapist saw this as helpful to John in broadening his self-awareness about the ways he was feeling and thinking about his multiple losses. It also provided a fuller clinical picture and one which allowed more accurate prioritising and focusing on the most pertinent elements in John's management of loss.

Qualitative amplification of responses to the scale provided clients, in both studies, with the opportunity to define the nature of their grief in more depth and in their own words. This enabled the practitioner to broaden the areas of therapeutic exploration and increased awareness in the client and the therapist about the nature of the grief being experienced.

Harry (2004 study), who had lost his son, was able to say as his therapy progressed, 'I'm getting better at facing the pain' (AAG item 1) and 'My inner strength is coming back' (AAG scale item 3).

Repeat use of the scale was also found to provide a very helpful measure of the changes taking place and gave clients and practitioners insight into the movements in grief.

'Going through the questions again helped me see how much I'd grown in strength'; 'I feel freed by gaining confidence and thinking things through'.

Eileen, a client in the 2007 study, said, 'I had to pick up the pieces after my husband died suddenly. The scale made me think about my situation and what I needed to do to get on. With help from my counsellor I felt, when I did the scale a second time, as if I'd moved on and I was able to see that.'

The significance of change was noted by a number of counsellors (2007): 'Movement can be monitored'; 'A valuable record of each change and the overall depth of change'; 'The scale provides an easy way to see the change for the counsellor and the client'.

The social influence upon attitudes to grief

In listening to the perspectives being expressed through the AAG scale (2004), it became clear to the therapists that clients were often expressing attitudes which were not their own. Sometimes their responses were constrained by the views, perspectives and pressure from other people. The capacity to retain some independence of thought or action was reliant upon a number of factors; the need to retain the support of others, the self-confidence of the mourner, etc. Clearly, the social context of attitudes to grief became another important area for separate exploration:

- How far are attitudes learned and absorbed as part of socialisation?
- How far are attitudes formed as a result of personal experience of loss?
- How far do other people's attitudes shape the expectations of the client?
- How far is there a combination of these elements?

Looking at the social context of clients' grief provided the practitioner with a sense of how far dissonant attitudes, as seen in the response to the scale, reflected inner ambivalence or conflict within their social network. As social support is crucial to resilience, this was an important element to explore. For two-thirds of the clients in the 2004 study, past or present pressure came from other people who believed that the expression of grief should be controlled. For clients in the 2007 study, similar constraints were noted: 'I do believe I must be brave for my family' (item 4)'; 'Yes, I keep my grief under control because my family come first' (item 6); 'I have to keep going for my son's sake' (item 8).

Ann (2004 study) described how her mother and father employed different parenting styles (such as emotional vs unemotional; approving of open affection vs disapproving of open affection). Over the years, gaining the approval of others, therefore, had become a confusing attempt to clarify what others expected of her; a process in which she was always liable to get it wrong. This was experienced in her current situation as a sense of incongruity in which she felt/thought that 'I ought to stop grieving' (for her dead daughter), while feeling a deep inner grief. Attempts to reconcile different life perspectives prompted a predisposition to procrastination and anxiety, which became a chronic feature of her psychological state. As the AAG scale was used to explore the varied dimensions of her loss, Ann began to recognise the acceptability of her own felt grief, and her therapist observed that the notions in the scale gave her permission to grieve. As she felt more able to accept the pain of her grief, she was less distressed by it, which was seen in her diminishing agreement with the overwhelming items on the AAG scale. The progress made in therapy with Ann was more accurately reflected in the retest scores on the AAG scale, than on another psychometric test (Hospital Anxiety and Depression scale – Zigmond and Snaith, 1983), which did not show any change.

When bereaved people attempt to satisfy the expectations of family and friends and do so by hiding their own feelings and thoughts, their grief is compounded by a sense of aloneness and social separation.

Mary in the second study (2007) said, 'The hardest statement was about facing the loss [item 1 on the scale]. I find that so painful. But other people thought I was brave. How you're feeling is different from how others see you.'

The impact of currently discrepant perspectives were evident for William and his wife Joan (2004 study).

William had suffered some visual impairment following a stroke and had unrealistic expectations about being able to continue to drive. The medical view, and that of Joan, was that he no longer had the capacity to take his car out. Joan became very anxious about his ability to look after himself, and very agitated when he went out. In this case, the AAG scale was used with both William and Joan. The item which pointed to greatest attitudinal discrepancy between them, was item 2: 'For me, it is difficult to switch off thoughts about [the stroke]'. William strongly disagreed and was able to focus on the things he could still manage, while Joan strongly agreed with the statement and was full of apprehension about the practical implications of her husband's disabilities. Clearly, losses arising from William's stroke were being keenly felt by his wife and this was affecting her resourcefulness as his carer. Roos (2002) describes the sorrow felt by those people living with an ongoing loss, such as a stroke, as a 'self-loss', and the sorrow felt by those people who are in close relation-ship with them as 'other-loss'. This distinction was evident in the different responses made to the AAG scale by William and Joan, and revealed a significant difference in their capacity to cope with Williams' illness and its consequences. The points of dis-crepancy in their response to the scale provided the therapist with clearly different agendas to be addressed in supporting William and Joan with the consequent losses arising from William's stroke.

Reflections on the practice use of the AAG scale

Each study (2004 and 2007) demonstrated that by using the initial responses to the scale and the qualitative amplification to the attitudinal statements, there was a structure for telling the 'story' of grief. Reconstructing a new narrative to embrace the loss and to find new meanings was possible when it was clear which were the areas most pertinent to the concerns of the client and which were particular dimensions of distress and dissonance.

Does the AAG scale fit naturally into clinical work? The question of the face validity of the AAG scale was an issue throughout the two studies and practitioners were alert for possible negative reactions by clients. While there was some initial hesitation in its use by therapists/counsellors, the uncovering of key concerns/problems flowed very naturally from the attitudinal items and themes associated with them. This gave confidence in making greater use of the scale: 'Gives form to what is going on for the client'; 'I was sur-prised how accurate the scale was in showing how people handle their emotions'; 'Raised points to explore, especially after working out the score, which they [clients] all agreed was an accurate reflection of their grief'. Clients felt relief that the items on the scale gave recognition to their disparate responses to loss; it normalised the conflicts and contra-dictions in their experience of grief – 'I feel happier and can understand my own feelings more'(2007).

While the practitioners in the two clinical studies all agreed it was easy to administer and there were no contraindications, some adjustments to the scale were made in response to the discussion between clients and their counsellors. As the review process progressed (2004), consideration was given to the way in which learning gained by those practitioners involved in the study might be communicated to those new to the idea of working with the AAG scale. Guidelines were produced and these have been updated regularly (Machin, 2005/6/7) with new thinking emerging from both practitioners in the field and the second practice study (Machin, 2007a). The methods and procedures for using the scale will be discussed in the next chapter.

The possibility of using the AAG scale as an outcome measure has emerged from a separate study (Lydon, Ryan-Woolley and Amir, 2007). A revised version of the AAG scale, for use with young people (see Appendix 5), was used to assess the efficacy of intervention in a Child Bereavement Service, following varied support and therapeutic interventions. These interventions included peer groups, individual counselling and work with the child in the context of the family. Statistical analysis of the data for 52 children who had completed the revised AAG scale before and after intervention, showed that:

- Children/young people had become less overwhelmed by the death of their relative (mainly a parent).
- They had developed a more balanced/resilient view of life.
- They were less controlling of their emotions and more able to be open in expressing their feelings regarding the loss.

Increasingly, services are being expected to give evidence of the effectiveness of the interventions they use with patients/clients. The scale, used as an outcome measure, may have practical application within a wide variety of health and social care settings. Clearly, all of the practice applications of the AAG scale, described in this chapter, will benefit from further research and practitioner debate.

Conclusion

Based upon research and the clinical experience of working with bereaved people, the Range of Response to Loss model was developed as a theoretical framework for describing the spectrum of grief reactions – overwhelmed, balanced/resilient, controlled. These notions of difference have parallels with other classic theories of grief. In particular, there is a relationship with Attachment Theory, which persists in its central influential position in the field of bereavement studies, and with the contemporary theory contained in the Dual Process Model of grief.

A new measure, the Adult Attitude to Grief scale was devised to test the validity of the concepts of categorical difference proposed in the RRL framework (Machin, 2001). Test results indicated that the AAG scale provided a good measure of the three categories – overwhelmed, balanced/resilient, controlled. However, more importantly, the study demonstrated that the range of attitudes to grief could most appropriately be applied to understanding the diverse reactions taking place within individuals rather than as an account of categorical difference. This suggested that the AAG scale might be useful in clinical practice. This has been tested in a range of settings, amongst diverse populations. Practitioner experience of working with the AAG scale has confirmed its merit as a tool of assessment, as a structure for telling the story of grief, as a measure of change taking place in grief, and as an indicator for therapeutic focus. The practice application of the scale is explored in the following chapters.

6

Exploring the Individual Territory of Loss – Mapping Grief

In the last chapter distinguishable grieving characteristics were framed within the Range of Response to Loss model. What emerged from the 2001 study, exploring the concepts within the model, was that the overwhelming, resilient and controlled reactions function interactively, not as discrete grieving states (Machin, 2001). The nature of this grief dynamic became visible through the responses to the Adult Attitude to Grief scale. In this chapter the RRL model will be used as the conceptual framework for exploring the grieving dynamic more fully. This will be the base for considering two different ways of working with grief; the first, using the theoretical perspectives of the RRL model, and the second, using the AAG scale as a practice tool.

In the first of these approaches the theoretical concepts in the RRL model will be used to understand how core emotional, cognitive and behavioural responses to loss are mediated (or not) by factors of personal and social resourcefulness, or their absence. The RRL model is used as a theoretical compass to gauge the direction and intensity of grief in an individual client/patient. The second practice approach uses the AAG scale to provide a structure for mapping detailed personal reactions to loss and charting the changes in grief taking place over time. Both methods are used as the basis for more effective therapeutic engagement with grief. These themes are divided into three sections:

- The Range of Response to Loss model as a way of understanding the dynamics of grief: core grief states; resilience; vulnerability.
- The RRL model as a theoretical compass to guide practice.
- The AAG scale as a structure for mapping grief in practice.

The Range of Response to Loss model as a way of understanding the dynamics of grief

When first conceptualised, the RRL model looked at clearly defined categorical differences in loss response. While the overwhelmed, resilient and controlled themes were validated as distinguishable elements, individual responses to the AAG scale made visible the complexities of the biases and blends across the three categories described in the model (Machin, 2001). By exploring this dynamic, through case studies in the research and further practitioner use, the concepts of overwhelmed, resilient and controlled components of grief can be understood as interacting elements.

Core grief states

Within these interacting elements, two states can be seen to lie at the heart of a grief reaction; feelings of anger, guilt, sadness, etc. may be seen, particularly in the early stages of a loss or bereavement, and in this emotion-dominated state feelings may be experienced as **overwhelming**. A natural counter to this emerges with a pull to divert from feelings and focus upon action, especially in those people for whom **control** is central to a sense of well-being (see Figure 6.1). These two elements are conceptualised in the Dual Process Model of grief as loss orientation or restoration orientation (Stroebe and Schut, 1999). One or other of these core states will dominate, for most people at some stage in their grief and for some people more persistently. Persistence of one or other of these states may be particularly evident following traumatic loss. Extreme experiences of intrusive feelings or avoidant thinking strategies, often unknowingly adopted, have been identified as Post Traumatic Stress Disorder (Hodgkinson and Stewart, 1998; Horowitz, 1997), and reflect the polarising of overwhelmed and controlled responses to loss.

Overwhelmed response: Focus on feelings – sadness, anger, guilt, etc.

Controlled response: Focus on action – doing, organising, caring, etc.

Figure 6.1   Core grief states

The conflict implicit in managing these core states is seen by Marris (1974) as representing the ambivalence of loss, and the working out of that conflict as a process of grieving. Shuchter and Zisook in their description of the attempts to balance the core components of grief describe the process as:

The human thrust toward homeostasis places the bereaved in an enormous conflict between very powerful and opposing forces. Faced with intense emotional anguish, a primary task is to shut off such pain. On the other hand, the disruptive changes that are the psychological and material reality of the survivor demand attention. Facing reality initiates pain, which in turn, sets off a variety of mechanisms to mitigate against it. (1993: 30)

Grief – the tension between powerlessness and attempts to regain power

The sense of internal (overwhelming) anarchy, associated with the psychological impact of a profound loss, is not only distressing in itself but is compounded by its dislocation from the normal mechanisms of control. Actual powerlessness arising, for example, from someone's death, generates anxiety and with it a possible sense of emotional disorientation ('Am I going mad?'), which can be brought to therapy as the need to be reassured about the normality of grief. It is produced by two layers of emotion; first, the reactive response to loss, grief; and second, anxiety about the normality and appropriateness of grief – feelings about feelings. The person who has learned to use control and feel safe within it, experiences a collision between the security of that state and the vulnerability of unbidden emotional and cognitive reactions. The battle to master feelings often does not result in subdued emotions but adds to the potency of powerlessness.

Acquired ways of regulating feelings and behaviour

How to balance the competing elements of feelings and behaviour are deeply embedded in the process of personality development and socialisation. In his theory, Freud (1957) saw the task as one of subduing instincts by the ego and superego. Erikson (1980) saw development in terms of crises generated by the tension between the meeting of individual needs and acquiring the capacity to function socially (see Chapter 2). As an adult, it becomes necessary to exercise self-control in respect of inner feelings and desires, when their expression would be disadvantageous personally or socially. Self-preserving skills in not exposing personal vulnerability or social skills in being diplomatic and tactful are ways in which people learn to function appropriately. Cultural mores may dictate, through conventions in behaviour and social etiquette, the acceptability (or not) of giving expression to feelings etc. For example, the visible keening for the dead in Middle Eastern cultures contrasts with the 'stiff upper lip' typifying the British response to loss.

Contemporary Western perspectives on powerlessness and power

In a society where education, economic stability, health care and professional opportunities, are available to many of its citizens, there is both a real and an illusory sense of control over much of life experience. Assertive decision making, use of personal and political power, cooperation, negotiation and even manipulation are ways in which people can exert control. For many people personal well-being depends upon feeling in charge of life. This can pose real problems when in a risk-averse society people have become less skilled in dealing with unexpected events and frustrated aspirations (Craib, 1994). Within modern, Western society, therefore, the capacity to adapt to loss has been weakened, as life contingencies such as illness and disease have been overcome, and in many circumstances death itself will be seen as avoidable. Frequent enquiries into apparent incompetence and litigation for alleged culpability in public services are evidence of a society unwilling to be reconciled to the ultimate vulnerability, human mortality. However, the range of losses which accompany developmental change and arise as unpredicted life contingencies (described in Chapter 2) will generate varying degrees of grief, and will clearly make attempts to be wholly in control problematic.

Resilience

Resilience is having the capacity to achieve a fine balance between the contradictory and competing forces of grief rather than being able to stay in control of life events. It is the ability to face the distress, tension, and uncertainties of loss, with courage, resourcefulness and optimism (Seligman, 1998), while recognising those areas of life where control and active choice are still possible and appropriate. The process of reconciling the tension between the core grief responses begins when the overwhelming feelings about a loss which cannot be changed are accepted and faced, and there is a revised understanding about those areas of life where control is possible. This synchronising of opposite forces is seen in the natural world where the rain and the sun coexist and produce the rainbow; a helpful metaphor for resilience. The Dual Process Model of grief describes the dynamic relationship between facing feelings and having a continued ability to deal with ongoing life demands as oscillation (Stroebe and Schut, 1999). Greene (2002) describes this as a self-righting mechanism, which promotes adaptation to loss.

Resilience and the RRL model

Resilience is the capacity to integrate and find a balance and coherence between the core elements of grief; overwhelmed feelings and controlling aspirations comfortably coexist (see Figure 6.2).

In addition to the inner processes of reconciliation and integration, the availability of appropriate **social support** is crucial for the promotion of resilience. The context of grief is the family and wider social/cultural networks, which potentially provide the necessary support to members suffering the consequences of loss (Rosenblatt, 1993). This may be available formally through ritual and shared expression of belief, and informally through the symbolic interactions taking place between people. At the formal level, ritual provides an opportunity for the chaos of distress to be expressed and redefined through the symbols and meanings used to address both the transitional and the new status of the bereaved (Shapiro, 2001). At the informal level, time taken to share memories and reconstruct the biography of the deceased with other mourners provides

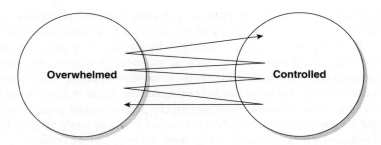

Figure 6.2 Resilience – reconciling and integrating the core dimensions of grief (described in the Dual Process Model as oscillation. Stroebe and Schut, 1999)

personally affirming and socially sustaining bonds in the early days of bereavement (Walter, 1996). At its best, therefore, ritual is a means of promoting resilience by embracing distress and providing symbolic actions, which enable the loss to be endured and managed.

Vulnerability

The process of reconciling the tension between the core elements of grief is often a lengthy one. Where a person lacks the innate qualities of resilience (courage, optimism, inner resourcefulness, social support networks, and a capacity to find meaning) or does not develop them as part of the journey through grief, they are likely to demonstrate some degree of **vulnerability**. Conceiving vulnerability as opposite in nature to resilience, implies that there will be an incapacity to balance the competing forces of grief.

In the past, two key risk factors (see Chaper 3) provided a way of identifying vulnerability. First, the predisposing resourcefulness (or not) of the person, and, second, the circumstances of the loss. The first of these factors is created by life events and personality, which have developed either to produce resilient coping mechanisms in the face of difficult life experience, or not in the case of risk. Attachment Theory suggests that insecure people who are anxious and fearful are at high risk following a major bereavement (Parkes and Weiss, 1983), although recognition should be given to the capacity for this to change over the life course (Feeney and Noller, 1996). Secondly, risk arises from the nature of the loss experience itself. The circumstantial factors producing risk have been identified as a loss which is sudden and unexpected, the death of a child, a stigmatised loss such as death by suicide etc., and where there are concurrent crises such as redundancy and divorce etc. (Sanders, 1993).

Stress theory looks at the relationship between the demands of the situation and the resources for coping with it. This is described in stress theory as 'a particular relationship between the person and the environment that is appraised by the individual as taxing or exceeding his or her resources and endangering his or her well-being' (Lazarus and Folkman 1984: 19). Where the demands are high and the resources low, Post Traumatic Stress Disorder may be the extreme manifestation of vulnerability, evidenced through an inability to regulate either intrusive feelings and thoughts or regulation by flight into avoidance (Hodgkinson and Stewart, 1998; Horowitz et al., 1980). The interplay of predisposing factors and loss experience are variably accounted for by stress theory and Attachment Theory (Stroebe and Schut, 2001).

Vulnerability and the RRL model

The extent to which a person is rendered vulnerable by their loss can be explored using the RRL model. While there is not a separate category in the model defined as vulnerability, it is evident as an absence of resilience, and is characterised by:

- Unresolved **tension** between the overwhelming powerlessness of grief and the strong pull to be in control, especially when being in control is central to a person's sense of well-being.
- **Overwhelming feelings** and thoughts are especially **powerful** and **persistent**.
- **Control** is the normal coping style but the usual strategies fail to **subdue distressing emotions** of grief.

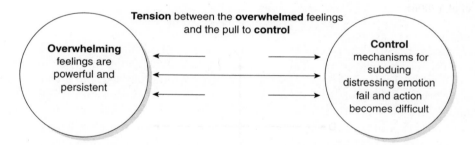

Figure 6.3   Vulnerability demonstrated by an incapacity to move comfortably between the core grief responses

Vulnerability, therefore, is seen as an inability to manage and reconcile feelings, thoughts and actions in a satisfactory way, that is an inability to oscillate between the core grief dimensions. It also indicates that the resources of the mourner are being taxed beyond the capacity to sustain wellbeing (Folkman, 2001; Lazarus and Folkman, 1984). Figure 6.3 shows how extreme elements of overwhelmed emotion or anxious attempts to exert control produce vulnerability as well as a tension between those two core modes of grief.

It is important, however, to recognise that transitory distress, an overwhelmed response, or aspiration for control, are not in themselves indicative of vulnerability. These responses are likely to be evident soon after a loss has occurred, when the reality of the loss has not been absorbed and the mechanisms of adjustment are not yet operating. One or other of these extremes may be seen, for example, at a funeral when the mourner automatically responds in a way that is typical for him/her, such as distressed sobbing or a blank emotionless demeanour.

The RRL model as a theoretical compass to guide practice

The RRL model provides a way of looking at the core states of grief, overwhelmed (feelings) and the desire for control, and at mediating factors – personal resources and circumstantial demands – which lead to a resilient or vulnerable outcome. These intersecting dimensions provide a conceptual compass for observing the grief dynamic (see Figure 6.4).

More detailed characteristics of grief response associated with the four dimensions – overwhelmed, controlled, resilient and vulnerable – are shown in Figure 6.5. The 'compass' shows how both overwhelmed and controlling responses are not of themselves indicators of vulnerability but it is how they are managed and what other personal and circumstantial factors prevail to produce vulnerability or resilience. This depiction of the grief dynamic echoes the integrative risk factor framework proposed by Stroebe et al. (2006).

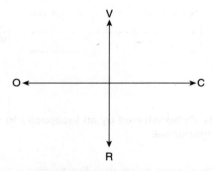

Figure 6.4   The intersecting dimensions of overwhelmed and controlled grief, and factors which produce resilience or vulnerability

The 'compass' used as a way of demonstrating detailed variability in loss response

Overwhelmed and vulnerable – Overwhelmed feelings are likely to be powerful and persistent when a person has acquired few personal strengths for meeting stressful life events, such as relationship difficulties, financial problems, sickness, bereavement, etc. This may lead to a general pessimism about the loss situation itself or about the personal capacity to cope with it. There may also be a limited ability to make sense of what is happening which adds to the feeling of powerlessness. Social support may be limited or the grieving person unable to engage with it. Overall, these factors will produce a situation in which demands exceed the capacity to manage change and this will produce some degree of vulnerability.

Overwhelmed and resilient – Where a person has developed personal resourcefulness and can access effective social support, which is adequate for meeting the circumstantial demands of a loss, resilience is likely to be evident. In resilience, overwhelming feelings of grief can be faced and tolerated and are recognised as an appropriate but temporary reaction to loss. The grieving person is more able to make sense of events without perceiving them as permanent, all pervasive or the result of personal culpability (Seligman, 1992). The resilient response is characterised by acceptance of emotions, which are embraced within the spectrum of reactions to loss.

In the same way, the controlling reaction to loss will be manifest in different ways depending on personal coping style and other personal and circumstantial factors.

Controlled and vulnerable – Where personal capacity is limited and circumstantial demands are high, the normal strategies for remaining in control may be defeated and the anxiety of powerlessness will be very dominant. The struggle to reassert control may show itself in difficulty in accepting the reality of the loss or being defensive about its consequences, for example, by not accepting the need for support. In spite of the need to suppress emotion, some reactions, such as irritability, inappropriately targeted anger etc., may demonstrate that the attempt to achieve control is problematic.

Controlled and resilient – Where the aspiration for control is not undermined but is reinforced by adequate personal resources and manageable circumstantial factors, control may be seen as a functioning response to loss. Functioning will be based on a realistic appraisal of changed circumstances and a practical focus will distinguish those aspects of life in which choice and active agency are possible. Clear strategies will be used to confront the loss and counter the sense of powerlessness.

Practitioners in health and social care need to be able to distinguish these variable manifestations of resilience and vulnerability when they are working with clients/patients, in order to identify those most in need of support. Using the 'compass' perspectives of the RRL model, the matrix (see Figure 6.5) has been developed as guidance for palliative care workers who, during the period of caring for a dying patient, will appraise the likely need relatives and friends might have for bereavement support following the death (Relf, Machin and Archer, 2008). Multiple agreement with factors in the top half of the matrix will indicate the potential need for loss/bereavement support, while evidence of a bias towards responses in the bottom half of the matrix will show that the need for bereavement/loss support is less likely. These, however, are not fixed realities but full recognition needs to be given to how grief and the circumstances surrounding it change over time. Support would not/should not be denied to people who self-refer for support, on the basis of their own perceived need.

The matrix provides a way of understanding the interplay of factors which contribute to the Range of Response to Loss. The manifestation of these variable responses will be

	Vulnerability	
Overwhelmed and vulnerable **Feelings:** Continual and/or high levels of distress. **Thoughts:** Preoccupied with the loss. Views self as a victim of circumstances. **Behaviours:** Confused, unpredictable. **Life perspective:** Generally negative outlook. **Social support:** Perceives support as lacking or makes poor use of it.	**Personal capacity reduced**, for example, by physical or psychological problems, difficulty in dealing with past stresses. **Circumstantial risk heightened** by concurrent factors such as difficult death, caring for children, elderly parents, relationship/ financial/housing problems.	**Controlled and vulnerable** **Feelings:** High anxiety about losing control or expressing strong feelings. **Thoughts:** Has difficulty in accepting reality. Cognitive defences may not effectively control emotions. **Behaviours:** Finds it hard to cry – temper or irritation under pressure. **Life perspective:** Believes in being strong but struggles to maintain this. **Social support:** Reluctant to make use of support or disclose personal needs.
Overwhelmed Powerful emotions are central to the experience of grief.	Vulnerability O/V C/V O ◄——— Core dimensions of grief ———► C O/R C/R Resilience	**Controlled** The desire to (re)establish control is central to grief.
Overwhelmed and resilient **Feelings:** Experiences feelings but not continually dominant. **Thoughts:** Able to understand and acknowledge impact of loss. **Behaviours:** Generally functions well. **Life perspective:** Has hope for the future even when currently distressed. **Social support:** Uses available support well.	**Personal capacity**: inner resources are adequate to meet the demands of the loss (for example, positive past experience, confidence, hopeful outlook). **Circumstantial factors** are positive, for example, events surrounding death, support available, additional demands manageable.	**Controlled and resilient** **Feelings:** Not visible **Thoughts:** Thinks clearly regarding strategies to manage loss. **Behaviours:** Functions practically and effectively. **Life perspective:** Believes in importance of being strong. **Social support:** Makes few demands on social support.

Figure 6.5   Matrix showing the intersection of the core grief responses with the personal and circumstantial factors which may produce resilience or vulnerability (Relf, Machin and Archer, 2008)

Table 6.1 A Narrative interpretation of the elements within the Range of Response to Loss model

Narrative Process (Angus and Hardke, 1994)	Range of Response to Loss (Machin, 2001)		
	Overwhelmed	Balanced/Resilient	Controlled
External narrative (what happened, when and how…)	Story told in great detail with emphasis upon the awfulness of experience.	Story told with coherence and attention given to the positive and negative aspects of experience.	Story told with minimum detail and with an emphasis upon factual aspects of experience.
Internal narrative (the impact of events upon the teller)	The engulfing nature of grief is described (2) and the teller may assume the role of victim.	The pain of loss (1) is countered by a positive sense of personal resourcefulness (3)	The desire for control (6) and bravery (4) dominates and accounts of pain are minimised.
Reflexive narrative (a process of making sense of experience)	A lack of hopefulness about the outcome of grief (5) and difficulty in finding a sense of meaning within it (7). Personal identity may be defined in terms of the loss.	A sense of optimism in spite of the pain (9), a capacity to find meaning, and awareness of the strength which might result from an experience of loss.	A diversion from the painful elements of loss and a need to find meaning in the stoical meeting of adversity (8).

Although this approach does not make direct use of the AAG scale it can be useful to see how the attitudinal statements in the Adult Attitude to Grief scale (Machin, 2001) are located within narrative accounts of loss – AAG scale item indicated by the numbers.

heard when listening to the stories of loss told by grieving people. Table 6.1 applies the concepts of the RRL model to the narrative process. The external and internal narrative make up the story which the therapist/counsellor will hear, and the reflexive narrative is the dimension in which therapeutic focus will primarily take place.

In a narrative which is dominated by overwhelmed feelings, an ability to find areas of life where control can be exercised is yet to be achieved. The reflexive narrative will be characterised by a lack of hopefulness, difficulty in finding a sense of meaning within the events of loss and personal identity defined in terms of the loss, for example, the woman whose husband committed suicide, the family whose son was killed, etc. When this perspective is brought to therapy the focus of narrative reconstruction will be towards enhancing a sense of hopefulness, developing resourcefulness and finding meaning.

A controlled narrative will lack focus upon emotional distress and attend to the factual aspects of experience. The reflexive narrative will emerge as one in which meaning is found through meeting adversity stoically. For some people this will be achieved through cultural and religious beliefs, which value stoicism and discourage emotional expression of grief. For other people, however, a significant loss may prompt a fundamental revision of life perspectives and strategies for feeling more able to deal with emotion, this is a task for narrative reconstruction.

Potential vulnerability is present in both of these story themes and will be clearly evident in a narrative which shows an incapacity to face distress, a lack of connection to personal or social resources and overall pessimism or false optimism. It is also seen as the direct opposite of a resilient narrative, which is told with coherence and recognition given to both positive and negative aspects of the story (Dallos, 2006). The capacity to recognise and make use of personal and social resources and find meaning within experience is present in the resilient narrative but absent from the vulnerable one.

In listening to the clients/patient's narrative, it is important to remember that grief is a shifting dynamic and any conclusion about how an individual might be grieving must be subject to reappraisal and revision during the course of clinical work.

Alongside the attention given to individual grief reactions, it is necessary to consider how the social context of family and friends contributes to personal resourcefulness. What is the nature of comfort giving or tension within family/friendship relationships and are the different grieving styles within these relationships compatible or in conflict? Additionally, what are the social responsibilities carried by each family member, and what are the mechanisms for support? Pressures generated by limited finance, inadequate housing, health problems, employment difficulties, etc. should all be taken into account when understanding the emotional and social resources of an individual (Scharf et al., 2006; Scharf, Phillipson and Smith, 2007).

The following is an account of counselling work in which the RRL model was used as a theoretical compass for understanding the grief dynamics of the client.

Case Study 6.1

The counsellor's initial encounter with Sally came as the result of a referral, which described her as struggling with grief following the death of her mother. Using the RRL model to provide compass bearings for assessment and intervention in counselling, the counsellor was looking for the extent to which Sally's bereavement was overwhelming and how control featured in her response to loss. Additionally, how were these core grief states mediated by personal resourcefulness, or its absence, and by wider circumstantial stress?

Initially, Sally was clearly overwhelmed. Distress was dominant; Sally was very tearful and she described herself as being overwhelmed (her word) with grief. Her thinking was preoccupied with distress and distorted her sense of being able to manage life demands as a wife and mother. This was self-fulfilling to the extent that she had difficulty in functioning and spent a good deal of time playing computer games and aimlessly wandering around the house. All of these factors contributed to a sense of hopelessness not least because she perceived her own situation as echoing that of her mother, who had been subject to serious bouts of depression. Sally was part of a busy family and social network but at the time she was first seen she was not able to access this network for her own support.

Alongside Sally's distress was an account of a woman who had successfully held some demanding professional jobs. Sally's previous confident, positive self-image seemed to have disappeared, and the things which were crucial to her sense of well-being were hidden by her grief. This produced a secondary layer of anxiety about her currently unrecognised self and her capacity to recover her old competencies.

For Sally there was an uncomfortable struggle between the overwhelming nature of her grief and the desire to have some control in her life. This same pattern was repeated some time later when her brother committed suicide. In both situations the therapeutic object was to help reconcile these competing forces and nurture her facility for resilience.

When Sally was first seen she was clearly vulnerable. It was evident in the struggle between the overwhelmed feelings and her desire for control, a state which had persisted for over two years. She had also found it difficult to acknowledge the persistence of her grief with family and friends and so effectively access their support. It was important, therefore, for the counselling to explore the extent to which this could be reversed by helping her engage with her own innate resilience and the personal strengths and social connectedness, which had typified her pre-bereavement functioning. Sally's story will be picked up in Chapters 7 and 8 as she gives an account of her bereavements and the counselling process is described in more detail.

The AAG scale as a structure for mapping grief in practice

The AAG scale, having been used as a tool for research, emerged as a measure capable of providing an individual profile of grief (Machin, 2001). While psychometric testing is not unusual in the setting of a psychology service (Machin and Spall, 2004), the type of counselling used in working with grieving people in other settings may make a questionnaire feel an inappropriate tool for some practitioners. The clinician needs to be able to distinguish between personal resistance and professional sensitivity, in order to reach a rational decision about the appropriate/inappropriate use of a measure such as the AAG scale. Many counselling practitioners, especially those trained in a person-centred approach, would regard the use of a measure/questionnaire as an anathema. However, Joseph and Linley assert that, 'there is no reason not to use tests and measure within the person-centred framework ... it is not what the therapist does that is important, it is how they do it' (2006: 86). As was confirmed in the previous chapter and will be shown in case study 6.2, sensitive use of the AAG scale does not compromise the integrity of practitioners who use a person-centred approach. Rather, it can enhance the ways in which the client's story is facilitated (Machin, 2007a).

The studies into the practice use of the AAG scale (Machin, 2007a; Machin and Spall, 2004) provided evidence of four areas in which the scale was a helpful therapeutic tool:

1   **Assessment** of the nature of grief may be pertinent to many practitioners in health and social care, where a clear understanding of the manner of client/patient response to loss will determine subsequent support/intervention/treatment.
2   **Clarification** of complex grief symptoms is often necessary when a client/patient presents a lengthy story which may be confused and overlaid with conflicting emotions.
3   **Therapeutic exploration** develops as the structure of the scale provides both prompts for telling the story of loss and opportunity to look more deeply at experiences, meanings and desired outcomes.
4   **Measurement of change** is possible with the repeat use of the scale. It reveals the changing perspectives over time.

Guidance for using the AAG scale in practice

A six-stage process suggests a pathway for using the AAG scale quantitatively and qualitatively (Machin 2005/6/7)– see Figure 6.6.

Stage 1

The client/patient completes his/her response to each of the nine items on the self-report questionnaire. This may be done alone or with the assistance of the practitioner.

The scale might be introduced in the following way (adjusted for bereavement or other losses):

> The term grief is usually associated with our reactions when someone important has died. The kind of feelings and thoughts (such as anger, sadness, guilt, etc.) which we have when we are bereaved can occur with many other losses (for example separation from someone who is important to us, illness, disability, redundancy, etc). The nine statements in this questionnaire are a way of exploring what your experience of loss is like and how you are reacting to it. This will help your counsellor/therapist/nurse etc. understand the aspects of your bereavement (or other loss) which are important to focus on in the process of offering you support. It may also help you understand more about your own reaction to your loss.

Stage 2

This is a self-report questionnaire and so the involvement of the client in as much of the process, as is possible, should be attempted.

• Scores are applied to the responses, by the practitioner – see Appendix 3. This might be done in the session where the immediate insight of the client would be helpful, or after the session if this is thought less intrusive to the counselling process.

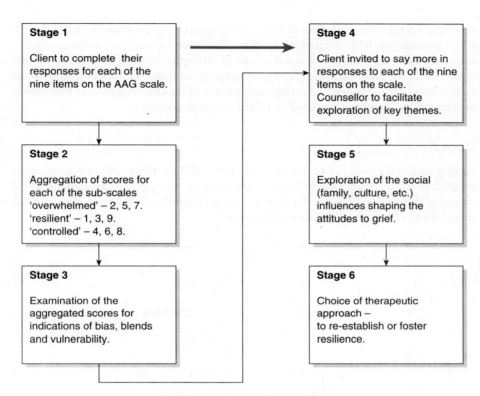

Figure 6.6   A six-stage process for working with grief using the AAG scale

While the process consists of six steps, where practitioners choose to use the AAG scale only as a qualitative tool, steps 2 and 3 are omitted (move from stage 1 to 4 – see the block arrow).

Plus numbers (+2 and +1) indicate strong agreement and agreement, respectively.

Minus numbers (−2 and −1) indicate strong disagreement and disagreement respectively.

Zero (0) indicates neither agreement nor disagreement.

This method of scoring allows equal importance to be given to responses at each end of the scale. Disagreement with the items on the scale is as significant as agreement, for example, disagreement with the resilient factors is indicative of vulnerability. A 0 score indicates some degree of ambivalence.

- Scores for the three items in each of the three categories are aggregated:
Overwhelmed items: 2, 5, 7 are added together.
Balanced/resilient items: 1, 3, 9 are added together.
Controlled items: 4, 6, 8 are added together.
- By looking at the scores (use the record sheet – Appendix 3) for strong agreement (+2) or agreement (+1), can you see a clear categorical bias? That is, do scores +2 and/ or +1 appear for one category but not for the others? Do scores −2 and −1 appear for one category more than another?

Simple aggregation of clusters of scores give a general indication of whether there is a bias towards one RRL category or another. This process is not one in which + and − scores are used in a mathematical way to cancel each other out but as a qualitative definition of the extent of agreement and disagreement; information from both ends of the scale is important. It provides a preliminary picture of the characteristics of the respondent's grief but should not be used as a fixed categorical 'diagnosis'.

Stage 3

Having looked for evidence of general association with the three RRL categories, more detailed attention is paid to the variable combination of responses by looking at the nature of the overlap between the three categories identified in the scale. The complex permutation of responses is shown in Figure 6.7.

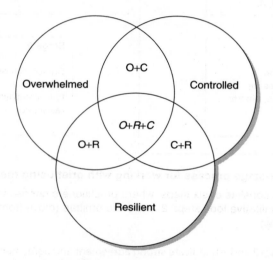

Figure 6.7   Combination and permutation of overwhelmed, resilient and controlled responses

Different combinations suggest different levels of vulnerability:

High levels of vulnerability

1) O + C = maximum distress/tension
2) O = high distress/persistent distress

Moderate levels of vulnerability

3) O+R+C = an undifferentiated response reveals some ambivalence and there may be anxiety about the conflicting aspects of grief
4) O + R = distress tempered by some qualities of resilience

Lower levels of vulnerability

5) C = controlled management of loss which may demonstrate some capacity to function well but it is necessary to be aware that this could be fragile and subject to change
6) C + R = mix of control and resilience, which may show a good coping capacity
7) R = capacity to deal with feelings and manage the consequence of loss

The process of examining these scores and interpreting them is suggested in the following steps:

- It is very unlikely for there to be a totally clear bias, that is, where there is agreement with one category but not with the other two. In the absence of a clear bias look for the ways in which the categories overlap. Are the responses undifferentiated, a true mix of O+C+R or are there two visible elements – O + C or O + R or C + R? See Figure 6.7 to help in your assessment of the degree of evident vulnerability.
- Examine the items on the scale where the scores show disagreement (−1) or strong disagreement (−2). Disagreement with statements on the scale can add to the picture of the client's grief by defining how far, for example, the client is not able to concur with the resilient statements, a demonstration of vulnerability.
- Consider scores which stand outside the overall pattern of response. For example, is there one item within a category where there is agreement but for the other two items there is disagreement? What might the client/patient be saying?
- Interpreting the responses to the scale requires attention not simply to the scores but also to what agreement or disagreement, reveal in a qualitative sense, about the nature of the grief reaction (see Appendix 3).

These three stages can usefully be repeated at points throughout the therapeutic process. This will provide indications of the direction of change (if any), which is helpful for both the practitioner and the client/patient (see Chapter 5). The repeat use of the AAG scale might also be employed as an outcome measure (Lydon, Ryan-Woolley and Amir, 2007).

Stage 4

The first three stages focus on the numerical scoring of the responses to the scale as a way of quantifying the degree of agreement or disagreement with the AAG items. The purpose is not to statistically process the responses but is a way of creating an individual profile in which the nuances of grief can be visible through the extent of agreement/disagreement with each item on the scale. At Stage 4 the focus is a qualitative one. It might follow immediately from Stage 1 if the scale is intended primarily as a structured cue for exploring the story of grief brought by the client/patient (see Appendix 4). Or it might follow the more detailed scrutiny of the numerical scores at Stages 2 and 3.

The exploration of themes associated with the items on the scale provides an opportunity to listen to the more detailed client perspective as he/she begins to qualify his/her agreement/disagreement with the nine statements. By elaborating on the responses to each of the nine items in the AAG scale, greater depth will be given to the story of grief. This might flow quite naturally as the client reflects on his/her reaction to the statements

Adult Attitude to Grief scale (numbered as on the scale)	Themes for therapeutic exploration
Overwhelmed statements	
2 For me, it is difficult to switch off thoughts about the person I have lost.	2 The unwelcome intrusion of grief, or the the chosen desire to remain focused upon it.
5 I feel that I will always carry the pain of grief with me.	5 The persistence of grief – an incapacity to see beyond the current pain/distress.
7 Life has less meaning for me after this loss.	7 A sense that life's meaning has been lost and life has changed fundamentally.
Resilient statements	
1 I feel able to face the pain which comes with loss.	1 The ability to confront the loss and deal with the emotional reactions to it.
3 I feel very aware of my inner strength when faced with grief.	3 A sense of inner resourcefulness including a capacity to access and use social support.
9 It may not always feel like it but I do believe that I will come through this experience of grief.	9 A positive outlook which can see beyond the current pain/distress.
Controlled statements	
4 I believe that I must be brave in the loss.	4 A value put upon courage and fortitude. This may be for its own sake or in order to support/ protect other people.
6 For me, it is important to keep my grief under control.	6 The importance of keeping emotions in check. Fear of the power of unleashed emotions.
8 I think it's best just to get on with life after a loss.	8 The need to divert and focus on the future.

Figure 6.8   Linking the items on the AAG scale with themes for therapeutic exploration

or it might be prompted by the counsellor as the nature of grief is examined more fully. The counsellor/therapist may initiate the general themes suggested by the items in the AAG scale (see Figure 6.8).

It will soon become clear that some themes are more pertinent to some clients/ patients than others but they will readily choose to explore and elaborate those which are most significant and/or difficult for him/her. The sensitive practitioner will be able to pick up cues given by the client/patient about the dimensions of grief which are most problematic.

Stage 5

Wider social influences impact upon individual grief reactions and attitudes. This needs to be recognised in the therapeutic context.

- How far are cultural and religious values and beliefs reflected in the attitudes of the client/patient?
- Does the client/patient feel supported by opportunities to express his/her grief – formally through ritual, informally through social/cultural networks, etc.?
- Do the family and friendship groups provide appropriate support?
- Do any of the cultural or interpersonal perspectives on loss (past or present) conflict with those of the client/patient?
- Is a difference of perspective shown in personal discomfort and/or social alienation?

Where there is evidence of dissonance between the personal and social way of looking at loss it might be helpful for significant others as well as the client to complete the AAG scale in order to explore the grieving social dynamic within a family. (See the example of William and Joan (Machin and Spall, 2004) in Chapter 5.)

Stage 6

The AAG scale aids the telling and the exploration of the story of loss. As the practitioner actively engages with the change processes of narrative reconstruction, choices will be made about the most appropriate therapeutic route to be taken. A desired overall therapeutic objective might be defined as one in which there is increased capacity to deal with the emotional distress of loss and a greater facility to manage the cognitive and social consequences of it (Shaver and Tancredy, 2001), that is, the fostering of 'resilience'. This is done within the context of a supportive relationship in which client/patient and therapist join to co-construct a preferred narrative – a story to be lived by and lived with (McLeod, 1997). For some clients/patients this may be a wish to restore the status quo, by subduing the 'overwhelming' emotions of grief, or being back in 'control'. For other people, the experience of loss may be a catalyst for a more fundamental change in life perspective, what Joseph and Linley (2006) call 'adversarial growth'. A therapeutic repertoire will be necessary to facilitate the exploration of emotion, thinking, behaviour and meaning-making. A range of therapeutic approaches was discussed in Chapter 4, and illustrative case examples will be used in Chapters 7, 8 and 9.

Case Study 6.2

The AAG scale was used as a means of exploring the grieving state of Jean, a 55-year-old widow, and as a way of following the changes taking place in her grief reactions. Table 6.2 shows the comparative responses to the scale on the four occasions it was used.

Jean had been referred to a counselling service by her GP who was concerned about the considerable emotional distress she was experiencing following the death of her husband. She had an assessment interview before she started counselling. With Jean's

(Continued)

(Continued)

Table 6.2   Four uses of the AAG scale during the process of counselling

Adult Attitude to Grief scale	Time1		Time 2		Time 3		Time 4	
O 2 For me, it is difficult to switch off thoughts about the person I have lost.	+2		+1		+2		+1	
5 I feel that I will always carry the pain of grief with me.	+2	+6	+1	+3	+1	+5	+1	+2 & −1
7 I believe nothing will ever be the same after an important loss.*	+2		+1		+2		−1*	
R 1 I feel able to face the pain which comes with loss.	−1		+2		0		+2	
3 I feel very aware of my inner strength when faced with grief.	−2	−4	+1	+4	0	0 &	+1	+5
9 It may not always feel like it but I do believe that I will come through this experience of grief.	−1		+1		+1	+1	+2	
C 4 I believe that I must be brave in the face of loss.	−1		−1		−1		−1	
6 For me, it is important to keep my grief under control.	+2	−2 & +2	−1	−2 & +0	−1	−2 & +2	+1	−1 & +2
8 I think it's best just to get on with life after a loss.	−1		0		+1		+1	

* 7 was changed to 'Life has less meaning for me after this loss' and was used at Time 4. The scores are shown for each of the nine items and the associated aggregated score for each sub-scale, shown in the following column.

agreement, the counsellor used the scale at her first counselling session, in order to look systematically at the nature of her grief. The dominant dimension of her grief was exemplified by her strong agreement with all the items on the overwhelmed sub-scale. She had managed to function for the first nine months of her bereavement by retaining control through deflected activity and business. Responses to the scale showed that she still believed it was important to keep her emotions in check, but she had come to realise that being brave and getting on with life no longer worked for her. The tension between overwhelming emotion and the desire for control, together with disagreement with the resilient attitudinal statements confirmed the clinical evidence, that Jean was having considerable difficulty in coping with her grief.

At the second time of use, the intensity of Jean's sense of being overwhelmed was less, and she was clearer about not having to be in control. She felt able to confront the pain and was more certain of her resourcefulness and a positive outcome. This changed grief profile indicated a considerable shift in perspective. Jean could release the hold on her feelings as she became more aware of her own strength in doing this, and as she recognised that it did not involve falling apart. Her improved functioning was the result of a move from a strategy based upon control to one in which the consequences of her loss could be faced and dealt with.

On the third occasion there was a reversal in the trends of Jean's responses, compared with those at time two. An increase in agreement in the overwhelmed items was matched with ambivalence about both the controlled and the resilient items. 'Getting on with life' was the strategy employed in the face of the upsurge in Jean's grief, which resulted from some difficult family circumstances and the prospect of facing her first Christmas without her husband.

On the final occasion when the scale was used, six months after its first use, the category with which there was clearest agreement was that of resilience. Some (overwhelmed) pain persisted, and while not needing to be brave, the other dimensions of the controlled sub-scale were important for Jean. At this stage not only were the resilient elements dominant in Jean's grief reaction but she was using these resilient qualities to reconcile both the pain of grief (overwhelmed) by accepting it and its management (control) as a realistic practical strategy.

During the period of counselling, while circumstances caused her grief to fluctuate, Jean's inner strength grew as did her self-confidence. She was able to be more assertive, exercise appropriate control, while being able to face her emotions honestly and deal with them. The scale was an important catalyst in the helping process and a useful measure of change.

This case example uses the responses to the AAG scale as a way of mapping the nature and changing shape of Jean's grief. Her story and the therapeutic process will be explored more fully in Chapters 7 and 8.

Discussion

The RRL model provides a theoretical 'compass' to guide the appraisal of the core characteristics of grief and the mediating factors which interact with it as they are manifest in individual reactions to loss. It is a structured way of understanding individual nuances in client/patient grief as it is observed and as it is heard in the story of loss told in therapy. It is a synthesis of other grief theories and is particularly applicable to practice.

Use of the AAG scale affords a more precise way of examining the characteristics of current grief and of tracking its progression during the course of therapy. The choice about whether to work with or without a tool such as the AAG scale may be determined by therapeutic preference. For some practitioners, a person-centred approach might preclude a structure which is derived from a process of exploration external to the agenda brought by the client, although Joseph and Linley (2006) suggest that there is not necessarily a conflict between these different ways of working. However, even where the scale is seen as a possible therapeutic tool there may be some circumstances in which its use would be inappropriate. This may be in situations where the physical or mental health/capacity of the client suggest that short exchanges, which avoid emphasis on cognitive approaches to distress, are the most helpful. Heightened distress itself is likely to limit cognitive functioning, if only for a limited period. During such times listening to the emotional pain without the need for structure and process is essential. At other times, client bias towards resilience or control are so obvious that use of the scale may be superfluous.

Whether the RRL model is used as a theoretical 'compass' or the AAG scale is used as a 'mapping' tool, the therapeutic focus seeks to facilitate a move from the limitations of vulnerability to the possibilities of resilience. Dallos sees this as requiring the encouragement of coherence and integration. In those people who are dismissive of emotion, the aim is to help them 'get nearer to their feelings rather than taking the distancing position they have learnt' (2006: 128). In contrast, for those people who are emotionally preoccupied, the aim is to assist them 'to gain some distance from the immediacy of their feelings and to be able to reflect on and develop narratives which can locate experiences in causal and temporal connections' (ibid.: 129).

Conclusion

This chapter has developed the concepts begun in the last chapter by looking in more detail at how the dynamics of grief can be understood, using the RRL model as a theoretical compass. This account of the complexities of grief provides the basis for the first of two different ways of working with loss. The first approach explores the stories brought to therapy, for information about how the tension between overwhelming and controlling states of grief are being managed, and it looks at how personal and circumstantial factors combine with this process to produce vulnerability or resilience. The second approach makes use of the Adult Attitude to Grief scale to provide a more structured way of identifying the variations and complexities within the grief response. Illustrative case examples demonstrate the contrasting ways of working in these two modes.

The flexibility of the practitioner is essential to effective therapy, and central to the process is listening to the narrative of loss told by the client. A therapeutic repertoire is necessary to match the varied grief reactions with the method best suited to help restore a sense of equilibrium. Chapters 7, 8 and 9 will look in more detail at the ways of working with the core grief reactions, and the therapeutic challenge of promoting resilience and engaging with vulnerability.

7

Listening to Personal Grief Narratives

In the preface to *Narrative and Psychotherapy,* McLeod says:

> story represents the basic means by which people organise and communicate the mean-
> ing of events and experiences. Not listening to *stories* deprives both the therapist and the
> client of the most effective and mutually involving mode of discourse available to both.
> (1997: x)

Exploring the grief story through listening to the narrative account of loss provides the
counsellor/therapist with an entrée into the private world of feelings and thoughts, and
the wider social context, in which the client/patient is trying to make sense of experience. A person-centred approach (Rogers, 1961, 1980) is necessary to provide the opti-
mum therapeutic conditions for the client/patient to tell their loss story.

This chapter will look at starting to engage with the grief narrative, using the RRL
model as a theoretical compass for helping recognise the core components of grief, or
the AAG scale as a story telling structure. The external and internal narrative processes
(Angus and Hardke, 1994) will be used to consider the place of overwhelmed and controlled themes in the story (see shaded area Table 7.1). In those people who seek therapeutic help or are referred for support, the core grief responses are likely to have
produced some degree of vulnerability. The place of resilience and vulnerability will
have a more central focus in Chapters 8 and 9, as therapeutic engagement with the
reflexive narrative is used in the process of reconstruction.

Case examples will be used to illustrate the different approaches to hearing and
understanding the variable qualities of grief experienced by four clients/patients. The
first will be that of Tom, a young person, and the characteristic manifestations of grief
proposed in the RRL model will be seen in his drawings. The second and third will pick
up the stories of loss described in Chapter 6, that of Sally and Jean. In Sally's case, the
RRL model provided the conceptual background to counselling while in Jean's case the
AAG scale was a central practice tool. In the fourth case example, the AAG scale was
used as a tool to engage with Rob's complex grief reactions.

Table 7.1   The dimensions of grief, narrative structure, therapeutic approach and narrative process in listening to the nature and impact of loss

Dimensions of grief (RRL model/AAG scale)	Narrative structure (Angus and Hardke, 1994)	Therapeutic approach	Narrative process (McLeod, 1997)
Core grief responses: Overwhelmed	External	Person-centred	Construction
Controlled	Internal		Deconstruction
Balanced/ resilient	Reflexive	Psychodynamic Cognitive Meaning-making	Reconstruction

The shaded area identifies the focus for the initial storytelling process.

1   Tom aged 10 – death of his father.
2   Sally aged 38 – death of mother and brother.
3   Jean aged 55 – death of husband.
4   Rob aged 67 – death of wife.

Therapeutic engagement with grief stories

The narrative approach to counselling, described in Chapter 4, is concerned with:

- Listening to the client's story (external narrative).
- Exploring the unsatisfactory (painful) aspects of the story (internal narrative).
- Finding a more satisfactory (meaningful) story (reflexive narrative).
- Absorbing the new meanings of the story into the wider life of the client.

This chapter will focus on the first two of these narrative processes, evident through the external and internal narratives (Angus and Hardke, 1994). The external narrative will reveal the initial factual elements of the story, and the internal narrative will attend to the (painful/disturbing) impact of the loss experience on the teller. In practice, these may be woven together, with the therapist's role variably that of 'audience, witness, director, editor, interpreter, co-author' (Clarkson, 1995). The counsellor needs to be able to accept, hear and understand (Howe, 1993) in order to help promote the unfolding narrative.

How the story is told will indicate something of the nature of the grief reaction (see Table 6.1, p. 101). In listening to the personal descriptions of loss (the external and internal narratives), the counsellor will begin to understand how the bereavement/loss is being experienced. The characteristic responses within the RRL model will become visible.

- **Overwhelming grief** is evident when –

   The story of loss lacks coherence.
   Grief is experienced as emotionally engulfing.
   Distress is persistent.
   There are no signs of relief from distress.
   Life doesn't seem to make sense or have a purpose.
   The storyteller assumes the role of 'victim'.

- **Controlling grief** is evident when –

   The story is told with minimum detail.
   Bravery and stoicism are important values.
   Accounts of pain and suffering are avoided.
   Control is central to well-being.
   Supporting other people is an important goal.
   Receiving support is resisted.

Difficulty in coping/functioning may result from excessive emotions and/or defeating attempts to regain control, which will alert the counsellor/therapist to either temporary or more prolonged **vulnerability**. The practitioner also needs to be aware of other circumstantial pressures which are contributing to heighten vulnerability. The evidence of the contrasting responses to loss will fluctuate over time. Reaching a point where there is comfortable coexistence between the feeling, thinking, and behaving responses to loss is the goal of therapy, which will be addressed through a focus on resilience in Chapter 8.

- **Resilience** is evident when –

   The story is told with coherence.
   There is a sense of personal and social resourcefulness.
   Painful emotions can be faced and accepted.
   Action can be based on realistic appraisal of what is possible.
   There is an overall sense of optimism.

How do the core elements of grief show themselves in the narrative process? Four narrative journeys

While adults may find it difficult to describe their grief, children are even more likely to find talking about their loss problematic. However, increased knowledge about the nature of grief in childhood and the therapeutic ways of addressing it, have been developed (Christ, 2005; Machin, 1993; Munroe and Krause, 2005; Stokes, 2004). Unlocking the intense emotion and complex thinking about the person who has died requires patience and sensitivity. Moving to a stage where this can all begin to make sense to the child or young person can be a lengthy process.

Case Study 7.1   Tom, aged 10

In this first case example 10-year-old Tom gives an account of his grief story following the death of his father.

External narrative – a factual account of the events of Tom's loss

Tom's father died of a brain tumour. He was in his late 30s and during the period of his illness and increasing physical deterioration, Tom and his younger sister had been aware of the seriousness of the situation and fully involved in observing his care and treatment. He had been at home most of the time but as his death drew near he was admitted to hospital. At this stage other family members came to say their farewells and began to take over general decision making from Tom's mother, who was continually by her husband's side. An uncle decided that Tom and his sister should not see their father in this final stage of dying and so arrangements were made for them to be looked after by friends.

Internal narrative – the impact of the dying and death upon Tom

The circumstances surrounding the death made Tom angry and upset. He found it difficult to articulate his feelings but described the situation as 'not fair'. His counsellor invited him to draw a picture with 'it's not fair' as the title (see Figure 7.1). He began with what might be seen as a Freudian slip – 'it's not fear'. C.S. Lewis described his grief as

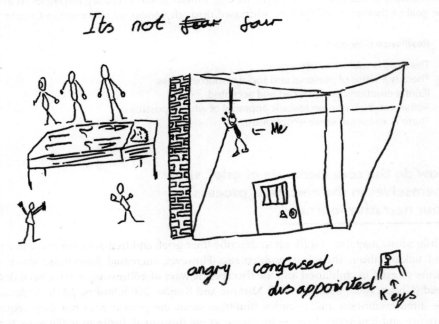

Figure 7.1   A picture of Tom's grief

Sometimes I get angry because...

Putting anger on paper doesn't hurt anyone!

Figure 7.2   A picture of Tom's anger

being like fear (1961). Perhaps it is not surprising that in some way Tom was also find-ing fear to be a part of his emotional response to his loss. The counsellor sat beside him but made no comments or observations while he was drawing. He began by painstak-ingly drawing the brick wall in the middle of the page. On the left of the wall he drew, as he imagined it, his father's deathbed scene in which the family and priest surrounded the bed. On the right hand side of the wall was a locked room, secured by keys kept in a cabinet outside. Tom showed himself banging with his fists on the wall, wanting to be part of that last stage of his father's life. He felt that not only had he been excluded but that other people who were there had less right than he had to say goodbye to his dad. The picture conveys something more powerful than the words he used – angry, con-fused, disappointed. Tom was overwhelmed by the powerlessness he felt and desper-ate for the limited control he had previously had as a participant in the process of loss.

Initially, Tom found it difficult to express the anger he felt especially as his inclination was to blame God for his father's illness. Tom had been brought up in a strong religious tradition, attending Catholic church and a Catholic school. It was alien to his learned beliefs that God could be anything but benevolent. His counsellor, while not undermin-ing what were key religious and social influences and support systems, encouraged Tom to feel safe in acknowledging his anger (Heegaard, 1988). He drew another picture of the globe with a clear outline of Britain in which a huge hand was lifting off the map a matchstick representation of his father (see Figure 7.2). Again, his powerlessness and lack of control were acknowledged and heard.

The counsellor's perspective

The overwhelming sense of powerlessness is very clear in Tom's account of his father's death. The pictures were an important way for him to convey his distress and showed the intensity of his overwhelmed feelings and his lack of control. They provided their own story form and helped the counsellor to see both Tom's pain and the ways in which he felt out of control. In Chapter 8 we will look at how Tom's counsellor worked with his grief.

Case Study 7.2   Sally, aged 38

Sally's story of grief, much of it told in her own words, is divided into two sections: a) following the death of her mother, and b) following her brother's suicide.

A) External narrative – a factual account of Sally's bereavement

Sally's external narrative contained five topic areas:

1   Sally's mother's death.
2   The way Sally coped with bereavement.
3   Practical changes in Sally's life post-bereavement.
4   How Sally managed home life.
5   The counselling option.

1)   Sally's mother died of a brain haemorrhage brought on by high blood pressure. 'I think she knew she was going to die but wasn't able to make anyone else do anything about it.'
2)   Nine months after the death, and at a point when Sally had finished a work contract, she felt the need to get some help and went to her GP. The medication took away the intensity of Sally's depression but induced a 'bland and unanimated' state in which there were 'few lows but also few highs'.
3)   Eighteen months after the death, Sally and her family moved some considerable distance from the town in which she was brought up to their 'dream house'. At this point Sally came off the antidepressants.
4)   In spite of her new situation, Sally found coping with the everyday life of her family difficult so enrolled on a parenting course, believing that there was some deficit in her mothering. She found the course did not meet her needs so she stopped attending. The inner turmoil became evident when Sally was with friends and couldn't stop crying. At this stage Sally accepted that she might benefit from counselling.
5)   Two and a half years after her mother's death Sally was pleased to consider an option other than medication, believing that 'the drugs were merely masking the grief, which ultimately meant that if I stayed on the tablets I would always be this person who was somehow dimmed down on them.'

A) Internal narrative – the impact on Sally of her mother's death

Sally described herself as OK when working but 'I was very depressed at home and became unable to manage normal things like looking after the children, the house and generally organising my life.' Managing these reactions to her loss through medication dulled all her responses and her husband felt that she was not the woman she used to be. 'I just wanted to go to bed and pull the covers over my head. For me, depression was an unfeeling state.' However, off the medication 'my grief was seeping into all areas of my life and I was unable to cope with very much at all.' However, at the beginning of counselling, Sally recalls that, 'I remember explaining how I was feeling (to my counsellor) but being pretty much in control of myself.'

The counsellor's perspective

Underneath the initial controlled account of her loss, Sally's grief for her mother was overwhelming, as was her sense of not coping with the ongoing demands of everyday life. Sally was tearful and distressed. Her focus was upon not being a good-enough daughter; she was consumed by guilt, regret and some degree of anger. In this early narrative, Sally was clearly feeling out of control, and described herself as being 'unable to sort my head out'. She also saw the symptoms of her grief getting in the way of managing the demands of her household, a husband and two small children. Sally had previously held some demanding jobs and had functioned as a very capable and confident person. All of this positive aspect of self was lost within the grief. Although in an emotion-dominated state, Sally was having difficulty in facing her feelings, not least because her mother had suffered from depression and she feared that rumination on her own emotional pain might become a long-term problem for her too. Sally was overwhelmed by grief but unable to manage the powerful feelings which emerged.

Sally had always been in control of most life situations at both a personal and a professional level. Her mother's death confronted her with being totally out of control, no longer having the positive presence of a loved mother, nor able to set old hurts to right. She was overwhelmed by grief and sought help through medication but found that while it afforded some control of her depressed feelings it also distorted her overall emotional response to life. The tension between Sally's desire for control and the overwhelming distress of her grief are clear in the story she told of her loss. The inability to manage this tension made Sally feel very vulnerable. We will look in Chapter 8 at the therapeutic engagement with Sally's grief.

Three months after Sally finished counselling, her brother, aged 40, committed suicide. She sought counselling help immediately.

B) External narrative – a factual account of Mark's death and its consequences

1 Mark's illness and death.
2 Sally's children's reaction to their uncle's death.
3 Seeking help.

1) Sally's brother suffered from schizophrenia and had been depressed for a long time. 'He had never been given any talking therapy by the NHS who persisted in giving him more and more drugs. He would sit and think and think, trying to work out a way to become well. But he couldn't manage to make himself do anything. His 40th birthday was five days before his death. I think he just saw the rest of his life stretching out in front of him with no cure or joy and decided to end it all. It wasn't a surprise, although you never actually believe they will do it.'

2) From the beginning, Sally was open in discussing Mark's death with her two children. 'Dan wanted to know how and why Mark died and we told him the truth. In hindsight, maybe we should have tempered the discussion to help him understand, but I didn't want him to feel ashamed about what had happened.' Counselling was sought for Dan, aged eight, who was finding it difficult to deal with his uncle's death.

3) Sally knew immediately that counselling rather than medication was the help she wanted for herself.

B) Internal narrative – the impact of Mark's death upon Sally

1 Staying in control.
2 Feelings of grief.
3 Coping with day-to-day life.

1) Sally talked about her brother and his death and felt rationally that the nature of his illness had lead almost inevitably to this outcome and that now he was at peace from his many years of distress. Sally minimised the impact of Mark's death early in her bereavement – 'At first, just as previously, I felt in control and able to manage.'

2) A little time elapsed before Sally could acknowledge within herself the feelings of grief. 'I realised that I had been keeping my emotions locked away and had been doing so for some time. I became depressed once again and realised that this was caused by me not dealing properly with the grief and just keeping it inside me. I was determined not to go back to the antidepressants. I felt out of control with the house and to a lesser extent with the children once again. There were times when I felt angry with Mark for what he had done, in particular to Dan (killing himself on Dan's birthday).'

3) Sally had counselling support throughout the early days of her bereavement. Having already been through the therapeutic process in relation to her mother's death, she said, 'I knew how I would be likely to react, but I still became unable to cope with my home life and my children.'

The counsellor's perspective

The second period of counselling with Sally began immediately after Mark's death and so much of the work was in taking that journey alongside her, rather than looking retrospectively at her loss, as was the case following her mother's death. The agendas were much the same and the interconnection between feeling overwhelmed by grief and feeling overwhelmed by life were repeated. The RRL model provided a helpful theoretical compass for the counsellor, as an aid to understanding the emotional and cognitive tensions and conflicts which characterised Sally's response to loss. It was important to listen to her second loss story and consider how she was managing the core elements of grief; the pain of her sadness and loss (overwhelming aspect) and her capacity to find ways of managing her life and make active choices (control aspect). The strengths and insights gained from the first bereavement were able to reassure Sally that her vulnerability was temporary. She knew that she had the capacity to cope effectively with this second traumatic loss. Sally was able to understand the nature of her grief more quickly and used the insight acquired in her previous bereavement to find strategies to regain control where possible, while accepting and embracing the realities of those situations where control was not possible. Sally's developing resilience will be discussed more fully in Chapter 8.

Case Study 7.3   Jean, aged 55

Jean's story of her husband's death and of her bereavement experience.

External narrative – the facts of Jean's loss

In the overall telling of Jean's story the external and internal narrative were woven together but they are examined separately here to clarify the content of the narrative process.
   Jean's external narrative can be divided into five topic areas:

1   The story of Jean's husband's last illness and death.
2   The bereavement response by other family members.
3   Jean's account of herself and her usual style of coping.
4   The emergence of Jean's grief.
5   Jean's experience of counselling.

1)   This is the story which 55-year-old Jean brought to counselling. Her previously fit husband was diagnosed with lung cancer and while he responded well to chemotherapy this was not the case with radiotherapy. He deteriorated very quickly and spent the last two and a half weeks in a hospice. Jean stayed with him during those final weeks, sleeping in the same room and caring for him. Brian did not speak

(Continued)

(Continued)

about his illness or its outcome and a few days before his death he was discussing getting a new car and planning holidays.

2) After his death Jean kept going for her family not least because her 5-year-old granddaughter was suffering sleep disturbance and emotional distress following her grandfather's death, and was consequently receiving counselling. Their relationship (Brian and his granddaughter) had been very close and the counsellor said the impact had been as great as for the loss of a parent. Jean's children, two daughters and a son, coped in different ways but her son in particular was stoical and was unable to talk about his father's death.

3) Jean had held a senior job in a bank, being responsible for a lot of people and large sums of money. She saw her capabilities as being especially able to manage situations by compartmentalising things and remaining in control. In the early days of her bereavement she tried to deal with Brian's death in the same way.

4) After Brian's death there was a lot to be sorted out practically and financially. When she had completed these tasks (eight or nine months after the death), Jean went on holiday with some friends. Things changed for Jean on her return; her grief emerged for the first time. This was what took her to counselling. Initially she had two sessions of Reiki therapy at the hospice but she was not comfortable with the process. The GP referred her to a voluntary counselling organisation (the base from which this story is told).

5) Jean related well to her counsellor and agreed that the Adult Attitude to Grief scale be used as the basis for exploring her grief. The scale was used at the beginning and at several points in the counselling (see Table 6.2, p. 110).

Internal narrative – the impact of Brian's death upon Jean

Jean's story of the impact of Brian's death are explored through the same topic areas as those for the external narrative.

1) Jean described what her husband's last illness and death were like for her. The initial diagnosis came as a tremendous shock. The disbelief was compounded because of his apparent good health. When the radiotherapy was clearly not working, the reality of the nature of Brian's illness and life prospect began to hit Jean. However, Jean described the hospice experience as 'brilliant'. Other life demands were put on hold and Jean and the family could make the most of the time that was left. The kindness of the hospice staff enabled the family to fully concentrate on Brian and his needs and to recognise that – 'He was still himself, it was only his body failing'. One of her daughters, who is a nurse, undertook some of his nursing care. However, Brian's inability to talk about the reality of the situation and his continued focus on the future meant that Jean felt cheated of an opportunity to talk about some of the poignant things that might have been part of saying goodbye. This was especially difficult for Jean to deal with after his death.

2) There was a spectrum of grief responses to Brian's death, from the distressed crying and screaming of her granddaughter, to her son who was unable to talk about his father and his death. Jean's energy was taken up in being strong and sensitive to the varied ways in which her family was grieving. Her own grief remained unexpressed.

3) Jean stood outside her grief in order to show the strong and competent person she was, and as she had been in the world of work. She saw this as exemplifying the strategies she used to care for Brian in his illness and to care for her family after his death. This was a significant way for Jean to define herself and she felt it was important to justify the denial of her own grieving needs in order to be strong and supportive for her family. 'I kept this front going.'

4) Jean took a holiday after the extended period of caring for other people and sorting the practical things associated with Brian's death. On her return, she describes herself as 'a different person. I didn't want to get out of bed. I didn't care whether I was here or not. It was as if everything had shut down – it was awful.' Her family were concerned and arranged for her to see the doctor. He prescribed antidepressants and sleeping tablets, 'as a crutch', and referred her for counselling.

5) Jean felt able to 'get it all out because my counsellor was there for me without being related to me and I didn't have to hold anything back. He was an approachable person and I couldn't have had anyone better.'

The counsellor's perspective

Jean was able to give a very clear account of her husband's last illness and death and the consequences for her family. It was evident from this narrative that she had always been the person to care, support and organise. The impact of the bereavement on Jean was deflected initially because of the concern for her distressed granddaughter. The control theme dominated and it took time before she was able to confront the overwhelming feelings of grief. It was when the normal mechanisms for control were exhausted that Jean felt unable to cope and the emotional impact was considerable. For a time this made her very vulnerable and it was only as the counselling (and the use of the AAG scale) provided her with some understanding of the full spectrum of contradictory characteristics of overwhelmed and controlled grief, that she was able to move forward. The therapeutic help process is explored through the reflexive narrative in Chapter 8.

Case Study 7.4   Rob, aged 67

External narrative – the facts of Rob's loss

Rob was receiving psychological support following the death of his wife. A community psychiatric nurse, who thought that he was a suicide risk, had referred him for in-patient care.

Rob was unable to engage with the reality of his wife's death and the facts surrounding it. The loss was denied and contained in a blank period in which the events of

(Continued)

(Continued)

Alice's death could not be recalled and Rob felt himself to be in a dream. 'I have a three-week blank period after she died: I went to the funeral and the burial of the ashes but I can't remember being there.'

Internal narrative – the impact of Alice's death upon Rob

The metaphors which Rob used serve to tell a story of his disbelief about the death and his disengagement from the world. The incongruity between the reality and his perceptions are demonstrated by his statements about Alice's (as he saw it, alleged) death:

'If it were true that she was dead, then I would want to be with her.'
'I loved her; I don't think I could live without her'. Rob was indicating that facing Alice's death was something he could not do and his words suggested the potential for suicide.
'If it were true that she died here [the hospital unit where Alice had died and where Rob was having therapy], I wouldn't be able to relax or even come here'.

A blank period

Rob felt as if he was still located in the time before his wife died – 'It's March 31st [the day before his wife died] when I go to sleep.' As with the death, Rob recalled going to a wedding two days after the funeral – 'I've got the photos but I can't remember being there.'

In a dream

'To me none of this is real. When I wake up everything will be all right again.'
'Everything is still a dream and I can't waken up from it.'
'If I can wake up we shall be together again … Soon this nightmare will end: I shall wake up and we will be able to laugh about it together.' (Part of a letter written to his wife.)
'I heard my wife say, "stay in your dream, you're safer".' (Said a few weeks after her death.)
'I feel safe in my dream; it's as if the dream is protecting me.'

However, the mismatch between disbelieving Alice had died and inhabiting a world without her was highly disturbing to Rob. Even his dreams did not provide the protection he craved but confronted him with his loss – 'In my dreams I'm in a long dark space and locked in, or in a big black hole and there's no way out'.

In a cocoon/a wall between me and the world

In some ways the in-patient treatment centre did more to provide a distance between himself and the reality he wished to avoid. 'I feel I'm in a cocoon, wrapped up safe. There's no challenge [in hospital]'. 'It feels like there is a brick wall between me and the world, there is a wall all the way around myself.'

Nothing clicks or fits into place

Rob's denial of reality was not total and he was able to register a sense of incongruity within himself. 'Nothing seems to click. Nothing slots into place any more.' 'I sat in the place where we were last together. I hoped it would make something click, that it would spring a magic lever and wake me up out of this dream, so we would be back together again.' For Rob there was only one reality with which he could live and that was with his wife restored to him. 'Where is she? I can't think where she is.' The metaphors of the dreams, the cocoon, a wall between self and the world tell a very vivid story of the vulnerable need to hide from reality. This is compounded when Rob wants to recapture the pre-bereavement reality only to realise that his search is in vain and the magic lever does not bring his wife back.

The therapist's perspective

The route into Rob's grief was problematic; while demonstrating considerable psychological distress he was unable to provide an account (external narrative) of Alice's death, in other words, the starting point for his story of loss was missing. The ambiguity in how he experienced the period after the death (internal narrative) was captured in the varied metaphors he used and was a powerful way of glimpsing Rob's distress. The linguistic images, though telling stories of their own, served to demonstrate that Rob had not embarked on the first task of mourning (Worden, 2003), that of accepting the reality of loss.

Working with Rob's almost complete denial of Alice's death was extremely challenging. The AAG scale was used (Table 9.3, p. 156) to help the therapist gain greater access to the processes making up Rob's grief. Rob strongly agreed with all the overwhelmed and the controlled items on the scale. This confirmed the clinical manifestations of his grief, as a state in which there was high tension between the desire for control and real emotional distress. The therapeutic engagement with Rob's grief is explored through the reflexive narrative in Chapter 9.

Conclusion

In this chapter we have begun looking at four grief stories told in counselling/therapy (and they will be developed in Chapters 8 and 9). A person-centred approach provided the principles and the practice base from which the client/patient's story of loss and its impact was heard and facilitated. The RRL model provided a theoretical compass in the work with Tom and Sally and the AAG scale was used with Jean and Rob. Listening to their stories, whether told in words or pictures, helped to identify the ways in which the core grief responses interact with each other to produce a very individual grief reaction.

In all of the cases, we have seen the way in which powerlessness is profoundly disturbing and produces a feeling of being overwhelmed.

Tom was overwhelmed not only by his father's death but by the power adults had to exclude him from saying a final farewell. Sally and Jean's identity was strongly bound by a self-perception of being in control. When they were defeated in maintaining control both became overwhelmed by the grief from which they could no longer hide. The battle for control seemed lost and resulted in depression. Medication was used to help restore emotional equilibrium but this felt like another form of losing control. For Rob, the need for control operated at both a conscious and unconscious level and was evident in his emotional disengagement from reality.

The battle to restore emotional and cognitive equilibrium can be seen through these external and internal narrative accounts of bereavement, which variably demonstrated some degree of vulnerability. In the next two chapters the reflexive narrative will focus on the process of reconstructing new stories in order to achieve increased strengths and coping skills, resilience (Chapter 8), and as a way of working to address more persistent forms of vulnerability (Chapter 9).

8

Engaging with the Grief Narrative –
Focus on Resilience

In the last chapter we looked at how the core grief themes, characterised by overwhelmed feelings and the strong desire for control, are central to the stories of grief brought to counselling/therapy (see Figure 8.1). Listening for the infinitely variable way in which those elements might be experienced is crucial to understanding the individual nature of grief. The RRL model, as a theoretical compass, and the AAG scale, as a mapping tool, provide particular ways of accessing the grief narrative.

The overwhelmed and controlled reactions represent two of the three dimensions of grief proposed in the RRL model. The third dimension is a response indicating a balance between the core elements of grief (see Figure 8.2). This equilibrium is characterised as **resilience** and is a mediating component, reconciling the feelings, thoughts and actions which stem from the tension between being overwhelmed and desiring control.

In the same way that overwhelming distress and an anxiety to regain control are central to grief so is the capacity to adapt to adversity. For many people qualities of resilience have developed naturally over the life course and researchers agree that a large proportion of people ultimately adapt well to the consequences of loss and bereavement (McCrae and Costa, 1993; Raphael, Minkov and Dobson, 2001; Sanders, 1993). Greene

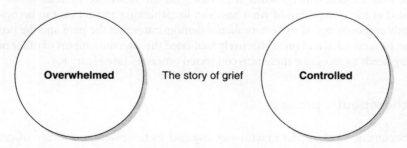

Figure 8.1   The key components within the grief narrative

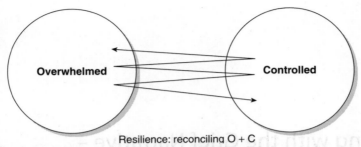

Figure 8.2 Finding a balance between the competing forces of grief

sees resilience as an 'innate self-righting mechanism', that assists in the adjustment and change demanded of 'disadvantageous or stressful circumstances' (2002: 4). Researchers and theorists (Greene, 2002; Grotberg, 1999; Seligman, 1998) have used different ways to define resilience but there are three common elements, which are important for practitioners to look for and nurture in their clients/patients (Machin, 2007b):

- **Personal resourcefulness**, characterised by qualities of flexibility, courage and perseverance.
- **A positive life perspective**, characterised by optimism, hope, a capacity to make sense of experience and motivation in setting personal goals.
- **Social embeddedness**, evident when support is available and there is a capacity to access it.

These qualities, though sometimes taking a lifetime to achieve, are natural to the human condition and Moskovitz challenges practitioners 'to rethink the idea that adversity inevitably leads to negative outcomes' (1983: 201). In working with loss it is important, therefore, to retain resilience as a focus (Cutcliffe, 2004; Joseph and Linley, 2006), both in observing existing coping strengths and in promoting the 'self-righting' or 'self-actualising' tendency. Figure 8.3 focuses on the meeting of the core grief responses with the resilient properties (shaded areas) needed to cope with them.

The emotion focus of grief may for a time feel overwhelming but where feelings are not persistently dominant, can be accepted and faced, and integrated into the fuller spectrum of grief responses, a movement towards resilience will be evident. Achieving a sense of control may be problematic when it is based on an avoidance of reality, but when grounded in full recognition of what has been lost, thinking and action can become significantly empowering. At its best, resilience demonstrates that the pain and the possibilities can be reconciled and most effectively facilitated through the support of other people. Therapy needs to recognise these interconnected processes (see Figure 8.4).

The therapeutic process

The therapeutic work of the practitioner engaged in the psychosocial care of grieving people is to navigate the client/patient through the complex and changing territory of grief.

Overwhelmed and vulnerable	Vulnerability	Controlled and vulnerable
Overwhelmed Emotions are central to the experience of grief.	**Vulnerability** 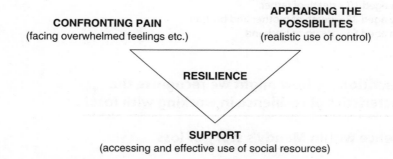	**Controlled** The need to (re)establish control is central to grief.
Overwhelmed and resilient • The dominance of distress feelings is a temporary part of the reaction to loss. • The pain of loss can be confronted and addressed. • Can begin to make sense of experience. • Makes good use of support.	**Resilience** a) A good innate capacity to deal with life losses; is able to face the pain of loss; is optimistic; can make sense of experience. b) Circumstantial demands do not exceed the personal capacity to locate inner resourcefulness. Can make good use of support.	**Controlled and resilient** • Thoughts and action successfully counters the powerlessness of grief. • An ability to function well. • Confronts changed realities and recognises where control is still possible. • Can rationalise experience.

Figure 8.3   The core grief responses and the resilient mediating factors

CONFRONTING PAIN
(facing overwhelmed feelings etc.)

APPRAISING THE POSSIBILITES
(realistic use of control)

RESILIENCE

SUPPORT
(accessing and effective use of social resources)

Figure 8.4   Promoting resilience by supportively confronting the pain and appraising the possibilities

The theoretical perspective of the RRL model and/or use of the AAG scale provide ways to identify the characteristics and the dynamics of grief in individual loss stories. Within the narrative structure, the **reflexive** element moves beyond the account of grief (the external and internal narrative used in Chapter 7) and explores and engages with the meanings attached to who (or what) has been lost. It also seeks new perspectives, which can be more comfortably integrated into the feeling, thinking, acting and believing life view of the grieving person. The process of reconstruction will make variable use of a range of therapeutic approaches, which will focus on the most troubling area of grief (see Table 8.1). Cognitive approaches can counter emphasis on (overwhelming) feeling; diversion into thinking/acting (control) can be countered by a psychodynamic approach in which personal attachment history and relationships will address the connections between emotion and experience. A person-centred approach and a focus on meaning-making strategies will crucially underpin the other methods as they facilitate the process of reconstruction.

Table 8.1 The dimensions of grief, narrative structure, therapeutic approach and narrative process in working with loss

Dimensions of grief (RRL model/AAG scale)	Narrative structure (Angus and Hardke, 1994)	Therapeutic approach	Narrative process (McLeod, 1997)
Overwhelmed/ controlled	External		Construction
	Internal	Person-centred	Deconstruction
Balanced/resilient	Reflexive	Psychodynamic	
		Cognitive	Reconstruction
		Meaning-making	Rehearsal

Four counselling/therapy case studies are used in this chapter to explore existing evidence of resilience (Mandy) and the way in which a balance was achieved in the face of the competing core elements of grief (Tom, Sally and Jean).

* Mandy aged 12 – death of brother.
* Tom aged 10 – death of father.
* Sally aged 38 – death of mother and brother.
* Jean aged 55 – death of husband.

As practitioners, how might we recognise the characteristics of resilience in working with loss?

Resilience within Mandy's story of loss

Mandy, aged 12, was referred for counselling help following the death of her brother, Craig, in a road traffic accident. He had been killed just outside their house when he had gone to the local shop for some bread. Her parents were devastated and believed that Mandy needed help. After a few sessions what became clear to her counsellor was that Mandy was coping well with the loss and that the parents' request for help was more indicative of their need for support. Mandy, in spite of being described as a 'slow learner'

Figure 8.5   Mandy says 'goodbye'

at school, was able to talk openly, if with limited vocabulary, about her feelings and thoughts, and demonstrate empathy for her parents. Her articulation of grief was most powerfully seen in her drawings (see Figure 8.5).

Mandy had been given the option of whether or not to go to Craig's funeral. She decided not to go. Her counsellor, in exploring how the funeral day had been for Mandy, asked her to draw a picture. Mandy chose the title herself – 'Goodbye Craig'. She positioned herself as observer and through the speech bubbles combined a farewell with feelings of anger and blame. These represent typically observed grief responses (Parkes, 1996). Mandy seemed able to accept that Craig was dead and expressed her feelings for her brother in a sad 'goodbye' alongside the strong feelings of anger and blame.

The drawing of her parents in the hearse gave Mandy an opportunity to show her recognition of what their grief was like. She highlighted two classic grief responses, of wanting to know why it happened and the anguish of not saying goodbye. The empathy extended further as she identified her aunt and uncle's response to the situation – 'Bet his mum and dad are very sad, they need all the help we can give them'.

The counsellor's perspective

Mandy's grief reaction could be seen to demonstrate resilience in a number of ways:

- She was able to give a coherent account of her loss through words and pictures.
- She could clearly identify her own thoughts and feelings.

- Her feelings and thoughts were not constrained by any sense of 'how I ought to be'.
- She could accurately identify the thoughts and feelings of other family members.
- She had a secure sense of her place within the family.
- She was functioning well at school, that is, her work and social relationships had not been adversely effected by her bereavement.
- She was able to say 'goodbye'.

Table 8.2   Mandy's story of grief and evidence of her resilience

Narrative structure (Angus and Hardke, 1994)	Therapeutic approach	Narrative process (McLeod, 1997)	Mandy's grief story
External	RRL model as	Construction	Story of Craig's death.
Internal	theoretical compass	Deconstruction	Feelings of anger, blame, sadness.
Reflexive	Person-centred Cognitive Meaning-making	Reconstruction Rehearsal	Courageous facing of the loss; acceptance of her feelings; a goodbye told in pictures; empathy for her parents; good use made of support.

Mandy demonstrated understanding and insights which suggested that she had some capacity to face the family tragedy. Her counsellor tried to build on this evident resilience by encouraging growth in her coping and in her self-awareness, through the telling of her loss story and exploration of her grief. While the short course of counselling was an important source of support at a time when the resources of Mandy's parents were limited by their own grief, the focus of the work was to reinforce her existing capacity to manage the consequences of Craig's death. Mandy showed courage and flexibility, she was positive and was part of a large caring family – all indicators of resilience (see Table 8.2).

Discussion

The care needs of young people and adults are different. Young people need particular kinds of support in the years of formative experience and this was the case with Mandy. However, it was important to recognise the clear signs of her resilience and work to reinforce this rather than undermine it by implying there was a deeper grief 'problem'. In adults, there is increasing evidence that offering therapy to people who are resilient may be harmful rather than helpful (Schut and Stroebe, 2005). It is important, therefore, that practitioners look for evidence of resilience and recognise when intervention might only be required if other support systems are limited or unavailable.

As practitioners, how might we promote resilience in those who seek our support?

Traditionally, work with grief has focused predominantly on personal vulnerability resulting from loss and bereavement. The newer orientation to resilience works with existing strengths and also seeks to promote the development of those resources, internal and external, which will not only meet a current loss with increased equanimity but will be available to meet future losses.

Initially, the external and internal narrative will reflect the core themes of unprocessed grief (see Chapter 7). A predominantly overwhelmed perspective will be one in which meaning is yet to be achieved. The narrative is likely to be characterised by a lack of hopefulness, difficulty in finding a sense of meaning within the events of loss, and personal identity defined in terms of the loss, for example, the woman whose husband committed suicide, the family whose son disappeared, etc. While these perspectives are indicative of vulnerability and most clients will see this as a reason to seek therapy, for others the status of victim may have psychological or social benefits which resists revision. However, working with overwhelming distress requires a process of reconstruction in which clients/patients can discover some of their own resourcefulness in the face of powerlessness; achieve a sense of hopefulness and meaning in their life; and make good use of support systems in their own network as well as through professional help.

An initially controlled narrative will emerge as one in which meaning is found through meeting adversity with fortitude. This may hinder the expression of emotion or limit the willingness to revise beliefs about oneself and the world through introspective reflection. Such a perspective may be encouraged by some cultural and religious belief systems which value stoicism. For example, a belief in an afterlife may be used to deny the pain of loss and discourage the emotional expression of grief. For some people however, a loss may so significantly undermine earlier controlling aspirations that a more fundamental revision of life perspectives may be undertaken through the reflexive narrative process. In these circumstances, newly addressing feelings and revising life meanings will create a temporary vulnerability which requires the counsellor to ensure that a safe and 'secure' base can be provided for the client. The desired outcome is to provide a potentially more satisfactory attunement with feelings, greater flexibility to respond to life losses and new ways of arriving at meaning(s) which can be understood and accepted.

The **reflexive narrative** is considered separately as a means of identifying the processes of change taking place in therapy. Three case studies, introduced in the last chapter, will be used illustratively.

Tom – finding new meaning and understanding following his father's death

In the last chapter we saw how the story Tom told was crucially shaped by his feelings of powerlessness at the time of his father's death. His pictures articulated what Tom found hard to put into words. The counsellor's aim in that early phase of their work together was to accept, hear and understand (Howe, 1993) the external and internal narratives. From a person-centred perspective, and reflecting the attachment theory objective of creating a safe base, this aim is intrinsically empowering.

As the counselling progressed, Tom's counsellor encouraged him to elaborate on his story by talking about his father, their relationship, the shared journey of his illness and what he was thinking and feeling about all of these things. This process both encouraged and allowed Tom to begin to think differently about his experience. As he talked about his dad before his illness, their shared love of football and fishing, and the day-to-day ways in which they had related to each other, Tom began to use alternative story-lines which countered his earlier grief narrative. He was also able to think of ways in which the specialness of their relationship was important as his dad became less able to do things; Tom would sit on his bed and chat or cuddle up to him as they watched television. Tom would look more relaxed and smile as he talked about these aspects of shared experience and came to see for himself that all these things were more important not only to him but also to his dad, than were the last hours of banishment from the hospital.

Tom struggled with the religious concepts which might have given him comfort, expressing in his own way the contradiction between a loving God and one who might so cruelly take his father from him. Again by making it safe to express these feelings, while looking at what sources of comfort did exist within his church community, Tom began to accept some of the things he could not change.

The counsellor's perspective

While feelings dominated at the beginning of the counselling process, helping Tom to think about his father, his feelings and coping with a new life without his dad enabled him to make choices about how he could understand and cope in this new situation. Tom became able to reflect and find in words, rather than pictures, a new place for his dad and a new sense of his own resourcefulness. He could also contextualise this new perspective within the religious frame which was important for Tom. The task of supporting Tom was not that of the counsellor alone but was collaborative work with his mother. She was being seen separately for counselling and this gave her the capacity, in spite of her own grief, to recognise the particular areas of pain for Tom (and his sister) and to provide loving support to them in their grief. After 12 sessions Tom was able to confront his feelings, act confidently in everyday situations and feel the place of his dad was still appropriately fixed within his thoughts, feelings and family conversations. The reflexive narrative had become the means by which Tom had replaced the earlier story, which had been too difficult to live with, with a reconstructed story which could be more comfortably incorporated into his changed life situation (see Table 8.3).

Table 8.3 Tom's story of grief and developing resilience

Narrative structure (Angus and Hardke, 1994)	Therapeutic approach	Narrative process (McLeod, 1997)	Tom's grief story
External	RRL model as theoretical compass	Construction	His father's death and dying
Internal		Deconstruction	Powerlessness, anger, confusion, disappointment.
Reflexive	Person-centred Attachment Cognitive Meaning-making	Reconstruction Rehearsal	Putting his loss into the perspective of the good and happy relationship he had with his father; working out what he understood about God; beginning to find new resources for coping at home and school; making good use of support.

Key aspects of Tom's developing resilience:

- Tom became less afraid of his feelings, especially the powerful ones like anger.
- The dominant distress at being denied access to his father as he was dying reduced, as he could locate his feelings within the wider context of experiences shared with his dad.
- He could recognise how through the sharing of memories and reflecting on what his dad might have done or thought in certain situations, he was integrated into Tom's ongoing life situation (Continuing Bonds).
- He became stronger in dealing with other people's (unhelpful) reactions to his bereaved state, at school.
- The family grew stronger in supporting each other.

Discussion

Children and young people grieve within a family context, which may promote or inhibit the expression of grief in a number of ways (Machin, 1993). In some families, grief will be openly acknowledged and shared. This was the case in Tom's family and they could grieve together and share the good memories of a loved father and husband. This makes the work of the counsellor/therapist more straightforward in that collaboration can take place and there is consistency of support offered between home and therapy. In other situations, expressions of grief, tears, fretfulness, anger, etc. may be perceived as appropriate responses for children but not for adults who see control as strength. Here the family may focus on the need of the child/young person, who may vicariously carry the burden of expressing the pain of other family members. The real need within the family may be more complex than is at first apparent, and as with Mandy it was her parents who were most in need of counselling support. A further variation in the dynamics of family grief may be seen when the adults are so consumed by their own grief that the needs of their children go either unnoticed or unaddressed. This may be the case when parents lose a child after a long or distressing illness, over the course of which the needs of their healthy children have been marginalised. The challenge for the counsellor/therapist is to help the adult(s) see the needs of their grieving children. Working with young people always demands a clear appraisal of their family dynamics (Zaider and Kissane, 2007). This systemic approach is necessary in order to target support to the most appropriate person/people and in order for the process of therapy not to create conflicting messages of permission/prohibition in the mind of the child (Dallos, 2006). According to Goldman (1994), for children to adjust to loss there is a need for understanding, grieving, commemorating and going on.

Sally – finding new meaning and understanding following her mother's death

Throughout the counselling process Sally's grief was reflected not only in her emotional response to her mother's death but was manifest in a reduced capacity to function in the way she wanted to, as a wife and mother. Addressing both of these elements was central to the reflexive narrative.

The initial focus was Sally's self-doubt as a daughter. 'I thought I should have done things differently and then maybe she would have lived or maybe we would have had a better relationship. For a long time I felt angry about her dying and also the way she had been with me and John [Sally's husband]. Then when the counsellor summarised what I had been telling her about my relationship with my mother by saying, "it sounds as if you thought you weren't a good-enough daughter" I just broke down and couldn't stop crying. She had gone straight to the most raw part. I noticed (in the early days of counselling) that I was unable to deal with any of these raw emotions other than when I was in a counselling session. However, I found that the more counselling I had the better I felt and the more I felt back in control of my life. The counselling gave me a safe place to deal with the emotions of grief without anyone judging me or feeling offended by what I said.'

'Early in the counselling process I began to realise that Mum wasn't always right and that if she and John didn't see eye-to-eye, I was not responsible for that. I found that I had been feeling I ought to be in control of the situation between them and help Mum realise that John did like her.'

As the counselling progressed, a journaling process (Progoff, 1975, see Chapter 4) was introduced to Sally in which, through writing, she reflected on the paths taken in her own life and those taken by her mother (stepping stones – significant life events). This was a prelude to engaging with a free-flowing written dialogue between herself and her mother. 'It was illuminating. I felt as if I had spoken to her and it helped explain how I felt about my relationship and my husband's relationship with her. She was able to

---

reply and explain why she felt the way she did and to say sorry. It was a real turning point in my counselling.'

As the guilt about the quality of her relationship with her mother subsided so did her anxiety about her parenting skills and household management. 'Gradually I became more tolerant and less angry. I was expecting the children to be perfectly behaved and that wasn't realistic. I was also obsessed with the state of the house and my inability to keep it perfectly. Every small job became like a mountain that I couldn't climb and so I became addicted to playing solitaire on the PC. I found out that I was doing that to stop my mind having to think about the pain. As I tackled my grief, I began to feel less stressed about the children and the house. I adopted a mantra we discussed in counselling: "good enough is better than perfect". It's on my mobile to remind me. The confusion in my head was mirrored in the house. Out of control with my grief meant out of control with my home and my children.'

Sally recalls that 'I did eventually feel well enough to stop the counselling. I know now that my mother and I actually had a great relationship with the usual mother–daughter conflicts now and again. I began to feel that I had been a reasonable daughter. What surprised me about this was that at the start I wanted all the hurt to go away and for me to be "over" my mum's death. But actually, at the end, I felt it was OK to feel sad when I thought about her. I still sometimes feel sad and have a little cry but it doesn't take me over anymore.'

The counsellor's perspective

The reflexive process took Sally from talking about and expressing her feelings of grief, to a deeper articulation of what it meant to lose her mother. The counselling became a context in which she began to reappraise her thoughts and feelings about their relationship, and to consider alternative ways of looking at the bond between them. Reflecting on the mother–daughter experiences and ways of communicating, especially unresolved issues between them, suggested that the Progoff journal approach (1975) might be a helpful way of addressing some of these issues (see Chapter 4). It was used to explore Sally's own history and that of her mother and moved on to a written dialogue between them. The content of her writing produced a great deal of emotion but also insight. She began to be much more forgiving of herself and accepting of those parts of the relationship with her mother which she thought could have been better; she modified her expectation of perfection.

Sally worked hard processing her feelings and the meanings associated with her loss. The more she was able to make sense of both her relationship with her mother and her death, the more she began to function satisfactorily in all dimensions of her life. As she began to 'sort her head out' (Sally's phrase) she became more able to cope with the practical aspects of housekeeping and looking after the family.

Through counselling, Sally found new resources within herself – emotional, cognitive and spiritual – which allowed her to confront the pain, understand it, and come to recognise the need to accept the things which she could not change while retaining control in other life situations. The reflexive narrative had been a rich journey of exploration in which Sally's own capacity to reach an alternative version of her grief story was facilitated by the

Table 8.4   Sally's story of grief and developing resilience following the death of her mother

Narrative structure (Angus and Hardke, 1994)	Therapeutic approach	Narrative process (McLeod, 1997)	Sally's grief story
External	RRL model as theoretical compass	Construction	Her mother's death and dying.
Internal		Deconstruction	Powerlessness, guilt, self-doubt as a daughter, depression, practical inability to function.
Reflexive	Person-centred Attachment Cognitive Meaning-making	Reconstruction Rehearsal	Exploring the history of her relationship with her mother; looking at what was important to her; finding a new sense of control by accepting the things she couldn't change; recognising that perfection and control are not always possible or desirable; discovering new capacities to deal with feelings; an increased sense of spirituality; good use made of support.

counselling. Attachment issues were explored along with cognitive approaches to revising corrosive beliefs about her relationship with her mother and what that loss meant to her. Sally was also able to locate her reconstructed story within a wider frame of religious belief, which assisted her acceptance of herself and the loss of a loved mother (see Table 8.4).

Sally's resilience could be seen in:

- Her capacity to tell her grief story coherently.
- Her willingness to face and accept painful emotions and difficult relationship issues.
- Her cognitive ability to revise perspectives, especially on previously entrenched views about perfection and being in control.
- A new found integration of accepting what could not be changed but acting effectively in those areas where agency is possible.
- Her overall optimism contained within a spiritual frame of reference.

Sally – finding new meaning and understanding following her brother's death

In her second bereavement, Sally was dealing with many contradictory feelings about her brother's suicide.

Sorting out the conflicting feelings was partly facilitated by using the (Progoff) journal approach again, in which Sally undertook a dialogue with her brother. This did not immediately bring about a change in her perspective but her written dialogue was used at various points throughout the counselling to explore the coexistence of apparently opposite grief reactions. 'When Mark died, I felt that maybe if I'd stayed living in the same town as him, I may have been able to stop the suicide. I also felt that maybe I'd said something to him the week before he died that had made him feel really depressed and that may have pushed him over the edge. Once I recognised that it was his decision and I didn't have any effect on it, I felt better. One of the difficult things I learned was that it is ok to have two contradictory feelings at once. For example, when Mark died I felt very sad about his death but I also felt a bit of relief at no longer having to worry about him. This made me feel guilty until I was able to accept this as a normal part of grieving.'

Sally found that she was much more able to confront her feelings of grief after Mark's death than was the case when her mother died. She accepted the painful emotions and rather than attempting to control them through medication, as she had done in her first bereavement, she sought out counselling as a way of staying fully engaged with all her feelings. These were not only emotions of grief but a real sense of connection with positive emotions too. She recalled, 'One day I was driving down the road when I saw a magnolia bush in full bloom. They are my favourite and it made me cry a little. About two weeks later in the same place I saw a massive number of starlings wheeling, twisting and turning. It was a fantastic show of God's creation. I had to stop the car because I was crying. I began to see that I was getting back in touch with my (good) feelings again. I was allowing myself to feel great joy which had been locked away since Mark died'. Sally saw how facing the overwhelming feelings in the safety of counselling not only made the grief more manageable but also liberated her suppressed happiness. She was building on her capacity for resilience by holding feelings and a sense of agency in balance.

'As I began to improve (from the overwhelming pain of grief) I started writing down the small jobs I had done, rather than making a to-do list. This helped me focus on the things I could do (and had done) rather than the long list of what I couldn't do. I stopped making a mountain out of a lot of small molehills and recognised that tackling one molehill at a time was the only way to handle it. Rather than being angry or frustrated with the children, I began to involve them in domestic tasks. This helped me enormously because they felt involved and so would do their bit of tidying and I felt less out of control with it all.'

'I find it amazing that all these issues seem to link back to my feeling out of control either with emotions or with my home life. It seems quite a contradiction that I finally felt more in control when I accepted that the things I was unable to control were not for me to worry about and that being in control meant letting go of the level of perfection my previous standards required. When I started the counselling I wanted a cure for the grief. Now at the end of the process, I'm not cured and indeed don't want to be. However, I am able to control the grief as a normal part of my life now. I do feel that I have less grief but I don't believe it will ever go away totally, and that's OK.'

Table 8.5   Sally's story of grief and developing resilience following the death of her brother

Narrative structure (Angus and Hardke, 1994)	Therapeutic approach	Narrative process (McLeod, 1997)	Sally's grief story
External	RRL model as theoretical compass	Construction	Her brother's illness and his dying.
Internal		Deconstruction	Powerlessness, guilt, self-doubt as a sister, some practical inability to function.
Reflexive	Person-centred Attachment Cognitive Meaning-making	Reconstruction Rehearsal	**Exploring the history of her relationship with her brother; reaffirming her sense that control comes from accepting the things she couldn't change; being realistic about the things she could change; discovering new capacities to deal with feelings, living with pain and being open to good things; an increased sense of spirituality; good use made of support.**

The counsellor's perspective

Having worked reflexively on her earlier bereavement, Sally was quickly able to engage in the process of confronting her loss and reflect, with self-awareness, on the way in which grief was rendering her powerless in all aspects of her life. Bringing this process to consciousness again, reactivated her strategies for managing both her own attitude to being in control and the way she approached the practical aspects of day-to-day living. Sally responded well to counselling and it was undertaken as a collaborative enterprise of narrative reconstruction (see Table 8.5).

Evidence of Sally's resilience was seen in:

- An immediate willingness to make use of (counselling) support.
- Ready re-engagement with the strategies she had used in her previous bereavement, to reappraise and revise views and assumptions about herself and her relationship with her brother.
- Revisiting her tendency to aim for perfection and control by recognising what is realistic.
- Reaching a sense of meaning in which she accepts her feelings as part of the person she is.
- Feeling a sense of optimism about the future.
- Now functioning effectively and happily in her home and work life.

Discussion

In both her bereavements, Sally acknowledged a link between her grief and her failure to cope with everyday life. Both generated a powerlessness which was profoundly disturbing to her need to be in control. Managing her grief and her children sometimes seemed overwhelming and all strategies for dealing with inner pain and practical tasks defeated her. Sally needed to recognise how important control was to her sense of well-being and how that self view needed to be adjusted to fit with the reality of her loss and everyday life. As she began to look with her counsellor at her sense of powerlessness and at those things over which she did have control, Sally's depression became less. She began to look at ways of encouraging the family's cooperation in practical ways, and gradually her sense of agency became stronger.

Reconciling the inner tensions of Sally's grief with the outer demands of her family life was achieved by (cognitive) exploration of the experiences and perspectives which were not serving her well. Faulty beliefs about the need for absolute control and perfection were challenged. The sense, brought to consciousness in the context of counselling, that she was not a good-enough daughter, that she was responsible for the way her mother and husband related to each other, and that she might have some culpability in her brother's suicide, all needed to be tested in reality. The counselling process gradually helped Sally 'reconstruct' her dominant narrative and focus on a reality which could be operationalised in her day-to-day life. The opportunity to ventilate feelings of grief and to cognitively reappraise the meaning of her losses enhanced Sally's resourcefulness in facing pain and in accepting the consequences of loss. Her resilience was evident by the time counselling ended. Person-centred therapy underpinned other therapeutic approaches, which included use of Attachment Theory as a way of exploring past and present relationships, and cognitive reconstruction to facilitate new ways for Sally to understand and experience her losses. Making sense of her experience was explored within the context of Sally's Christian beliefs. Through an understanding of faith she could see how many aspects of life are beyond comprehension or control and have to be accepted. The prayer of serenity captured for Sally the elements of powerlessness, control and personal agency (and reflect the notion of resilience in the RRL model) which she felt could guide her handling of present and future grief:

> God grant me the serenity to accept the things I cannot change, the courage to change the things I can, and the wisdom to know the difference.

Jean – finding new meaning and understanding following her husband's death

> The process of being supported and having a structure within which to explore her grief (the AAG scale) challenged Jean to consider new perspectives on her situation. 'The scale made me think about things which I did and I thought about lots and lots of things which hadn't come into my head. It made me focus on what had happened. It made me look at my situation and I realised that I hadn't allowed myself to grieve. It was like with my job I had had to be in total control.' The combination of having to respond to the items on the scale and then to have her perspective explored further by the counsellor made Jean say, 'Yes, why did I think that. I am a thinking person so it was switching me back on if you like – it was making me be me – it was allowing me to be
>
> *(Continued)*

141

(Continued)

me'. The thinking process was not a denial of her feelings but was a natural way for Jean to begin to understand them and therefore accept them. Jean's daughters benefited too as they saw their mother find a structured and safe way to deal with her grief.

Working with feelings was difficult for Jean. She had exhausted her own capacity to be in control and was functioning 'on automatic pilot'. As she found safety in exploring her grief, 'It was easier to talk about Brian and take him off his pedestal. I'd think, God he used to drive me crazy doing X. I would have felt disloyal if I'd said anything like that before but that is how it is in relationships. I probably drove him insane. Then I'd get angry with him about why he wouldn't let me talk about things. I know it was his way, trying to protect us. There were things I wanted to say that I never got the chance to say. Since the counselling, when I go over to his grave and change the flowers, I say the things I would have said: "How dare you leave me here on my own with this lot – stupid pension problems etc." It all comes out. To begin with I was very low but as we worked on the way I was feeling I could see light at the end of the tunnel and I started to feel more alive'. In counselling Jean realised that she needed to acknowledge and process her distress and anger before she could re-engage with her new life without Brian.

As Jean started to engage with her feelings and think through her situation she became more able to respond positively to friends and their wish to include her in social activities. She also found it easier to make it safe for them to talk about Brian and include him in their conversations. She saw this movement in her own response after reaching a low point in her grief, as 'milestones' in doing things for the first time without Brian. 'It was difficult but I did it.' She described her feelings about planning her daughters' weddings – 'At the beginning I really couldn't have cared less but I began to feel more able to face all this and thinking about things has helped me begin to not only get on with it but to enjoy it'. Jean is also finding care of her grandchildren something she enjoys but something she can now negotiate to suit her other activities. She no longer subdues her own needs to be the ever-present carer of others.

'I'm much more able to talk about Brian now but I have to believe that some day I'm going to see him again. I have to believe that.' She still feels unable to go to the church where Brian's funeral was held. However, Jean gains support from the minister of another local church, and enjoys the social companionship which she gets from people at that church. Someone within that congregation said to Jean 'You're strong and you will come through this'. That felt inspirational to Jean as it was said by someone who had experienced tragedy in her own life – her son had been shot in the street. Jean saw these changes in perspective as indicative of a growing spirituality – 'I think I'm more spiritual than I was'.

The safety of the counselling context and the awareness of the normal spectrum of grief responses represented in the AAG scale gave Jean permission to grieve. She said, 'I realised that I had to get it [grief] out of me because if I hadn't I don't think I would have gone forward. Other people were saying you have to move on but I said "Where to?" You don't get over a loss like this but I've learned to deal with it differently. I think about him every day but I think more about the positive aspects. I think that is a strength in itself, dealing with the grief, thinking about the person but still able to function.' Jean could identify this as a stronger place than when she was desperately trying to retain self-control and control of events around her.

The counsellor's perspective

The AAG scale was used in the first session as a way of helping Jean explore her grief (see Table 6.2, p. 110). A lot of discussion followed from each item on the scale. Jean described how she usually thought things through in order to be in command of difficult situations but that this was not working for her in her present bereavement – it was not possible to be brave, and she had no desire to get on with life. The antidepressants had helped blot out some of the intrusive elements of her grief but in spite of that she was now feeling out of control and that was very troubling to her. Looking at the aggregated scores for the three categories on the scale, Jean was able to see that she had a high level of agreement with the overwhelmed items, strong agreement with one of the controlled items (the others seemed to indicate she was weary with trying to maintain control) and considerable disagreement with the resilient items. Jean's reaction to this account of her grief was to say that it was like a 'hammer hitting her' – the realisation of how low she had become. She described how she had functioned over the past months by being totally emotionally cut off and shut off and now she was dead to everything. She said that 'If I died tomorrow that would be fine'. Putting her overwhelming sense of grief, from which she could no longer hide, into words horrified her as she realised that she had been saying some desperate things about how she was feeling to her daughters. The scale, in addition to providing a way of telling her story, became a kind of mirror which reflected the reality of Jean's grief to her in a way she had not previously recognised.

Three weeks later the scale was used again. Jean spoke of Brian's death and described it as 'not calm' and that she had felt traumatised by it – a new recognition of its impact. She was still finding her grief difficult but was able to face some aspects of her loss in a way that she could not do a short time ago. This was shown in the changes in Jean's reaction to the AAG scale; a slight reduction in the severity of her overwhelmed response but also strong agreement with the resilient item 1, 'I feel able to face the pain which comes with loss'. Her perspective on control had also changed; she held a neutral view about getting on with life (item 8) but she recognised that if she were to deal with her grief, it was important not to be brave or to keep her emotions in check. This was a significant shift of coping style from someone who had functioned both before and after bereavement by remaining in control of situations and her own feelings. The most significant change came in her response to the resilient items on the scale. She was able to put in her own words her readiness to face her grief, a belief that she had the resources to cope and that she would come through the grief, although she did not know when. For Jean, it seemed like a massive change was taking place. The scale provided a picture of how she was in her bereavement and a marker for how her grief was changing. Jean used the time between sessions for a considerable amount of self-reflection.

On the third occasion when the scale was used, three months later, events in her personal life had knocked Jean back quite badly and she was facing the prospect of Christmas without Brian. These factors were reflected in her responses to the scale, which reverted almost to the position of her first session. Jean was finding her grief difficult again and reported, 'the happy part of me has gone'. She was dependent upon other people's encouragement rather than her own sense of optimism. She began to recognise the circumstances which had triggered a reversal in her emotions, 'feeling rough', and trusted that she would weather the situation. She believed that it would not knock her back as far as she initially believed it would because she came to realise what might help her move forward – 'I've done it once I can do it again'. She was more able to deal with her feelings and rather than packing them down and having them ferment inside, she 'could take them out and look at them'.

Two months later the scale was used for the final time. Jean had recovered a greater degree of resilience and it was agreed that she was ready to end the counselling. She had dealt with the painful trigger which had emerged in the middle of counselling, and Jean was in a much better place, able to re-invest in new interests and resume some old friendships. She knew that there would be times when her grief would resurface, such as at anniversaries, but she had clear strategies for dealing with these.

A person-centred approach was used alongside the AAG scale (see Table 8.6). The scale was a central tool in the counselling process. As a self-report measure, Jean was actively involved in describing the nature of her grief and could clearly see the changes taking place over time, and how the counselling process was facilitating those changes. It was a collaborative process in which both client and counsellor could explore the dynamics of grief and work together on addressing it. The reflexive narrative process is clearly evident in both Jean's account of the counselling process and in that of her counsellor. They were both able to demonstrate the shift in perspective and the development of a more resilient coping style. As Jean began to confront her feelings and feel safe in doing so, she could think and act in a way that reconnected her with her own strength. Her inner strength grew, as did her self-confidence, and she was able to make sense of her memories of Brian and come to a satisfying life perspective in which he remains a part. The AAG scale was an important catalyst in engaging with the reflexive narrative. It provided clear direction for the dimensions in which Jean might choose to reconstruct her story of loss.

Evidence of Jean's resilience:

- The coherence of her loss story.
- Courageous facing of painful emotions and acceptance of them as part of her grief.
- An emerging ability to be proactive in undertaking new life directions.
- A strengthening sense of self in changed circumstances.
- An optimism about the future.
- New discoveries of spiritual meaning.
- Location within a strong and supportive family.

Conclusion

In this chapter we have focused on the resilient dimension of loss response, conceptu-alised in the RRL model and the AAG scale. Resilience is a quality of personal resource-fulness, which serves to reconcile the competing core elements of grief. It is a coping mechanism, which might naturally become operational in the face of loss or it might need to be facilitated by those who are supporting a grieving person. For practitioners,

Table 8.6   Jean's story of grief and developing resilience following the death of her husband

Narrative structure (Angus and Hardke, 1994)	Therapeutic approach	Narrative process (McLeod, 1997)	Jean's grief story
External	RRL model as theoretical compass AAG scale	Construction	Her husband's last illness and his dying.
Internal		Deconstruction	Control strategies failing to hold overwhelmed feelings at bay; not wanting to go on without her husband; depression.
Reflexive	Person-centred Cognitive Meaning-making	Reconstruction Rehearsal	**Exploring the positive things which live on from her relationship with her husband; exploring her grief responses through the AAG scale – discovering her capacity to choose to relax her control and engage fully with her feelings, locating her own resourcefulness; increased sense of spirituality; good use made of informal and counselling support.**

it is important to be able to recognise resilience and not to assume powerful feelings or controlling instincts are themselves evidence of vulnerability.

The circumstances of Mandy's bereavement might have suggested that she was likely to become vulnerable in her grieving but the evidence of her resilience was well articulated in her drawing and in her clear acceptance of her loss and its consequences. Her need for counselling help was to reinforce her existing coping abilities rather to address problematic grief.

For Tom, the quality of the relationship he had with his father and the general security with both parents were important sources of his resilience. This was gently activated in counselling as a way of reconnecting the past strengths with the present sense of vulnerability. Changing the focus from the anguish of the final separation from his father to the wider meanings of their relationship helped Tom develop new resources for dealing with his grief. Making sense of his experience was challenging to his existing beliefs about God but this was another dimension in which supportive collaboration between the counselling and home could help him discover new aspects to his religious understanding.

In the cases of Sally and Jean, the reflexive narrative was the framework in which the discomforting tensions of grief could be explored and reconciled. For Sally, the reflexive process was prompted by the dialogue with her counsellor and by the use of writing (Progoff, 1975). These helped her to deal with the grief-induced depression and her incapacity to manage her day-to-day life in the way she wished. In both these dimensions she became aware of the inner-grief processes, and was more able to reappraise her experience and construct an alternative narrative account of her loss. Within this, her Christian beliefs contributed to the way in which she made sense of her losses. The process of reconstructing her grief story was achieved more quickly with her second bereavement (her brother's death) as her awareness had been raised by the first (her mother's death). This is an example of how encouraging resilience in therapy can help develop new strengths, which emerge to meet subsequent losses.

For Jean, the AAG scale was the significant catalyst in reconstructing her grief story. Her responses to the scale and its use as a measure of change were held as a mirror to her. Whereas she began by controlling and blotting out the emotional elements of her grief, she later became able to use control as a cognitive mechanism to think differently and to choose how to behave in her new circumstances as a widow. New spiritual awareness dawned as Jean reflected on the deeper meanings of her loss. Both Sally and Jean saw the end point of their counselling not as one in which grief had been 'cured' but as a state which could be embraced and lived with. The meanings they had found within their new stories were more satisfying than the ones they first brought to therapy.

The theoretical concepts contained in the RRL model and in the self-report perspectives in the AAG scale have been explored through the reflexive narrative process and used to promote resilience – a journey of 'personal transformation' (Joseph and Linley 2006: 144).

9

Engaging with the Grief Narrative –
Focus on Vulnerability

In Chapter 8, harmonising the dissonant elements within the grief story was seen as a potentially natural mechanism of adjustment – resilience. The qualities of resilience, needed to achieve a balanced state following loss, are the qualities therapy seeks to facilitate. However, it is clear that sometimes the natural potential for resilience is not evident within grieving people and that cultivating it is difficult. While attention to resilience rightly counters the traditional emphasis upon problematic grief responses (often referred to as abnormal, pathological, etc.) it is important that vulnerability is recognised and understood as a state needing particular consideration. Vulnerability is the focus of this chapter.

Vulnerability has been conceptualised in traditional grief literature as a combination of personal characteristics and circumstantial factors which produce risk of a poor bereavement outcome. Chapter 3 looked at how Attachment Theory suggested a theoretical connection between insecure relationships and chronic grief (excessive intensity or duration) or delayed grief (too little intensity or duration). Another classification of a potential vulnerable response to loss is made by Roos (2002) who uses the term 'chronic sorrow' to define ongoing experiences of loss which is/are not capable of resolution, such as long-term disability. Sanders (1993) has identified a range of variable circumstantial factors which may contribute to a problematic grief response, for example, age, gender, relationship to the deceased (lost person), the nature and the manner of the death (loss), etc. However, Lazarus and Folkman (1984), Folkman (2001), and Stroebe et al. (2006) suggest a more complex interplay of factors contributing to potential vulnerability, in a theory of stress and coping. This theory proposes that vulnerability arises when a stressful situation, such as a loss, makes more demands upon an individual than he/she has the inner resources and social support to cope with. Where this is the case, personal well-being is put at risk, that is, the person is vulnerable. This concept, unlike earlier notions of risk, suggests that vulnerability cannot be predicted but has to be understood by looking at the mediating and moderating variables in individual coping – the resources/pressures and strengths/weaknesses in a particular context (see Figure 3.3). Grief support, therefore, needs to engage with the individual complexity of intrapersonal and interpersonal factors (Machin, 2007b).

Within the RRL model, vulnerability is an opposite state to that of resilience and is characterised by:

- **Tension** between an overwhelming sense of powerlessness and the pull to be in control, especially when control is central to the person's sense of well-being.
- **Overwhelming feelings** and thoughts are especially **powerful and persistent**.
- **Control** is the normal coping style but the usual strategies **fail to subdue distressing emotions** of grief.

These clinical symptoms demonstrate an inability to reconcile the competing tensions of grief (see Figure 9.1) Vulnerability is also evident whdere response to the AAG scale show strong disagreement/disagreement with the resilient/balanced items.

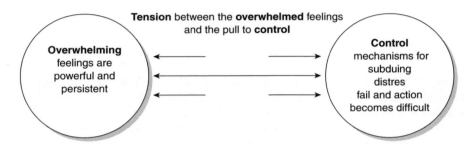

Figure 9.1   Vulnerability demonstrated by an incapacity to move comfortably between the core grief responses

While these characteristics may represent a temporary phase within grief, their persistence is likely to represent a level of vulnerability which requires (extended) therapeutic support. Figure 9.2 focuses on the meeting of the core grief responses and the factors likely to produce a vulnerable loss response (shaded area).

In circumstances of heightened vulnerability the same overall therapeutic objectives will apply as those described in Chapter 8 (see Figure 9.3). However, the level of skill required to achieve these aims will need to be greater.

Both the RRL model and the AAG scale can be used therapeutically to identify and respond to client/patient vulnerability. Within the narrative structure, the reflexive element allows for stories which are too painful to live with, and which disturb some part of emotional, cognitive, social or spiritual functioning, to be appraised and reconstructed. To counter this disturbance and to facilitate the integration of more effective functioning and a more satisfying life view, a range of therapeutic approaches are used (see Table 9.1).

- A person-centred approach facilitates full engagement with the client/patient's presenting concerns, heard through their loss story, and provides the quality of relationship which will nurture openness to changed perspectives.
- The psychodynamic approach is concerned with personal history and the link between emotion and relationships (Attachment Theory). This provides a way of reappraising the significance and meaning of past experiences and their influence on current circumstances.

Overwhelmed and vulnerable	Vulnerability	Controlled and vulnerable
Persistent and/or heightened distress seen as: • An incapacity to face the issues of loss. • Has few inner resources. • Is generally pessimistic. • Cannot make sense of what is happening. • Lacks social support or finds it difficult to make use of support.	a) Limited capacity – has few personal strengths for the meeting of loss. b) Experiences a considerable degree of need – arising from loss or impending loss and/or other life pressures, such as relationship difficulties, financial problems, inadequate housing, (un)employment, etc.	Normal strategies for managing loss are not able to quell the dominance of feeling, resulting in: • A defeating sense of powerlessness. • Heightened anxiety and/or depression. • Reluctance to make use of support.
Overwhelmed Emotions are central to the experience of grief.	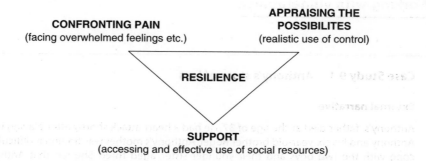	**Controlled** The need to (re)establish control is central to grief.
Overwhelmed and resilient	**Resilience**	*Controlled and resilient*

Figure 9.2 The core grief responses in relation to the factors likely to produce a vulnerable response (shaded area)

CONFRONTING PAIN
(facing overwhelmed feelings etc.)

APPRAISING THE POSSIBILITES
(realistic use of control)

RESILIENCE

SUPPORT
(accessing and effective use of social resources)

Figure 9.3 Therapeutic objectives for working with vulnerability and encouraging resilience

- A cognitive focus allows the distortions in thinking, which occur when people are distressed, to be understood, challenged and revised.
- At the height of vulnerability people may not be able to make satisfying sense of what is happening to them. The meaning-making process is more likely to follow when other psychological and cognitive distress has been resolved (if only partially). Nevertheless, it is a focus which counsellors/therapists need to consider when people are seeking solace from spiritual or religious perspectives, for example, a client/patient may derive comfort in extreme distress from religious observance or from the support of other people who can speak of certainties of their faith etc.

Table 9.1 The dimensions of grief, narrative structure, therapeutic approach and narrative process in working with loss

Dimensions of grief (RRL model/ AAG scale)	Narrative structure (Angus and Hardke, 1994)	Therapeutic approach	Narrative process (McLeod, 1997)
Overwhelmed/ controlled	External Internal	Person-centred Psychodynamic	Construction Deconstruction
Balanced/ resilient	Reflexive	Cognitive Meaning-making	Reconstruction Rehearsal

Case studies will be used to explore the evidence of vulnerability and the way in which this has been addressed therapeutically.

- Anthony aged 8 – death of father (external, internal and reflexive narrative accounts).
- Rob aged 67 – death of wife (see external and internal grief narrative in Chapter 7).
- Hannah aged 82 – death of husband and a stroke (external, internal and reflexive narrative accounts).

Working with vulnerability

Case Study 9.1 Anthony's story of loss

External narrative

Anthony's father died at the age of 37. He had a heart attack shortly after playing with Anthony and his six-year-old brother Roger. Anthony's mother was finding it difficult to cope with the two boys and their younger sister, aged three. She felt that Anthony would benefit from counselling.

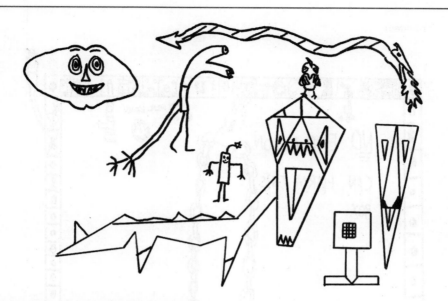

Figure 9.4　Anthony's nightmares

Internal narrative

Anthony was having nightmares and finding it difficult to cope with the taunts at school about his father having died. He wondered whether he had been the cause of his father's death because of their playful session of 'rough and tumble'. He was also very anxious about his mother and fearful that she might die too. His fears were compounded when a relative told Anthony that his mother needed him to be the man of the house now and that if he was naughty she might also die. His father's death brought many new responsibilities and anxieties for Anthony in addition to his missing a very loved father. This was a very sad little boy.

Pictures were used to help him tell his story. Figure 9.4 is the first picture he drew, showing something of the nightmares he was experiencing. Watching as he constructed his picture helped his counsellor see the coffin shape, which was his starting point, at the centre of the shapes representing his night-time terrors. He was asked to talk about his picture. The centrality of the coffin was related to Anthony having served as an altar boy at his father's funeral and undertaking that task while staring at 'the box with my daddy inside'. This image had been revisited in his dreams and caused him to awake fretfully.

Reflexive narrative

Anthony found it hard to communicate verbally and each session began with a picture. He always needed a ruler to construct his drawing and became upset on one occasion when asked to do some free-flowing lines as a base for exploring shapes and images to

(Continued)

(Continued)

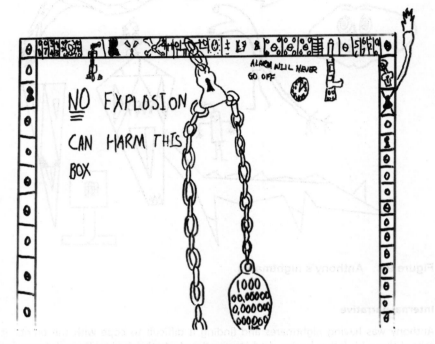

Figure 9.5   Anthony's locked away emotions

talk about. His counsellor, therefore, allowed him to choose the focus for his pictures. Figure 9.5 shows a very carefully constructed chest. Anthony took quite a long time to draw it and then described its invulnerability; locks, chains, radioactive protection, code numbers, etc. When asked what was inside the chest he said 'my feelings'.

Anthony was clearly communicating that emotion was something he could not talk about. His counsellor needed to provide the safety and sensitivity to convey her aware-ness of some of his fears without prematurely inducing him to share what felt too dan-gerous to disclose. At the beginning, therefore, the focus needed to be upon factual aspects of his situation – clear information about his father's death, and what grief is like for children and adults. It was not sufficient for Anthony, that his mother had told him, that his father's death was not his fault. This fact was reinforced in his counselling ses-sions when he was able to explore his reducing but still real sense of culpability. The connection between naughtiness and death was also challenged. This was more diffi-cult to negate when he felt that staying in control, that is, being 'good', was a safer option than risking the consequence of losing control. Anthony was a frequent observer of his mother's grief. She was distressed and found day-to-day functioning dif-ficult. This resulted in Anthony having to assume more responsibility, if only for himself.

His own grief was frightening and baffling and something he was having to undertake alone. Using books written for children, for example, *Badger's Parting Gift* (Varley, 1992) and workbooks (Heegaard, 1988; Machin, 1993), helped Anthony recognise that his grief reactions were normal and that his feelings were feelings that other children had had before him.

After six or seven sessions Anthony slowly became more certain that it was safe to describe his school situation and the daily dread of coping with pupils who said that they could do whatever they liked to him because he had no father to tell. He felt that he could not tell his mother because of the constraints on upsetting her. His counsellor helped him look at some practical ways of getting help from his teacher and responding to and/or avoiding the taunts of fellow classmates. In discussing these strategies, the counsellor helped Anthony to see that in spite of his mother's grief she would want to know how difficult it was at school and he agreed that together they would tell his mother what had been happening. Reaching a stage of involving Anthony's mother was a big step for him, not only in acknowledging what he had believed was unsafe to do, but in marshalling more support for his own grief. He moved to a more comfortable position finding through the different therapeutic approaches – pictures, stories and talking – that feelings, though painful, could be comforted and supported, and thoughts and actions could be made less scary when shared with other people. In a limited way, Anthony began to process his grief and relax the control which was keeping his emotions locked away and fermenting.

The counsellor's perspective

Anthony's was a situation in which he was rendered vulnerable for a number of reasons:

- His young age (limited inner resources – emotional immaturity, cognitive misunderstanding, etc.).
- The unexpected loss of his father.
- No previous experience of dealing with such a profound loss (undeveloped internal resources).
- The vulnerability of his mother (limited external resources).
- His misunderstanding about the reason for his father's death.
- The misinformation he had been given about his power to act destructively (negative external 'support').
- Bullying at school.
- Little effective social support (limited external resources).

These factors resulted in a considerable degree of powerlessness, and, together with a strongly perceived need to be in control, made Anthony's counselling needs very complex. Pictures and stories were a powerful way of helping Anthony describe, in his own way, the things which were troubling him. A person-centred approach was used to make Anthony feel safe. This was crucial to all the counselling work as his level of trust, in others and himself, was very fragile. Although Anthony could not freely disclose his distress

Table 9.2   Anthony's story of grief

Narrative structure (Angus and Hardke, 1994)	Therapeutic approach	Narrative process (McLeod, 1997)	Anthony's grief story
External	RRL model as theoretical compass	Construction	His father's death and dying.
Internal		Deconstruction	Guilt, fear, anxiety, powerlessness.
Reflexive	Person-centred	Reconstruction Rehearsal	Focus on practical steps to address, irrational fears, mistaken beliefs, etc.
	Cognitive		Strategies for dealing with bullying and to re-engage his mother with his needs.

it was very evident to his counsellor. His struggle to remain in control was a daily battle for him. It was necessary, therefore, to be alert for and make opportunities to move into areas which did not directly address feelings but which obliquely acknowledged them. Engaging cognitively allowed some of the irrational belief, generated by his own fears and the misinformation of other people, to be explored and challenged. A focus on thinking and behaving was a way of indirectly attending to Anthony's feelings. Reaching a stage of enabling Anthony to feel able to discuss some of his grief with his mother was a big step. He used the counsellor's support to decide and rehearse how he might tell her about some of the things which were worrying him. Reintegrating the support mechanisms of the family was important for all its members. Continued counselling might have been helpful, and it was clear that the tentative steps Anthony had taken in coping with his loss would be revisited as he reached other developmental milestones and raised new questions about his loss. A sense of meaning was not achieved and counselling ended when his mother believed that Anthony was coping adequately and the need to take him out of school to receive help was no longer required (see Table 9.2).

Discussion

Unlike Tom (Chapters 7 and 8), Anthony, who was younger, had little social support for his emotional needs at the time of his father's death. The suddenness of the death had not given any opportunity for preparation and Anthony's mother's own grief made her initially unavailable as a support for her children. The circumstances of the death and the management of it, therefore, heightened Anthony's problems in dealing with the loss; his own resources were limited as were his means of support. Although there were particular problematic aspects to Anthony's bereavement experience, children generally are likely to be vulnerable in loss situations. They have yet to develop the capacity to manage and understand the emotional consequences of grief. Schut et al. (2001) conclude from research evidence that while interventions to support bereaved adults may not be helpful, and in some circumstances may be unhelpful, work with children who by nature of their young age are likely to be at risk of complications is beneficial.

Bullying is an often-reported response to bereaved children in school. Bereavement services and organisations like Child Line, learn directly from children that their grief is made more unbearable by the reactions of their peers. Schools need to be alert for the taunting and ostracism of children who are already coping with traumatising loss experiences (Cross, 2002).

Case Study 9.2   Rob – finding a way to work with his grief following his wife's death

As we saw in Chapter 7, Rob was unable to engage with the reality of his wife's death. He was both emotionally distant from his grief and yet emotionally overwhelmed by his situation. The therapeutic work with Rob began to uncover more of his background history (external and internal narrative) which provided his therapist with a clearer understanding of the reasons for his current loss response.

External narrative (continued)

Rob's wife had a heart attack when she was 35, psoriasis for 15 years and mental health problems for 20 years. She had tried to commit suicide on many occasions (drinking bleach, cutting her wrists, taking an overdose of tablets with whisky).

Rob said that he and Alice had a good relationship and did everything together – 'We were a team, we used to battle it out together'. They didn't have much of a social life, didn't go out and mix, just saw their family. Very occasionally she had respite care but even then Rob visited her twice a day.

Looking at his early life, Rob revealed that his father was killed in a mining accident, when Rob was seven years old. He had a good relationship with his father. They had great times together, laughing and joking. His father was always in a good mood. He was 12 when his mother remarried. Rob reported that his stepfather was cruel to him and 'Saturday night was fright night when he had been drinking'. Subsequently, he stopped drinking and Rob got on better with him. His stepfather died one year before Rob's therapy began and his mother died two years before that. He got on well with his mother who was kind and supportive, and he had pleasant memories of her. She had been ill for a long time and Rob appeared to have anticipated her death and coped well when it happened.

Rob had occasional nightmares of when he was driving a lorry 25 years ago, and a woman jumped in front of his vehicle and was killed. It was believed to be suicide as she had attempted to take her life before.

After Alice's death, his sister and daughter provided practical help – washing, ironing, shopping, giving him his medication, etc. Rob saw his daughter each day. Occasionally he slept in the car rather than be in the bungalow alone.

(Continued)

(Continued)

Table 9.3   Rob's scores on the AAG scale at three points in his therapy

Factor	AAG Items	Score T = 1	Agg. score	Score T = 2	Agg. score	Score T = 3	Agge score
Overwhelmed	2	+2		+1		+1	
	5	+2	+6	+2	+4	−1	+2
	7	+2		+1		+1	−1
Resilient	1	−1		−1		+1	
	3	+1	+1	+1	+2	+2	+4
	9	−1	−2	+1	−1	+1	
Controlled	4	+2		+1		+2	
	6	+2	+6	+1	+3	+1	+5
	8	+2		+1		+2	

The scores are given for each item followed by the aggregated scores for each of the three sub-scales. Some of the aggregated scores fall in both a plus and minus direction – suggesting ambivalence.

Reflexive narrative

The use of the AAG scale was instrumental in understanding both Rob's complex grief reaction and in creating a therapeutic relationship with him. Table 9.3 shows Rob's responses to the scale at three points in the helping process.

The scores confirmed the clinical evidence; Rob was showing maximum agreement with both the overwhelmed items and the controlled ones, he was both attempting to block his grief and yet was deeply psychologically disturbed by it. However, Rob did agree with item 3 which hinted that he might be able to move away from denial of his wife's death, although he was still only making oblique references to his loss. 'I know I've got to face up to it eventually if it's not a dream. It will help me knuckle down and do the things I should be doing instead of being an in-patient.' His practical goal in adjusting to the recognised changes in his situation was to be able to stay in his bungalow and go shopping.

Two months after the initial assessment there was a significant change. There was a reduced level of intensity in his agreement with the overwhelmed and controlled items and a move to agree with item 9 (I do believe that I will come through this experience of grief). This seemed to be related to his achieving visits and an overnight stay at his bungalow. This step was very pleasing to Rob. There was other evidence of his feeling a little more optimistic in that he described being in a dream 90 per cent of the time, not all of the time, and this represented 'a little bit of a chink'. The therapeutic focus was on the two items (1 and 5), which were outside the overall trend in his responses. Strong agreement with item 5 (I feel that I will always carry the pain of grief with me) and disagreement with item 1 (I feel able to face the pain which comes with loss), showed the difficulty he was having in coping with his feelings. However, Rob reported in his diary: 'Saw therapist at the hospital, felt relaxed and able to talk. I didn't feel depressed during the session'. This suggests that in spite of his considerable emotional pain and tensions in managing his loss, Rob experienced the therapy positively.

By the third assessment two months later, Rob moved from strongly agreeing to disagreeing that he would always carry the pain of grief with him (item 5). However, it seemed unlikely that this was indicative of some resolution of his distress but was more consistent with his continued denial that he had suffered a loss. 'I'm in a dream, I've had no loss, I feel as if I've had no loss. I don't feel any grief. I'm in this dream, which is protecting me from grief.' This protection left him far from facing reality – 'How much she'll like the new bungalow when she sees it.'

Nevertheless, he felt sure he could cope but was frightened about what would happen if he couldn't cope. He said,' I'd built a wall all the way around myself and I've been able to break some of the bricks, about 40 per cent, down from it.' He equated achieving practical day-to-day things with the bricks coming down from the wall. The descriptions and the metaphors Rob used continued to give a picture of attempts to confront his loss, at least in practical ways, but was followed by speedy denials of it.

Rob felt bothered that he had not faced up to reality, as he had done with other problems in his life. Getting on with life (item 8) meant 'Trying to show people that I can but it's all an act really. Sometimes I feel like giving way to my feelings and showing them how I feel but I don't want to worry them. I've come through other grief but I don't believe she has passed away. I've not faced up to it, I don't believe she is dead. I'm still in this dream world and I want to be out of it and into reality.' He commented that nothing had shocked him into stepping into reality. Rob described his situation at this stage in therapy as being 'at a crossroads'. This metaphor was used by his therapist, to recognise that taking one route now didn't mean that he couldn't come back, and take another route in the future. His choice for the moment was to carry on in his dream. Rob described taking the fork in the road which allowed him to stay in his dream.

After a gap in therapy Rob still reported the continued dream-like quality of his existence. However, he felt that putting on an act was getting harder. Rob had developed some serious heart problems and he was concerned that if he was going to die he 'wanted to be in the real world when it happened'. Plans were made for Rob to rehearse specific thoughts when at the bungalow and when at the cemetery, with the aim of being able to help him on the road to acknowledging that his wife had died. He also kept a diary of his depressed feelings and activities. These included being frightened by angina attacks, wanting to be with his wife and occasional suicidal thoughts. He said 'Dying would be a relief, I would be with her again. It isn't worth going on and I don't want to be here.' Rob wanted to continue his therapy but his physical health deteriorated, requiring major surgery, and not long after he died.

The therapist's perspective

Rob's vulnerability was evident in a number of ways:

- Background complexity in attachment relationships as a child.
- Complex health needs of his wife over a lengthy period.

- His role as carer with few opportunities taken for respite.
- The symbiotic nature of his relationship with Alice.
- Anxieties evident in nightmares associated with an earlier traumatic event.
- Depleted inner resources for facing Alice's death.
- His own poor health.
- Limited capacity to engage fully with the social support available to him.

At some level, Rob appeared to find therapy helpful. However, from a therapist's point of view, he was particularly challenging. If denial was the best way for him to cope, then was it appropriate to push him to fully acknowledge his wife's death? How could leverage be found into an area that was closed down? How could unsafe things be looked at in a safe way? The therapist had noted after one of the early sessions, 'I think it is possible that he may not be able to let go of his wife. He may not be able to adjust well to living without her.' A note by the therapist after a later session said, 'the possibility that he may not be able to move out of his current denial must be kept in mind'. This situation generated a feeling of helplessness in the therapist, who was attempting to make full sense of Rob's difficulties and connect in a way that would be helpful to him.

The initial use of the AAG scale helped to build up a picture of Rob's complex grief, particularly the tension between his feeling totally overwhelmed and at the same time attempting to regain some control. It also highlighted his low levels of resilience. Repeat scores were also useful. This, in combination with qualitative comments amplifying his answers, made it possible to look at inconsistencies in his grief perspective.

Detecting small changes in Rob's psychological state was very important as a way of supporting him and encouraging him to move forward. However, the changes were not clinically significant and repeat use of the AAG scale generally confirmed the great difficulty Rob had in moving on in his grief. This led to the conclusion that it would be useful to have a gap in his therapy. The situation had not changed when he returned to see his therapist.

The use of the scale and focusing on small movements in Rob's perception about his loss, made most use of a cognitive approach to his grief. Practical ways of attending to day-to-day functioning allowed some progress to be made and observed, as he welcomed achieving some control within these situations. However, Rob's incapacity to sustain any belief in the reality of his wife's death meant that making sense of his experience was not possible. Not accepting the reality of the loss (Worden, 2003) prevented any real processing of grief (see Table 9.4).

Discussion

Rob's attachment history and the complexities of his 'good', though enmeshed, relationship with Alice are significant background factors to Rob's grief reactions. His continued denial suggested that he felt, largely at an unconscious level, that his inner resources and external support were not adequate to meet the enormity of what he had lost. Avoidance is recognised in Attachment Theory (Ainsworth et al., 1978; Bowlby, 1980)

Table 9.4 Rob's grief journey

Narrative structure (Angus and Hardke, 1994)	Therapeutic approach	Narrative process (McLeod, 1997)	Rob's grief journey
External		Construction	His wife's death.
Internal	AAG scale	Deconstruction	Disbelief, in a dream, distress.
Reflexive	**Person-centred Psychodynamic** **Cognitive**	**Reconstruction Rehearsal**	**Awareness of background attachments and experience. Focus on grief dynamic revealed through the AAG scale. Address management of day-to-day functioning. Affirming Rob's right to choose to how to be.**

and trauma theory (Horowitz, 1997) as a response to loss when a person is unable to confront their grief. While this was traditionally deemed a pathological response, it has more recently been recognised as a way of successfully managing traumatising experience (Bonanno et al., 1995). However, in Rob's case his strategy was not successful. He was not able to suppress his grief sufficiently to function in anything but a limited capacity and the mode of his denial, his sense of being in a dream, was itself a distressing state to be in. This rendered him very vulnerable, and the tension he demonstrated between overwhelming emotion and wanting to be in control, produced an intolerable pressure demonstrated by his suicidal tendencies. Clearly, Rob was a vulnerable client who needed support but who could not be helped beyond his own psychological need to hold at bay the reality of his wife's death.

Case Study 9.3 Hannah's grief journey

Hannah had been known by a hospital psychology service over a number of years. She was initially seen some time after her husband's death for problems with muscle contractions and headaches. She was referred again six years later following a stroke, when she was suffering from depression and anxiety. In addition to the therapy, she was prescribed long-term antidepressants. Four years later, she lost her confidence after a fall and was having difficulty regaining her mobility. Hannah had arthritis as well as limited mobility arising from the stroke. Deteriorating health problems triggered grief for her husband.

The AAG scale had been used in therapy when Hannah was an in-patient following her stroke and again following her mobility problems. Comparisons, over a period of time, could be made in her grief reactions for her husband and in relation to her stroke.

(Continued)

(Continued)

External narrative

Hannah's husband died 17 years ago and she had a stroke five years ago. She came into contact with the psychological services as she was having difficulty in coping with the physical and emotional consequences of her stroke. Her daughters thought that she had wasted her life since her husband died. Both daughters suffered from anxiety and depression and one had bereavement counselling. Hannah's mother, who was her confidante, stepfather and a brother also died during the period since her husband's death.

Internal narrative (bereavement)

Hannah's qualitative responses to the AAG scale (see Table 9.5) provided a picture of the impact of her husband's death. She reported a continued lowering of her mood at weekends and she attributed this to her husband having died at home on a Saturday. Hannah thought of her husband every day (item 2). She found it very difficult to get over his loss (item 5), believing that nothing would ever be the same (item 7) and feared that her grief might get worse, not better. This perspective led her to feel very depressed. However, Hannah tried to manage her feelings by being brave (item 4) for the sake of her children and concluded that, in spite of her feelings, she needed to get on with life (item 8) because 'there is nothing else I can do'. Trying to control her grief (item 6) was an emotional struggle but she kept reminding herself that 'I can't do anything about it so why keep crying about it'. The responses to the scale clearly showed the tension between her feelings and her attempt to suppress them.

Hannah said, 'It's difficult to face up to a loss [item 1] especially when on your own. I'm able to have happy thoughts but it still upsets me. In trying to face up to it I think about my daughters who are very good to me. I have come through [item 9] but there is deep depression and I don't think it will ever go away. It's taking a long time and I get upset if anybody talks about him. Anything sad, for example on the TV, can trigger it off. I don't think I'll accept it; it has gone on too long. Depression is worse when I'm alone. I thought it would get better with tablets but they have made no difference. I wish I could put it all to the back of my mind. Bad days equal being alone and wishing someone would come, wishing my husband was here. I don't think about him all the time and I do have pleasant memories, like holidays abroad, but I wouldn't want to go back to places we used to go to a lot. I don't have any regrets except failing to tell him not to smoke and feeling I didn't do enough for him but they're not guilt feelings. My only anger is about the delay in paramedics arriving and them not trying to resuscitate him in the home. I've always found comfort in talking to my husband about the children, grandchildren and great-grandchildren. I may talk to him if I've had a bad day but not sure if it's helpful then'.

As the stroke was a complicating factor in the depression linked with Hannah's bereavement, the modified version of the AAG scale was used to help look at the losses associated with her disability (see Table 9.6).

Internal narrative (stroke)

Hannah reported panic feelings, a poor appetite and occasional suicidal thoughts but with no specific plans to follow this through. 'If I hadn't had the stroke I don't think I

Table 9.5   Hannah's scores on the AAG scale, in respect of her bereavement, at four points in her therapy (across a five-year period).

Factor	AAG Items	Score 2002 T = 1	Agg. score	Score 2006 T = 2	Agg. score	Score 2007 T = 3	Agg. score	Score 2007 T = 4	Agg. score
Overwhelmed	2	+2		+1		+1		+1	
	5	+1	+5	+1	+3	+2	+5	+1	+3
	7	+2		+1		+2		+1	
Resilient	1	−1		0		−2		+2	
	3	−1	−3	−1	−1	−1	−4	+1	+5
	9	−1		0		−1		+2	
Controlled	4	+1		+1		+1		+2	
	6	+1	+3	+1	+3	+2	+4	+2	+5
	8	+1		+1		+1		+1	

The scores are given for each item followed by the aggregated scores for each of the three sub-scales.

would be like this [depressed]. I used to go out, shop, clean – you've got to cope there's no other alternative but it's very hard. You can't do much with one hand. I get bored, the same thing every day. I try to keep the grief about my stroke under control, there's nothing else you can do. It's not good if I moan to my daughters. It isn't living is it, sitting in a chair all day? I won't get back to how I was physically. I wish I could get up, do this, go here, go there – it's that that plays on my mind. Not coming through it is the hardest bit. I don't think you ever get over a stroke if it leaves you like this. You sit here and you're not going to get or feel any better.'

Hannah coped with her bereavement partly by keeping active, going shopping etc. The stroke became a key factor in constraining her coping mechanism and had a strong negative impact on her independence. Hannah's sense of resilience was absent from responses to the AAG scale in respect of both her bereavement and her stroke. In order to address her vulnerability the focus of therapy was upon building her capacity for resilience.

Reflexive narrative

Hannah was encouraged to reflect on her life and relationships and the ways in which she had coped well in the past. She talked of herself as a 'survivor'; 'I'm like my mother, she was a coper she had 11 children'. Hannah was the oldest child – 'I virtually reared the family before I got married'. She recalled her loving parents and happy home life. She worked from the age of 14 to 60. Hannah had known her husband from the age of 13/14 and she was married at 19. They had a good relationship and 'did everything together'. She also had lots of friends. Hannah was proud of the way she brought up her two daughters and proud of their families. She had coped with a number of deaths.

(Continued)

(Continued)

Hannah was asked to reflect on things which she was still able to do. She said that she coped by talking with a neighbour and her sister. She felt that she had determination and said 'I got to the Day Hospital even though I felt bad as I thought I would be better in company'. Her husband felt that she was a stronger person than he was. It also became clear to Hannah that she would be able to say 'no' to medication if this was offered in the future.

Reflection on her situation enabled Hannah to appraise the positive aspects of her situation more accurately and this was seen in the changed AAG scores (Time 4) in respect of her bereavement. She was able to agree or strongly agree with all the resilient items on the scale.

Hannah was able to admit that the intrusive thoughts about her husband decreased over the time she was having therapy and she felt that she could look forward to things. However, at the end of her last session she said 'I wish I could have had a bit longer with him'.

Table 9.6   Hannah's scores on the AAG scale relating to the losses associated with her stroke

Factor	AAG Items	Score 2002 T = 1	Agg. score	Score 2007 T = 2	Agg. score
Overwhelmed	2	+1		+2	
	5	+2	+5	+1	+4
	7	+2		+1	
Resilient	1	−2		−1	
	3	−1	−4	−1	−3
	9	−1		−1	
Controlled	4	+1		+1	
	6	+2	+4	+1	+3
	8	+1		+1	

The scores are given for each item followed by the aggregated scores for each of the three sub-scales.

The therapist's perspective

Hannah's vulnerability:

- Death of her husband.
- Stroke.
- Combined impact of these two major losses.
- Limited capacity to adjust to her changed situation because of her physical disabilities.
- Reduced social support leading to real and perceived isolation.

Table 9.7   Hannah's grief journey (bereavement and stroke)

Narrative structure (Angus and Hardke, 1994)	Therapeutic approach	Narrative process (McLeod, 1997)	Hannah's grief journey (bereavement and stroke)
External		Construction	Her husband's death and a stroke.
Internal	AAG scale	Deconstruction	Depression.
Reflexive	Person-centred Psychodynamic Cognitive	Reconstruction Rehearsal	Focus on grief dynamic revealed through the AAG scale. Focus on strengths and coping capacity. Perspective on loss story modified as strengths acknowledged.

The AAG scale and its modified version looked separately at the impact of Hannah's bereavement and her stroke, and helped to identify the components of her loss response. There were some positive movements (in resilience), seen in Hannah's reaction to her husband's death, but hardly any change in her responses to the AAG scale in relation to her stroke. This provided clear evidence, which was well supported by the clinical presentation of depression, that the stroke was a seriously complicating factor in Hannah's bereavement. The limited adjustment to the stroke brought the loss of her husband into fuller focus, as the strategies for 'getting on with life' were defeated. Her overall vulnerability could be seen in her disagreement with the resilient items on the scale (re-stroke) and the aim of therapy was to help her re-engage with her own resources and the support mechanisms available to her. Looking at her own history helped Hannah affirm the strengths which she had acquired during her life as daughter, caring sibling, good wife and mother, and as a hard worker. This approach allowed her to reflect on her situation and bring her strengths into focus, which had been lost in the overwhelming experiences of bereavement and a seriously disabling illness. Cognitive strategies included providing information about panic attacks and undertaking modified relaxation exercises. A more balanced perspective in her outlook was achieved, but fuller emotional equilibrium was not possible (see Table 9.7).

Discussion

Chapter 2 looked at the varied ways in which loss and change are experienced across the life cycle. Where people are coping with more than one loss simultaneously, the likelihood of vulnerability is considerable. This is especially the case if support is limited or inadequate. This could be seen in Hannah's case, where the sharpness of grief for her husband was reawakened by her illness and together produced long-term psychological disturbance. Nevertheless, within the innate constraints of her situation, Hannah was helped to reappraise her own life perspectives in a way which gave her some increased confidence in managing her physical limitations. By appraising the possibilities as well as confronting the difficulties and by looking for ways to make use of support (see Figure 9.3), the therapeutic focus addressed her vulnerability and looked to build her resilience, if only in a limited way.

Conclusion

This chapter has explored the ways in which vulnerability may result from an inability to reconcile the core elements of grief – the overwhelming feelings and the desire for control. The case examples identify three situations which might give rise to vulnerability – childhood experience of traumatising loss (Anthony), the severing of a symbiotic adult attachment figure (Rob), and the complexity of having to adjust to two losses alongside the natural ageing processes (Hannah). In each of these cases the social support was either inadequate or was not satisfyingly experienced in the meeting of emotional needs. Anthony, Rob and Hannah travelled a lonely journey, which obscured most of their innate coping capabilities from their own awareness. Counselling/therapy was used to redress some of the absences of support and to help in the reconstruction of a narrative that restored some sense of balance for them.

When working with a client/patient who is very vulnerable, there may be limitations to achieving a narrative which can be 'lived by and lived with' (McLeod, 1997). While resilience may seem elusive, it remains an overall therapeutic objective (see Figure 9.3). Counselling/therapy may necessarily be longer-term and the demands upon the practitioner are undoubtedly challenging.

10

Practitioner Perspectives – Maps, Journeys and Destinations

This book has brought together contemporary ideas about loss and grief and presented a new model for practitioner engagement with life-changing experiences. While the dominant focus has been on therapeutic practice, the theoretical perspectives and the proposed ways of working with grieving people are widely applicable in health and social care settings. This chapter will review the place of loss in practice by considering:

- Loss and its place within health and social care.
- A new model and working tool.
- Values and objectives in working with loss.

The challenge for practitioners working with grief is to apply knowledge and skill with awareness of the wide individual variations in loss response. This is personally demanding and if undertaken without sensitivity can reinforce the sense of isolation felt by grieving people. Awareness needs to operate in three dimensions of care:

1 Awareness of the professional perspectives and expectations which influence work with grieving people.
2 Awareness of how practitioners' own loss experiences and personal life perspectives are brought to practice.
3 Awareness of the need for support to maximise professional effectiveness and maintain personal resourcefulness.

Loss in practice

Loss and its place within health and social care

The knowledge base for working with loss and grief has emerged largely from research and literature on death and dying. The parallels between death and the grief produced by other life losses becomes visible when full consideration is given to loss across the life cycle. Chapter 2 sets out the landscape of loss and provides two different maps for recognising the centrality of loss to life's journey. First, the path from birth to death which is punctuated by psychosocial change and associated losses, and, second, the unpredictable and distressing circumstantial losses resulting from disturbance or disintegration in relationships, in health, in personal hopes and in traumatising experiences of death. This is a landscape which embraces the life contingencies brought to health and social care settings. In health care, in addition to provision being made for physical treatment and rehabilitation, recognition needs to be given to the emotional, intellectual, social and spiritual impact of physical/mental losses, such as the grief component of illness and disability. Similarly in social care, clients/service users within statutory and voluntary settings bring problems of finance, housing, relationships, etc., which are difficult to manage and which produce variable degrees of grief within their lives. Practice solutions for these losses often focuses upon alleviating symptoms and neglects attention to the full human impact of these events and circumstances. Adopting a loss perspective moves more deeply into personal grief and demands an engagement with the individual who is processing, for example, ageing, abuse, divorce, disability, disappointment, death, etc.

The cultural context in which loss is experienced shapes attitudes towards grief and determines the way it is expressed (Martin and Doka, 2000). It is important for practitioners to recognise the wider social influences which impinge on client/patient grief reactions.

The range of practice roles in working with loss and grief is diverse. Some practitioners will be involved with patients/clients as they approach a loss situation, for example, as medical investigations are being undertaken, as decisions are made about admission to residential care, etc; some may begin their work with the breaking of bad news or having conversations about life-changing events; others will travel the journey of loss, for example, from terminal diagnosis to death, (unsuccessful) fertility treatment, etc; others will work retrospectively with a client/patient who is seeking to adjust to a loss, such as bereavement, childlessness, etc. The nature and intensity, formality or informality of engagement will vary with the practice role:

- Psycho-therapeutic role – psychotherapists, psychologist, counsellors, etc.
- Medical role – doctor, nurse, physiotherapist, etc.
- Medico/psychosocial role – palliative care nurse, community psychiatric nurse, etc.
- Social care role – social workers, care managers, etc.
- Care support role – home care and residential care workers etc.
- Ancillary staff – ward orderlies, clerks, etc.
- Specialist workers with loss – funeral directors, clergymen/women, stone masons, etc.
- Volunteers in supportive roles – counsellors, visitors, providers of practical services, etc (associated with any of the above care settings).

Each of these roles is enhanced by knowledge about the nature of grief. Even where intervention is not implicit within the role, attending to the story of loss will carry some therapeutic benefits when the listener is able to convey an understanding of the nature of the impact of loss upon the client/patient. This may equally occur when a nurse is bathing a patient or a warden is making a daily visit to check residents in sheltered housing, as when a counsellor/therapist sits down with the specific intention of engaging with a person's grief. Theories of grief, described in Chapter 3, provide a knowledge base which can be used to help the listener sensitively attune to the individual account of loss.

The narrative structure (Angus and Hardke, 1994) described in Chapter 4, is an important way of identifying the components of the loss story, which practitioners might hear:

- The factual account of what been lost (the external narrative).
- The impact of the loss upon the grieving person (the internal narrative).

These two elements make up the grief stories most practitioners will hear in the course of their work. Case examples are used in Chapter 7 to illustrate these aspects of the narrative process.

More specific therapeutic engagement focuses on the processing of grief by exploring ways of accepting what cannot be changed, looking at new ways of thinking and behaving in response to the loss, and attempting to make sense of the loss experience. This is described as the third element in the narrative structure:

- Making sense of experience (the reflexive narrative).

This is a more specialist role and the methods, goals and examples describing the process of promoting resilience and working with vulnerability are given through case examples in Chapters 8 and 9.

Loss, as a human experience, is clearly central to the work of practitioners in health and social care settings and theories of grief and therapy can be usefully, but variably, applied across multiple care roles to inform good practice

A new model and working tool

The central focus of this book has been the account of the development (Chapter 5) and practice use (Chapter 6) of a model which emerged directly from research and practice experience with grieving people (Machin, 2001). The Range of Response to Loss model provides a framework for recognising and understanding the core grief reactions and the ways in which people experience the competing elements of distressed feeling (overwhelmed reactions) and the thoughts and actions (control) which are used to counter the sense of powerlessness. Where these two elements can be reconciled a newly emerging feeling of balance can be achieved (resilience), (see Figure 10.1). Sometimes the process of gaining equilibrium will occur naturally but at other times the practitioner has a role in helping facilitate it. Chapter 4 explores the therapeutic approaches and perspectives, which can be used to achieve this sense of balance.

The structure of the RRL model provides a theoretical compass for appraising the state of grief (bearing in mind that there are changes over time) and indicates the direction in which collaborative work with the client/patient can be undertaken in order to enhance or promote resilience. See Figures 10.2 and 10.3.

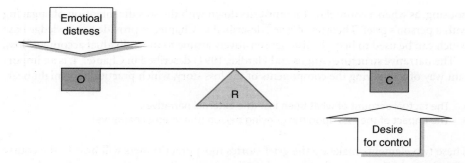

Figure 10.1   The competing elements of grief – Overwhelming distress and attempts to Control events and circumstances, mediated by the balance mechanism of Resilience

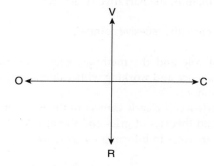

Figure 10.2   'Compass' showing the intersection between the core grief responses (overwhelmed and controlled) and the mediating factors (resilience and vulnerability)

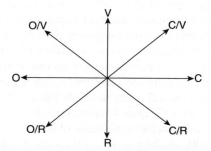

Figure 10.3   'Compass' showing additional bearings – overwhelmed and resilient/vulnerable; controlled and resilient/vulnerable

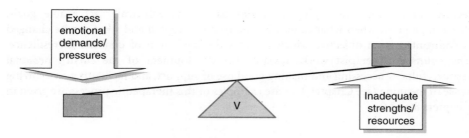

Figure 10.4   A lack of equilibrium where excessive demands and pressures outstrip strengths and resources producing Vulnerability

For some people, resilience is an already developed faculty for dealing with loss and some support will help activate it. For other people, limited personal resourcefulness and demanding circumstantial factors exceed their strength to meet a loss with equilibrium. Therapeutic help is especially pertinent when a number of factors are indicative of vulnerability, for example, history of difficulty in managing stressful events and concurrent losses. See Figure 10.4.

The Adult Attitude to Grief scale is a working tool which can assist in the clearer identification of the grieving dynamic. The nine self-report statements in the scale, made of three sub-scales which reflect overwhelmed, controlled and resilient perspectives (or their absence), provide the counsellor/therapist with a structure to facilitate the client/patient in the telling of their grief story. Elaboration of the story and the impact of loss emerges naturally from responses to the items on the AAG statements. Studies of its use in practice (Lydon, Ryan-Woolley and Amir, 2007; Machin, 2007a; Machin and Spall, 2004) show that the scale is a tool which can be used:

- For assessment.
- To help identify the components of complex grief reactions.
- To facilitate therapeutic dialogue.
- To identify the grief changes taking place over time.
- As an outcome measure.

Evaluation has become an important measure of the efficacy of practice interventions. While changes in grief can never be wholly attributed to the care process, as many other factors influence movement, the AAG scale provides one way of identifying shifts in grief response. Further studies of the varied practice use of the AAG scale would usefully build on earlier research.

Both the theoretical propositions within the RRL model and the AAG scale provide a way for the practitioner to access a picture of the client/patient's grief. This knowledge provides a basis for selecting therapeutic approaches to restore equilibrium. A bias towards overwhelmed feelings requires engagement with empowering strategies focused on the agency which comes from thinking and acting. A bias towards control, which is often defeated by the powerlessness of loss, requires a safe place in which to address feelings and reappraise coping strategies based on realistically achievable goals. Reaching a point when what cannot be changed is accepted and what can be changed is confronted is an objective which requires the mediation of qualities of resilience. The counsellor/therapist works towards the development of the client's personal resourcefulness, accessing and making good use of support, and facilitating an evolving sense of meaning (see Chapter 4). Case examples of this therapeutic process are given in Chapters 8 and 9.

Values and objectives in working with loss

The assumption which underpins the approach to working with loss described in this book, is based on a belief in the individual worth of each grieving person. Theories of grief, which provide an understanding of the common characteristics of grief, need to be applied with sensitivity to the individual variations in loss response. The RRL model as a theoretical compass, and the AAG scale as a mapping tool, provide ways of giving full recognition to the individual nature of grieving. The model and the scale are used with a person-centred approach, which stresses the value of individuals. Techniques are nothing if they do not engage with the lived experience of individuals and sensitively appraise the pain and needs of each person. John Smith in his poem, 'My Gift', poignantly depicts the fragility of what is brought to those who work in health and social care.

> Handle me with care,
> The wrapper's worn
> And held by threadbare string,
> Almost torn apart;
> Gaping edges
> Invite you to look with curious eyes.
> Worthless, you might think.
> So old, carelessly parcelled up.
>
> Just think before you touch
> Think where I have been,
> Seen, spoken, listened, touched,
> Hurt, born, and felt.
> Can't you feel the passion
> Left within me?
>
> Share it,
> Undo the string, slowly please,
> (I'm so slow now)
> undo the hurt
> (I hurt now)
> the guilt
> (aren't you guilty too?)

the hate
(as I hate what's happening now)
undo the love,
and let it go,
my gift to you.

[1989: 41–2]

A traditional focus for practitioners has been upon the risks associated with loss. A medical model of care has developed which has majored on symptomotolgy and the pathology of grief (Averill and Nunley, 1993). At the same time in the West, social structures, beliefs and rituals, which traditionally provided the way of understanding grief and its expression, have been weakened (Martin and Doka, 2000). Both these movements, professional and social/cultural, have lead to ambiguity about the normality of grief and a tendency to label anything but a fairly reserved, short-term reaction as problematic. However, a new emphasis has grown with the development of positive psychology (Joseph and Linley, 2006; Seligman, 1999). This perspective seeks to move from 'preoccupation only with repairing the worst things in life to also building positive qualities' (Seligman and Csikszentmihalyi, 2000: 5). For practitioners, this means helping clients/patients reconnect with their innate human capacity to flourish in spite of those experiences which might appear to detract from growth, but which provide through challenge, strengthening opportunities to realise human potential. This perspective is gaining ground in health and social care as attention is given equally to resilience as to risk (Munroe and Oliviere, 2007). This book has set resilience within the spectrum of grief responses and encourages practitioners to give major consideration to the appraisal of strengths as well as vulnerabilities in their clients/patients.

The challenge for practitioners

Awareness of the professional perspectives and expectations which influence work with grieving people

The culture in which care is offered to grieving people influences the nature of service provision. The 2004 study in practice (Machin and Spall – see Chapter 6) was undertaken in a medical setting in which both psychological and physical illnesses are treated by drugs and therapy, in order to alleviate symptoms of pain and distress. In a medical context a patient may feel it necessary to be good and cooperative, picking up the cues from medical staff about being in control. Bravery and stoicism may be the qualities to display in settings where 'big boys don't cry'. At an unconscious level this may encourage unwanted feelings to be suppressed, and attitudes and thoughts which perpetuate vulnerability inhibited. Patients who do not conform to this script may be seen as troublesome, uncooperative, not wanting to get better, etc. There was evidence of strong aspirations for control in many of the participants in the 2004 research (Machin and

Spall). However, the attitudinal statements in the AAG scale reflected the spectrum of reactions a patient might experience, and the scale implicitly gave permission to describe, express and explore those reactions which might normally be inhibited.

In contrast, the study conducted within a voluntary agency (Machin, 2007a), where the service of care was focused upon the psychological and social consequences of loss, overt aspirations for control were much more mixed. Clients were able to report on their grief in the knowledge that this specialist service was familiar with loss reactions and, reinforced by the person-centred approach of their counsellors, could feel free to give an unedited account of their experience. The AAG scale reflected this diversity and while control was often a reflection of the wider culture's regulations of emotional expression, there was no similar organisational constraint on working with feelings.

At a time when greater attention is being given in many care settings to the potential impact of loss, it is important that care cultures themselves do not contribute to a process of inhibiting grief. Psychosocial care needs to be mindful of its own power to influence how grief is understood and expressed (McLeod and Machin, 1998).

Awareness of how practitioners' own loss experiences and personal life perspectives are brought to practice

All practitioners bring their own loss agenda to their work. Grief may already have been a significant life experience and listening to the loss narrative of another may reawaken existing or latent pain. Client/patient grief can also focus attention on potential future losses and arouse fears and anxieties about one's own mortality. These are combined with losses implicit in the caring role (Papadatou, 2000):

- Loss of a bond with someone when a significant shared therapeutic/treatment journey comes to an end.
- A sense of loss produced by identification with the pain of people who are grieving.
- Loss generated when professional goals could not be reached – for example, a patient dying before all possibilities for their treatment had been exhausted.
- A sense of loss when personal belief systems are challenged, for example, death of a child, elder abuse, etc.

When these inner processes are recognised and understood they can generate empathy but where they are a distraction (a process of counter-transference is taking place) the client/patient may receive seriously reduced care. In counselling and therapeutic tradition, practitioners are required to undertake personal therapy as a way of addressing those issues which might obstruct full engagement with the client/patient. Personal therapy also provides an experiential perspective on what it is like to be a client.

Practitioner awareness also needs to extend to recognition of our own coping styles in relation to loss, as this has the potential to influence the response made to clients/patients. Research by Papadatou (2000) looked at the grief responses in nurses working with dying children. The study concluded that where fluctuation between focusing on the experience of loss and moving away from it was observed, there was a capacity to provide competent care to other patients and their families. Conversely, the dominance of feelings about a patient's death or shutting out feelings and retreating into practical tasks, detracted from good care and the valuing of patients. Papadatou (2000) suggests that both of these tendencies produce 'stuckness' which has a disabling effect on the functioning of the care provider. This study highlights the same dynamic in carers as the RRL model has done in grieving people. The RRL model also looks for a balance between being absorbed by feelings of loss (being overwhelmed) and using controlled diversion from it.

In considering the importance of practitioner grieving styles the following questions suggest areas for personal reflection, and agendas for supervision:

1   In a crisis or when under pressure is my coping bias towards feeling or thinking/acting?
2   How do I respond to a client/patient whose feeling/thinking bias is opposite to my own?
3   How do I/can I restore some balance between feeling and thinking/acting?
4   Does the therapeutic approach I use reflect my coping style, that is, psychodynamic and person-centred – feeling focused; cognitive/behavioural – thinking/action focused?
5   How do I work with a client/patient who does not respond to my therapeutic perspective?
6   How can I expand my therapeutic repertoire to be responsive to individual difference?

Organisations have a responsibility to consider how staff reactions to loss affect their capacity to cope with the grief of others.

Awareness of the need for support to maximise professional effectiveness and maintain personal resourcefulness

Working with grieving people is demanding. Their distress can be disturbing especially when the client/patient's powerlessness is also felt by the people who are caring for them. There are no solutions for some losses, only adjustment to the reality of them. The concept of burnout has been to applied to the state of exhaustion reached by some professionals whose work has taken them beyond their functioning capacity to a depressed place where they have reduced enthusiasm, stagnation, frustration, apathy (Kirk, 1998). This may be especially true for those workers who are dealing, for example, with abused children, severely disfiguring illness, traumatic deaths, etc. in which they are also traumatised by what has to be absorbed from profoundly disturbing grief stories. Figley and Kleber, (1995) see this as secondary traumatic stress or compassion stress.

'Effective and improved coping strategies are those which enable the person to renew his or her sense of original purpose of helping people' (Coppenhall, 1995: 42). At a professional level supervision is crucial. Different styles of supervision provide opportunities for practitioners to have time for individual reflection and support, and group supervision can reduce a sense of isolation. Supervisors need to be experienced in the field of their supervisee's practice and be alert for signs of stress. Organisations, too, need to take responsibility for the management of practitioners' workloads and ensure training and support adequately meet their practice needs. The four factors which Papadatou et al. (1998) suggested are necessary for the support of health professionals working with dying children can be applied across all services offering care in stressful situations:

1   Informational support – being fully aware of all the factors pertinent to the care-giving role.
2   Clinical/practical support – experiencing the care team as one which is collaborative and is mindful of individual carer's needs.
3   Emotional support – recognition within the team, unit, department, etc. of the impact of working with loss, and where necessary providing opportunities for personal debriefing and/or time-out for its staff.
4   Meaning-making support – debriefing and reflection on practice, as a way of care teams coming to some shared sense of meaning about their work with loss and grief.

These support conditions demand that organisations have coherent philosophies and protocols in order to achieve fully operational staff care.

At a personal level, practitioners may have particular methods of countering their work with relaxation or reflection. A good balance of activities outside work is essential for the maintenance of healthy professional functioning. Social activities and relationships can help restore an exhausted and tarnished outlook on life. This ensures the maintenance of resilience in workers which echoes the central aspirations for coping with loss conceptualised in the RRL model and AAG scale.

Conclusion

This chapter has brought together the themes of the book and explored the implications for practitioners. The RRL model emerged from listening to grief stories and the AAG scale was developed as a way of entering more deeply into individual loss narratives. The concepts contained within the model and the measure provide practitioners, in wide health and social care settings, with practical tools to engage with loss and grief. The underlying assumption is that there is a common humanity between the cared for and the carer and that within the overall process the carer, at times, also needs to be cared for.

Those who grieve and those who care for them undertake a shared journey. It is both demanding and rewarding. The challenge is to work with the 'jagged fractures and distortions' of grief, and facilitate reaching a place which is not an ending, but is a location where there is 'harmony … pain and peace united'.

Let all its jagged fractures and distortions,
all unmeaning scattered scraps and
wrecks and random ruins, merge in
vastness of some evening stilled with
thy remembrance, filled with endless
harmony of pain and peace united.

Rabindranath Tagore (1923)

Appendices

Appendix 1   Adult Attitude to Grief scale

ADULT ATTITUDE TO GRIEF

Indicate (circle) your response to the attitudes expressed in the following statements.

1 I feel able to face the pain which comes with loss.
   Strongly agree / agree / neither agree nor disagree / disagree / strongly disagree

2 For me, it is difficult to switch off thoughts about the person I have lost.
   Strongly agree / agree / neither agree nor disagree / disagree / strongly disagree

3 I feel very aware of my inner strength when faced with grief.
   Strongly agree / agree / neither agree nor disagree / disagree / strongly disagree

4 I believe that I must be brave in the face of loss.
   Strongly agree / agree / neither agree nor disagree / disagree / strongly disagree

5 I feel that I will always carry the pain of grief with me.
   Strongly agree / agree / neither agree nor disagree / disagree / strongly disagree

6 For me, it is important to keep my grief under control.
   Strongly agree / agree / neither agree nor disagree / disagree / strongly disagree

7 Life has less meaning for me after this loss.
   Strongly agree / agree / neither agree nor disagree / disagree / strongly disagree

8 I think it's best just to get on with life after a loss.
   Strongly agree / agree / neither agree nor disagree / disagree / strongly disagree

9 It may not always feel like it but I do believe that I will come through this experience of grief.
   Strongly agree / agree / neither agree nor disagree / disagree / strongly disagree

Appendix 2 Adult Attitude to Grief scale modified for use with other losses

ADULT ATTITUDE TO GRIEF (modified)

Indicate (circle) your response to the attitudes expressed in the following statements.

1 I feel able to face the (emotional) pain, which comes with the loss of [for example, mobility, home, relationship, etc.]
Strongly agree / agree / neither agree nor disagree / disagree / strongly disagree

2 For me, it is difficult to switch off thoughts about [for example, my illness etc.]
Strongly agree / agree / neither agree nor disagree / disagree / strongly disagree

3 I feel very aware of my inner strength when faced with grief associated with [for example, my stroke, my lost job, etc.]
Strongly agree / agree / neither agree nor disagree / disagree / strongly disagree

4 I believe that I must be brave in the face of loss such as [example]
Strongly agree / agree / neither agree nor disagree / disagree / strongly disagree

5 I feel that I will always carry the pain of grief, associated with [example] with me.
Strongly agree / agree / neither agree nor disagree / disagree / strongly disagree

6 For me, it is important to keep my grief, associated with [example] under control.
Strongly agree / agree / neither agree nor disagree / disagree / strongly disagree

7 Life has less meaning for me after the loss of [example]
Strongly agree / agree / neither agree nor disagree / disagree / strongly disagree

8 I think it's best just to get on with life after a loss like [example]
Strongly agree / agree / neither agree nor disagree / disagree / strongly disagree

9 It may not always feel like it but I do believe that I will come through this experience of loss/grief.
Strongly agree / agree / neither agree nor disagree / disagree / strongly disagree

© *Linda Machin, 2001*

Appendix 3 Record chart for quantitative scores for the AAG scale

Client No: Date: Session No:

Use the grid below to record the responses of the client to the AAG scale (tick the appropriate box).

Strongly agree / agree / neither agree nor disagree / disagree / strongly disagree
   +2   +1   0   −1   −2

AAG scores	+2	+1	0	−1	−2
'O' 2 For me, it is difficult to switch off thoughts about the person I have lost.					
5 I feel that I will always carry the pain of grief with me.					
7 Life has less meaning for me after this loss.					
'R' 1 I feel able to face the pain which comes with loss.					
3 I feel very aware of my inner strength when faced with grief.					
9 It may not always feel like it but I do believe that I will come through this experience of grief.					
'C' 4 I believe that I must be brave in the face of loss.					
6 For me, it is important to keep my grief under control.					
8 I think its best just to get on with life after a loss.					

'O' overwhelmed items; 'R' resilient items; 'C' controlled items.

Appendix Figure 1   Score grid for responses to the AAG scale

Using the diagram showing the interlinking nature of grief responses (Figure 6.7) and the proposed Hierarchy of Vulnerability (p. 106) to guide your understanding of the scores consider the following questions:

1 By looking at the scores for strong agreement (+2) or agreement (+1) can you see a clear categorical bias? That is, do scores +2 and/or +1 appear for one category, but not for the others?
2 If there is no clear bias to one category, what is the nature of the blend of responses? Is it undifferentiated, a true mix of O+C+R or are there two visible elements – O + C, or O + R, or C + R?
3 What do you understand by the responses of disagreement (−1) or strong disagreement (−2)? How does this add to your picture of the client's grief?
4 Are there scores, which stand outside the overall pattern of response?

NB **Remember each client will be different and each journey of grief will follow a different route.** Grief fluctuates and the use of the scale will provide a snapshot of the current characteristics of grief. Repeat use of the scale will provide a picture of the changing dynamic of grief. The overwhelmed dimension is the one which is likely to show most variability. This aspect of distress is often the one which causes people to seek help.

Appendix 4   Record sheet for qualitative responses to the AAG scale

Clients should be invited to elaborate on their perspective on each of the items on the scale. However, a client is likely to give greater attention to those statements which touch upon aspects of grief that seem most pertinent to her/him. This choice of focus by the client will help lead the counsellor into fruitful areas of therapeutic engagement. Wider themes are likely to emerge and require exploration.

The counsellor may also invite the client to look further into those dimensions of grief which are shown by the scores on the AAG scale to produce particular difficulty for the client. For example, especially prompt those items with a score of +2 (strong agreement) and those with a score of −2 (strong disagreement). Also explore those aspects in which the client demonstrates strengths/resilience.

Use Appendix Figure 2 to record the issues raised by clients as they explore themes associated with the AAG scale.

Client No: Date: Session No:

Themes associated with the AAG scale	
'O' 2 The unwelcome intrusion of grief or the chosen desire to remain focused upon it.	
5 The persistence of grief – an incapacity to see beyond the pain/distress.	
7 A sense that life's meaning has been lost and life has changed fundamentally.	

'R' 1 The ability to confront loss and deal with the emotional reactions to it.	
3 A sense of inner resourcefulness including a capacity to access and use social support.	
8 A positive outlook which can see beyond the current pain/distress.	

'C' 4 A value put upon courage and fortitude. This may be for its own sake or in order to support/protect other people.	
6 The importance of keeping emotions in check. Fear of the power of unleashed emotions.	
8 The need to divert and focus on the future.	

Counsellor comments:

Appendix Figure 2   Record sheet for qualitative responses to the AAG scale

Appendix 5   Case example and client comments in response to the AAG scale

Janet, aged 72, was referred to a psychology service for help with 'low mood and occasional suicidal thoughts'. She had a difficult childhood, living with an aunt and uncle. There was a long history of difficult bereavements starting with the death of a very loved grandfather in 1951, when she lost a considerable amount of weight, was on medication and had several months off work. Janet had been widowed twice. Her first husband died in 1985 of a heart attack and her second husband died of cancer in 1999. Following this bereavement she moved a few miles to a small flat, where she was not very happy.

Janet strongly agreed with the 'overwhelmed' statements, agreed with the 'controlled' ones and disagreed largely with the 'balanced/resilient' ones. This produced a tension between her 'overwhelming' experiences of grief and her aspiration for 'control', especially as she was not able to identify her own resourcefulness ('balance/resilience').

Themes associated with the AAG scale (with scores)	Client Comments
'O'2 The unwelcome intrusion of grief. (+2)	Especially when I'm very down, I feel it more. Why am I on my own?
5 The persistence of grief – an incapacity to see beyond the pain. (+2)	Especially for my first husband and grandfather – could cry for him (grandfather) even though he died in 1951. Also my mother and uncle.
7 A sense that life's meaning has been lost. (+2)	That's how it is for me. When you think a lot of them – all gone. They all died suddenly, they were young, in their 60s. Why couldn't they stay longer?

'R' 1 The ability to confront loss. (0)	Sometimes can, sometimes can't. Miss my first husband more (that is than the second husband).
3 A sense of inner resourcefulness. (−1)	Sometimes even now I feel I can't cope. Sometimes I want him back, especially the first one [husband]. I have no strength most of the time.
9 A positive outlook which can see beyond the present pain. (−1)	Should do better, time is going on. I've not come through as much as I'd like to, as I should do. Yes, I think I do sometimes. The only funerals where I cried were my grandfather's and uncle's. For others, the tears came afterwards. You see couples happy – but me, I'm one on my own.

'C' 4 Valuing courage and fortitude. (+1)	For other people's sake I know I've got to be brave but I'm not very brave at times. Shouldn't dwell on the past. I think of them (relatives who have died) all of them every day.
6 Keeping emotions in check. (+1)	When I'm out I have to, for other people's sake.
8 The need to divert and focus on the future. (+1)	To a degree. You've got to but it's an effort.

Appendix Figure 3 Case example of numerical and qualitative responses to the AAG scale

Appendix 6   Young Person's Grief Perspective scale (a modification of the AAG scale)

Indicate (circle) your agreement or disagreement with the following statements.

1   I feel OK about being sad.
    Strongly agree / agree / neither agree nor disagree / disagree / strongly disagree

2   I can't stop thinking about [...]
    Strongly agree / agree / neither agree nor disagree / disagree / strongly disagree

3   Although I'm sad I also feel able to cope with life since [...] died (left).
    Strongly agree / agree / neither agree nor disagree / disagree / strongly disagree

4   I think I should be brave.
    Strongly agree / agree / neither agree nor disagree / disagree / strongly disagree

5   I feel as if this sadness will never get better.
    Strongly agree / agree / neither agree nor disagree / disagree / strongly disagree

6   I can't let other people see how sad I am.
    Strongly agree / agree / neither agree nor disagree / disagree / strongly disagree

7   I don't think anything will ever be the same since [...] died (left).
    Strongly agree / agree / neither agree nor disagree / disagree / strongly disagree

8   I think it's best to get on with life – (school, friends, etc.) – after someone has died.
    Strongly agree / agree / neither agree nor disagree / disagree / strongly disagree

9   I know it's bad at the moment but I think things will get better.
    Strongly agree / agree / neither agree nor disagree / disagree / strongly disagree

References

Ainsworth, M.D.S., Blehar, M.C., Waters, E. and Wall, S. (1978) *Patterns of Attachment: A Psychological Study of the Strange Situation.* Hillsdale, NJ: Erlbaum.

Angelou, M. (1984) *I Know Why The Caged Bird Sings.* London: Virago.

Angus, L. and Hardke, K. (1994) 'Narrative Processes in Psychotherapy', *Canadian Psychology*, 35: 190–203.

Angus, L., Levitt, H. and Hardke, K. (1999) 'Narrative Processes in Psychotherapeutic Change', *Journal of Clinical Psychology*, 55: 1255–70.

Antonovsky, A. (1988) *Unraveling the Mystery of Health: How People Manage Stress and Stay Well.* San Francisco: Jossey-Bass.

Attig, T. (1996) *How We Grieve: Relearning the World.* New York: Oxford University Press.

Averill, J.R. and Nunley, E.P. (1993) 'Grief as an Emotion and as a Disease: A Social-Constructionist Perspective', in M.S. Stroebe, W. Stroebe and R.O. Hansson (eds), *Handbook of Bereavement: Theory Research and Intervention.* Cambridge: Cambridge University Press. pp. 77–90.

Bartholomew, K. (1990) 'Avoidance of Intimacy: An Attachment Perspective', *Journal of Social and Personal Relationships*, 7: 147–78.

Bartholomew, K. and Horowitz, L.M. (1991) 'Attachment Styles Among Young Adults: A Test of a Four-Category Model', *Journal of Personality and Social Psychology*, 61 (2): 226–44.

Bartholomew, K. and Shaver, P.R. (1998) 'Methods of Assessing Adult Attachment', in J.A. Simpson and W.S. Rholes (eds), *Attachment Theory and Close Relationships.* New York: Guilford Press. pp. 25–45.

Bauby, J.-D. (2004) *The Diving-Bell and the Butterfly.* London: Harper Perennial.

Beck, A. (1976) *Cognitive Therapy and the Emotional Disorders.* Harmondsworth: Penguin.

Beck, A.T., Ward, C.H., Mendelson, M., Mock, J.E. and Erbaugh, J. (1961) 'An Inventory for Measuring Depression', *Archives of General Psychiatry*, 4: 561–71.

Bell, M. (1995) *In Harm's Way.* Harmondsworth: Penguin.

Berne, E. (1961) *Transactional Analysis in Psychotherapy.* New York: Grove Press.

Berne, E. (1964) *Games People Play: The Psychology of Human Relationships.* London: Penguin.

Berne, E. (1975) *What Do You Say After You Say Hello? The Psychology of Human Destiny.* London: Corgi.

Bertman, S.L. (1991) *Facing Death: Images, Insights and Interventions.* New York: Brunner-Routledge.

Bhutto, B. (1989) *Daughter of Destiny*. New York: Simon and Schuster.

Birtchnell, J. (1997) 'Attachment in an Interpersonal Context', *British Journal of Medical Psychology*, 70: 265–79.

Blythe, R. (1979) *The View in Winter*. Harmondsworth: Penguin.

Bonanno, G.A. (2001) 'Grief and Emotion: A Social-Functional Perspective', in M.S. Stroebe, R.O. Hansson, W. Stroebe, and H. Schut (eds), *Handbook of Bereavement Research*. Washington: American Psychological Association. pp. 493–515.

Bonanno, G.A. and Kaltman, S.A. (1999) 'Toward an Integrative Perspective on Bereavement', *Psychological Bulletin*, 125: 760–76.

Bonanno, G.A. and Keltner, D. (1997) 'Facial Expressions of Emotion and the Course of Bereavement', *Journal of Abnormal Psychology*, 106: 126–37.

Bonanno, G.A., Keltner, D., Holen, A. and Horowitz, M.J. (1995) 'When Avoiding Unpleasant Emotion Might not be such a Bad Thing: Verbal-Autonomic Response Dissociation and Midlife Conjugal Bereavement', *Journal of Personality and Social Psychology*, 46: 975–89.

Bond, T. (1993) *Standards and Ethics for Counselling in Action*. London: SAGE.

Bowlby, J. (1984) *Attachment and Loss. Vol. 1 Attachment*. Harmondsworth: Penguin.

Bowlby, J. (1980) *Attachment and Loss: Vol. 3 Loss: Sadness and Depression*. Harmondsworth: Penguin.

Bowlby, J. (1988) *A Secure Base: Clinical Applications of Attachment Theory*. London: Routledge.

Bowlby, J. and Parkes, C.M. (1970) 'Separation and Loss Within the Family', in E.J. Anthony and C.M. Koupernil (eds), *The Child in His Family*. New York: Wiley.

Brammer, L.M. (1992) 'Coping with Life Transitions', *International Journal for the Advancement of Counselling*, 15: 239–53.

Bright, R. (1996) *Grief and Powerlessness: Helping People Regain Control of Their Lives*. London: Jessica Kingsley.

Brittain, V. (1978) *Testament of Youth*. London: Virago.

Buckman, R. (1992) *How to Break Bad News*. London: Papermac.

Burr, V. (1995) *An Introduction to Social Constructionism*. London: Routledge.

Buss, A.R. (1979) 'Dialectics, History and Development: The Historical Roots of the Individual-Society Dialectic', in P.B. Baltes and O.G. Brim (eds), *Life-Span Development and Behaviour* (Vol 2). New York: Academic Press.

Canda, E. and Furman, L. (1999) *Spiritual Diversity in Social Work Practice*. New York: Free Press.

Christ, G.H. (2005) 'Interventions with Bereaved Children', in P. Firth, G. Luff and D. Oliviere (eds), *Loss, Change and Bereavement in Palliative Care*. Maidenhead: Open University Press. pp. 96–118.

Clarkson, P. (1995) *The Therapeutic Relationship*. London: Wurr.

Cleiren, M. (1991) *Bereavement and Adaptation: A Comparative Study of the Aftermath of Death*. Washington: Hemisphere Publishing.

Coppenhall, K. (1995) 'The Stresses of Working with Clients who have been Sexually Abused', in W. Dryden (ed.) *The Stresses of Counselling in Action*. London: SAGE.

Courtenay, T. (2000) *Dear Tom – Letters from Home*. London: Doubleday.

Craib, I. (1994) *The Importance of Disappointment.* London: Routledge.

Cross, S. (2002) *I Can't Stop Feeling Sad.* London: ChildLine.

Cutcliffe, J.R. (2004) *The Inspiration of Hope in Bereavement Counselling.* London: Jessica Kingsley.

Dallos, R. (2006) *Attachment Narrative Therapy.* Maidenhead: Open University Press.

Didion, J. (2005) *The Year of Magical Thinking.* London: Fourth Estate.

Doka, K.J. (ed.) (2001) *Disenfranchised Grief: Recognising Hidden Sorrow.* New York: Lexington.

Ellis, A. (1962) *Reason and Emotion in Psychotherapy.* Secaucus, NJ: Lyle Stuart.

Ellis, A. (1989) 'The History of Cognition in Psychotherapy', in A. Freeman, K.M. Simon, L.E. Beutler and H. Arkowitz (eds), *Comprehensive Handbook of Cognitive Therapy.* New York: Plenum Press. pp. 5–20.

Epstein, S. (1990) 'Cognitive Experiential Self-theory', in L. Pervin (ed.), *Handbook of Personality Theory and Research.* New York: Guilford. pp. 165–92.

Erikson, E.H. (1980) *Identity and the Lifecycle: A Reissue.* New York: W.W. Norton.

Fahlberg, V.I. (1994) *A Child's Journey Through Placement.* London: BAAF.

Feeney, J. (2000) 'Adult Romantic Attachment and Couple Relationships', in J. Cassidy and R.R. Shaver (eds), *Handbook of Attachment.* New York: Guilford Press. pp. 355–77.

Feeney, J. and Noller, P. (1996) *Adult Attachment.* Thousand Oaks: SAGE.

Figley, C.R. and Kleber, R.J. (1995) 'Beyond the "Victim": Secondary Traumatic Stress', in R.J. Kleber, C.R. Figley and B.P.R. Gersons (eds), *Beyond Trauma: Cultural and Social Dynamics.* New York: Plenum Press.

Folkman, S. (2001) 'Revised Coping Theory and the Process of Bereavement', in M.S. Stroebe, R.O. Hansson, W. Stroebe, and H. Schut (eds), *Handbook of Bereavement Research.* Washington: American Psychological Association. pp. 563–84.

Fraley, R.C. and Shaver, P.R. (1999) 'Loss and Bereavement: Attachment Theory and Recent Controversies Concerning Grief Work and the Nature of Detachment', in J. Cassidy and P.R. Shaver (eds), *Handbook of Attachment: Theory, Research, and Clinical applications.* New York: Guilford Press. pp. 735–59.

Frankl V. (1959) *Man's Search for Meaning.* Boston: Beacon Press.

Freud, S. (1957) 'Mourning and Melancholia', in J. Strachey (ed.), *Standard Edition of the Complete Work of Sigmund Freud.* London: Hogarth Press. (Original work published 1917.)

Gelcer, E. (1983) 'Mourning is a Family Affair', *Family Process,* 22: 500–16.

Gerhardt, S. (2004) *Why Love Matters: How Affection Shapes a Baby's Brain.* London: Routledge.

Goldman, L. (1994) *Life and Loss: A Guide to Helping Grieving Children.* New York: Accelerated Development.

Gould, R.L. (1978) *Transformations: Growth and Change in Adult Life.* New York: Simon and Schuster.

Greenberg, L.S., Rice, L.N. and Elliot, R. (1993) *Facilitating Emotional Change: The Moment-by-Moment Process.* New York: Guilford Press.

Greene, R. (2002) 'Holocaust Survivors: A Study in Resilience', *Journal of Gerontological Social Work,* 37: 3–18.

(1999) 'Countering Depression with the Five Building Blocks of Resilience', *lay's Youth*, 4 (1): 66–72.

Carpenter, B.N. and Fairchild, S.K. (1993) 'Measurement Issues in in M.S. Stroebe, W. Stroebe and R.O. Hansson (eds), *Handbook of* Cambridge: Cambridge University Press. pp. 62–74.

Harvey, J.H. (2000) *Give Sorrow Words*. Philadelphia: Brunner/Mazel.

Havinghurst, R.J. (1972) *Developmental Tasks and Education*. New York: David McKay.

Hazan, C. and Shaver, P.R. (1987) 'Romantic Love Conceptualised as an Attachment Process', *Journal of Personality and Social Psychology*, 52: 511–24.

Heegaard, M. (1988) *When Someone Very Special Dies*. Minneapolis: Woodland Press.

Hendry, L.B. and Kloep, M. (2002) *Lifespan Development: Resources, Challenges and Risks*. London: Thomson Learning.

Hodgkinson, P.E. and Stewart, M. (1998) *Coping with Catastrophe*. New York: Routledge.

Holmes, J. (1993) *John Bowlby and Attachment Theory*. London: Routledge.

Holmes, T.H. and Rahe, R.H. (1967) 'The Social Readjustment Rating Scale', *Journal of Psychosomatic Research*, 11: 213–18.

Horowitz, M. (1997) *Stress Response Syndromes*. Northvale, NJ: Aronson.

Horowitz, M., Wilner, N. and Alvarez, W. (1979) 'Impact of Events Scale: A Measure of Subjective Stress', *Psychosomatic Medicine*, 41: 209–18.

Horowitz, M., Wilner, N., Mamar, C. and Krupnick, J. (1980) 'Pathological Grief and the Activation of Latent Self-Images', *The American Journal of Psychiatry*, 137: 1137–52.

Howe, D. (1993) *On Being a Client: Understanding the Process of Counselling and Psychotherapy*. London: SAGE.

Irish, D.P., Lundquist, K.F. and Nelsen, V.J. (1993) *Ethnic Variations in Dying, Death and Grief*. Washington: Taylor and Francis.

Jordan, J.R. (1991–1992) 'Cumulative Loss, Current Stress, and the Family: A Pilot Investigation of Individual and Systemic Effects', *Omega*, 24 (4): 309–32.

Joseph, S. and Linley, P.A. (2006) *Positive Therapy*. Hove: Routledge.

Kastenbaum, R. (1993) 'Reconstructing Death in Postmodern Society', *Omega*, 27 (1): 75–89.

Kirk, K. (1998) 'The Impact on Professional Workers', in Z. Bear (ed.), *Good Practice in Counselling People Who Have Been Abused*. London: Jessica Kingsley. pp. 178–93.

Kirkpatrick, L.A. and Hazan, C. (1994) 'Attachment Styles and Close Relationships: A Four-Year Prospective Study', *Personal Relationships*, 1: 123–42.

Klass, D. (1999) 'Developing a Cross-Cultural Model of Grief: The State of the Field', *Omega*, 39, 153–78.

Klass, D., Silverman, P.R. and Nickman, S.L. (1996) *Continuing Bonds*. Washington: Taylor and Francis.

Kroll, B. (1994) *Chasing Rainbows: Children, Divorce and Loss*. Lyme Regis: Russell House.

Kubler-Ross, E. (1970) *On Death and Dying*. London: Tavistock.

Lakoff, G. and Johnson, M. (1980) (Afterword 2003) *Metaphors We Live By*. Chicago: University of Chicago Press.

Lapper , A. (2005) *My Life in My Hands*. London: Simon and Schuster.

Lazarus, R.S. and Folkman, S. (1984) *Stress, Appraisal and Coping*. New York: Springer.

Lee, J.A. (1988) 'Love-Styles', in R.J. Sternberg and M. Barnes (eds), *The Psychology of Love*. New Haven, CT: Yale University Press. pp. 38–67.

Levinson, D.J., Darrow, D.N., Klein, E.B., Levinson, M.H. and McKee, B. (1978) *The Seasons of a Man's Life*. New York: A.A. Knopf.

Lewis, C.S. (1961) *A Grief Observed*. London: Faber and Faber.

Lund, D.A., Caserta, M.S. and Dimond, M.F. (1993) 'The Course of Spousal Bereavement in Later Life', in M.S. Stroebe, W. Stroebe and R.O. Hansson (eds), *Handbook of Bereavement*. Cambridge: Cambridge University Press. pp. 240–54.

Lydon, A.M, Ryan-Woolley, B. and Amir, Z. (2007) *The Evaluation of a Macmillan Children's Bereavement Service Established in Bury, Rochdale, Heywood and Middleton*. Report published by Manchester University and Macmillan Cancer Care.

Machin, L. (1980) 'Living with Loss'. Research Report for the Lichfield Diocesan Board for Social Responsibility (unpublished).

Machin, L. (1993) *Working with Young People in Loss Situations*. Harlow: Longman.

Machin, L. (1998) 'Making Sense of Experience: Death and Old Age', *Journal of Social Work Practice*, 12 (2): 217–26.

Machin, L. (2001) 'Exploring a Framework for Understanding the Range of Response to Loss: A Study of Clients Receiving Bereavement Counselling'. Unpublished PhD thesis: Keele University, UK.

Machin, L. (2005) 'Research in Practice', in P. Firth, G. Luff and D. Oliviere (eds), *Loss, Change and Bereavement in Palliative Care*. Maidenhead: Open University Press. pp. 38–52.

Machin, L. (2005/6/7) *The Adult Attitude to Grief Scale: Guidelines for use in Practice*. (Unpublished).

Machin, L. (2007a) *The Adult Attitude to Grief Scale as a Tool of Practice for Counsellors Working with Bereaved People*. A study report sponsored by Age Concern, Tameside and Keele University.

Machin, L. (2007b) 'Resilience in Bereavement: Part 1', in B. Monroe and D. Oliviere (eds), *Resilience in Palliative Care*. Oxford: Oxford University Press. pp. 157–65.

Machin, L. and Holt, C. (1988) *All Change: Exploring Loss and Change*. Middlesex: CEM.

Machin, L. and Spall, R. (2004) 'Mapping Grief: A Study in Practice Using a Quantitative and Qualitative Approach to Exploring and Addressing the Range of Response to Loss', *Counselling and Psychotherapy Research*, 4 (1): 9–17.

McAdams, D.P. (1997) *Stories We Live By: Personal Myths and the Making of the Self*. New York: Guilford Press.

McCrae, R.R. and Costa, P.T. (1993) 'Psychological Resilience Among Widowed Men and Women: A 10 Year Follow-up of a National Sample', in M.S. Stroebe, W. Stroebe and R.O. Hansson (eds), *Handbook of Bereavement*. Cambridge: Cambridge University Press. pp. 196–207.

McLeod, J. (2003) *An Introduction to Counselling*. Buckingham: Open University Press.

McLeod, J. (1997) *Narrative and Psychotherapy*. London: SAGE.

McLeod, J. and Machin, L. (1998) 'The Context of Counselling: A Neglected Dimension of Training, Research and Practice', *British Journal of Guidance and Counselling*, 26 (3): 325–36.

Main, M. (1991) 'Metacognitive Knowledge, Metacognitive Monitoring and Singular (Coherent) vs Multiple (Incoherent) Model of Attachment', in C.M. Parkes, J. Stevenson-Hinde, and P. Marris (eds), *Attachment Across the Life Cycle*. London: Routledge. pp. 127–59.

Marris, P. (1974) *Loss and Change*. London: Routledge and Kegan Paul.

Martin, T.L. and Doka, K.L. (2000) *Men Don't Cry...Women Do*. Philadelphia: Brunner/Mazel.

Maslow, A.H. (1987) *Motivation and Personality*. New York: Harper and Row.

Mearns, D. and Thorne, B. (1988) *Person-Centred Counselling in Action*. London: SAGE.

Middleton, W., Raphael. B., Martinek, N. and Misso, V. (1993) 'Pathological Grief Reactions' in M.S. Stroebe, W. Stroebe and R.O. Hansson (eds), *Handbook of Bereavement*. Cambridge: Cambridge University Press. pp. 44–61.

Mikulincer, M. and Florian, V. (1998) 'The Relationship Between Adult Attachment Styles and Emotional and Cognitive Reactions to Stressful Events', in J.A. Simpson and W.S. Rholes (eds), *Attachment Theory and Close Relationships*. New York: Guilford Press. pp. 143–65.

Morley, B. (1996) 'Grieving for What has Never Been', *Contact*, 120: 22–5.

Moskovitz, S. (1983) *Love Despite Hate*. New York: W.W. Norton.

Mulkay, M. (1993) 'Social Death in Britain', in D. Clark (ed.), *The Sociology of Death*. Oxford: Blackwell.

Munroe, B. and Krause (2005) *Brief Interventions with Bereaved Children*. Oxford: Oxford University Press.

Munroe, B. and Oliviere, D. (2007) *Resilience in Palliative Care: Achievement in Adversity*. Oxford: Oxford University Press.

Neimeyer, R. and Anderson, A. (2002) 'Meaning Reconstruction Theory', in N. Thompson (ed.), *Loss and Grief*. Basingstoke: Palgrave.

Newman, B. and Newman, P. (1995) *Development Through life: A Psychosocial Approach*. Pacific Grove, CA: Brooks/Cole.

Nolen-Hoeksema, S. and Larson, J. (1999) *Coping with Loss*. Mahwah, NJ: Erlbaum.

Oliver, M. and Sapey, B. (1999) *Social Work with Disabled People*. London: Palgrave.

Papadatou, D. (2000) 'A Proposed Model of Health Professionals' Grieving Process', *Omega*, 41 (1): 59–77.

Papadatou, D., Papazoglou, I., Petraki, D. and Bellali, T. (1998) 'Mutual Support Among Nurses who Provide Care to Dying Children', *Illness, Crisis and Loss*, 7: 37–48.

Parkes, C.M. (1996) *Bereavement: Studies of Grief in Adult Life*. London: Routledge.

Parkes, C.M. (1991) 'Attachment, Bonding, and Psychiatirc Problems after Bereavement in Adult Life', in C.M. Parkes, J. Stevenson-Hinde and P. Marris (eds), *Attachment Across the Life Cycle*. London: Routledge. pp. 268–92.

Parkes, C.M. (1993) 'Bereavement as a Psychosocial Transition: Processes of Adaptation to Change', in M.S. Stroebe, W. Stroebe, and R.O. Hansson (eds), *Handbook of Bereavement*. Cambridge: Cambridge University Press. pp. 102–11.

Parkes, C.M. (2001) 'A Historical Overview of the Scientific Study of Bereavement', in M.S. Stroebe, R.O. Hansson, W. Stroebe, and H. Schut (eds), *Handbook of Bereavement Research*. Washington: American Psychological Association. pp. 25–45.

Parkes, C.M. (2006) *Love and Loss: The Roots of Grief and its Complications.* London: Routledge.

Parkes, C.M. and Markus, A.C. (1998) *Coping with Loss.* London: BMJ.

Parkes, C.M. and Weiss, R.S. (1983) *Recovery from Bereavement.* New York: Basic.

Pennebaker, J.W., Zech, E. and Rime, B. (2001) 'Disclosing and Sharing Emotion: Psychological, Social and Health Consequences', in M.S. Stroebe, R.O. Hansson, W. Stroebe and H. Schut (eds), *Handbook of Bereavement Research.* Washington: American Psychological Association. pp. 517–43.

Piaget, J. (1969) *The Psychology of the Child.* London: Routledge and Kegan Paul.

Prigerson, H.G. and Jacobs, S.C. (2001) 'Traumatic Grief as a Distinct Disorder: A Rationale, Concensus Criteria, and a Preliminary Empirical Test', in M.S. Stroebe, R.O. Hansson, W. Stroebe, and H. Schut (eds), *Handbook of Bereavement Research.* Washington: American Psychological Association. pp. 613–45.

Pritchard, J. (1995) *The Abuse of Older People.* London: Jessica Kingsley.

Progoff, I. (1975) *At a Journal Workshop.* New York: Dialogue House Library.

Rando, T.A. (1992–93) 'The Increasing Prevalence of Complicated Mourning: The Onslaught is Just Beginning', *Omega*, 26 (1): 43–59.

Raphael, B., Minkov, C. and Dobson, M. (2001) 'Psychotherapeutic and Pharmacological Intervention for Bereaved Persons', in M.S. Stroebe, R.O. Hansson, W. Stroebe, and H. Schut (eds), *Handbook of Bereavement Research.* Washington: American Psychological Association. pp. 587–612.

Read, J. (1995) *Counselling for Fertility Problems.* London: SAGE.

Read, S. (2007) *Bereavement Counselling for People with Learning Disabilities.* London: Quay.

Reason, P. (1988) *Human Inquiry in Action: Developments in New Paradigm Research.* London: SAGE.

Reese, H.W. and Smyer, M.A. (1983) 'The Dimensionalization of life-events,' in E.J. Callahan and K.A. McCluskey (eds), *Life-Span Developmental Psychology: Non Normative Life Events.* New York: Academic Press.

Relf, M., Machin, L. and Archer, N. (2008) *Guidance for Bereavement Needs Assessment in Palliative Care.* London: Help the Hospices.

Rholes, W.S., Simpson, J.A. and Stevens, J.G. (1998) 'Attachment Orientations, Social Support, and Conflict Resolution in Close Relationships', in J.A. Simpson and W.S. Rholes (eds), *Attachment Theory and Close Relationships.* New York: Guilford Press. pp. 166–88.

Rogers, C.R. (1961) *On Becoming a Person.* London: Constable.

Rogers, C.R. (1980) *A Way of Being.* Boston: Houghton Mifflin.

Roos, S. (2002) *Chronic Sorrow: A Living Loss.* New York: Brunner-Routledge.

Rosenblatt, P.C. (1993) 'Grief: the Social Context of Private Feelings', *Journal of Social Issues*, 44 (3): 67–78.

Rosenblatt, P.C. (1996) 'Grief that Does Not End', in D. Klass, P.R. Silverman and S.L. Nickman (eds), *Continuing Bonds.* Washington: Taylor Francis. pp. 45–58.

Rosenblatt, P.C. (2001) 'A Social Constructionist Perspective on Cultural Differences in Grief', in M.S. Stroebe, R.O. Hansson, W. Stroebe, and H. Schut (eds), *Handbook of Bereavement Research.* Washington: American Psychological Association. pp. 285–300.

Sage, L. (2000) *Bad Blood.* London: Fourth Estate.

Sanders, C.M. (1993) 'Risk Factors in Bereavement Outcome', in M.S. Stroebe, W. Stroebe and R.O. Hansson (eds), *Handbook of Bereavement*. Cambridge: Cambridge University Press. pp. 255–67.

Sandford, L. (1990) *Strong at the Broken Places: Overcoming the Trauma of Child Abuse*. New York: Random House.

Sapey, B. (2002) 'Disability', in N. Thompson (ed.), *Loss and Grief*. Basingstoke: Palgrave. pp. 139–148.

Scharf, T., Bartlam, B., Hislop, J., Bernard, M., Dunning, A. and Sim, J. (2006) *Developing Measures of Older People's Poverty in the UK*. London: Help the Aged.

Scharf, T., Phillipson, C. and Smith, A.E. (2007) 'Aging in a Difficult Place: Assessing the Impact of Urban Deprivation on Older People', in H.W. Wahl, C. Tesch-Romer and A. Hoff (eds), *New Dynamics in Old Age: Individual, Environmental and Societal Perspectives*. Amityville, NY: Baywood.

Schut, H.A.W., de Keijser, J., van den Bout, J. and Stroebe, M.S. (1996) 'Cross-Modality Grief Therapy: Description and Assessment of a New Program', *Journal of Clinical Psychology*, 52: 357–65.

Schut, H.A.W., Stroebe, M.S. van den Bout, J. and de Keijser, J. (1997) 'Intervention for the Bereaved: Gender Differences in the Efficacy of Two Counselling Programmes', *British Journal of Clinical Psychology*, 36: 63–72.

Schut, H.A.W., Stroebe, M.S. van den Bout, J. and Terheggen, M. (2001) 'The Efficacy of Bereavement Interventions: Determining who Benefits', in M.S. Stroebe, R.O. Hansson, W. Stroebe, and H. Schut (eds), *Handbook of Bereavement Research*. Washington: American Psychological Association. pp. 705–37.

Schut, H. and Stroebe, M.S. (2005) 'Interventions to Enhance Adaptation to Bereavement', *Journal of Palliative Medicine*, 8: 140–46.

Seligman, M.E.P. (1992) *Helplessness: On Development, Depression and Death*. New York: W.H. Freeman and Co.

Seligman, M.E.P. (1998) 'Building Human Strength: Psychology's Forgotten Mission', *American Psychological Association Monitor*, 29 1.

Seligman, M.E.P. (1999) 'The President's Address', *American Psychologist*, 54: 559–62.

Seligman, M.E.P. and Csikszentmihalyi, M. (2000) 'Positive Psychology: An Introduction', *American Psychologist*, 55: 5–14.

Shapiro, E.R. (2001) 'Grief in Interpersonal Perspective: Theories and their Implications', in M.S. Stroebe, R.O. Hansson, W. Stroebe, and H. Schut (eds), *Handbook of Bereavement Research*. Washington: American Psychological Association. pp. 301–27.

Shaver, P.R. and Hazan, C. (1988) 'A Biased Overview of the Study of Love', *Journal of Social and Personal Relationships*, 5: 473–501.

Shaver, P.R. and Tancredy, C.M. (2001) 'Emotion, Attachment and Bereavement: A Conceptual Commentary', in M.S. Stroebe, R.O. Hansson, W. Stroebe, and H. Schut (eds), *Handbook of Bereavement Research*. Washington: American Psychological Association. pp. 63–88.

Shuchter, S.R. and Zisook, S. (1993) 'The Course of Normal Grief', in M.S. Stroebe, W. Stroebe and R.O. Hansson (eds), *Handbook of Bereavement*. Cambridge: Cambridge University Press. pp. 23–43.

Simpson, J.A. and Rholes, W.S. (1998) 'Attachment in Adulthood', in J.A. Simpson and W.S. Rholes (eds), *Attachment Theory and Close Relationships*. New York: Guilford Press. pp. 3–21.

Smith, J. (1989) 'My Gift', in J. Eisenhauer (ed.), *Travellers' Tales*. London: Marshal Pickering. pp. 41–2.

Snyder, M. (1984) 'When Belief Creates Reality', in L. Berkowitz (ed.), *Advances in Experimental Social Psychology*, (Vol. 18). New York: Academic Press.

Spall, B. and Callis, S. (1997) *Loss, Bereavement and Grief: A guide to Effective Caring*. Cheltenham: Stanley Thornes.

Spall, B., Read, S. and Chantry, D. (2001) 'Metaphor: Exploring its Origins and Therapeutic use in Death, Dying and Bereavement', *International Journal of Palliative Nursing*, 7 (7): 345–53.

Stanworth, R. (2003) *Recognising Spiritual Needs in People who are Dying*. Oxford: Oxford University Press.

Stokes, J. (2004) *Then, Now and Always … Supporting Children as they Journey Through Grief*. Cheltenham: Winston's Wish.

Stokes, J. (2007) 'Resilience and Bereaved Children: Helping a Child to Develop a Resilient Mind-set Following the Death of a Parent', in B. Monroe and D. Oliviere (eds), *Resilience in Palliative Care: Achievement in Adversity*. Oxford: Oxford University Press. pp. 39–65.

Stroebe, M. (1992–93) 'Coping with Bereavement: A Review of the Grief Work Hypothesis', *Omega*, 26 (1): 19–42.

Stroebe, M. and Schut, H. (1999) 'The Dual Process Model of Coping with Bereavement: Rationale and Description', *Death Studies*, 23: 197–224.

Stroebe, M.S. and Schut, H. (2001) 'Models of Coping with Bereavement: A Review', in M.S. Stroebe, R.O. Hansson, W. Stroebe, and H. Schut (eds), *Handbook of Bereavement Research*. Washington: American Psychological Association. pp. 375–403.

Stroebe, M. and Schut, H. (2005–06) 'Complicated Grief: A Conceptual Analysis of the Field', *Omega*, 52 (1): 53–70.

Stroebe, M.S., Stroebe, W. and Hansson, R.O. (1993) 'Bereavement Research and Theory' in M.S. Stroebe, W. Stroebe, and R.O. Hansson (eds), *Handbook of Bereavement: Theory, Research and Intervention*. Cambridge: Cambridge University Press. pp. 3–19.

Stroebe, M.S., Folkman, S., Hansson, R.O. and Schut, H. (2006) 'The Prediction of Bereavement Outcome: Development of an Integrative Risk Factor Framework', *Social Science and Medicine*, 63: 2440–51.

Stroebe, M., Gergen, M., Gergen, K. and Stroebe, W. (1996) 'Broken Hearts or Broken Bonds?', in D. Klass, P.R. Silverman and S.L. Nickman (eds), *Continuing Bonds*. Washington: Taylor Francis. pp. 31–44.

Stroebe, M.S., Hansson, R.O., Stroebe, W. and Schut, H. (2001) 'Introduction: Concepts and Issues in Contemporary Research on Bereavement', in M.S. Stroebe, R.O. Hansson, W. Stroebe, and H. Schut (eds), *Handbook of Bereavement Research*. Washington: American Psychological Association. pp. 3–22.

Stylianos, S.K. and Vachon, M.L.S. (1993) 'The Role of Social Support in Bereavement', in M.S. Stroebe, W. Stroebe, and R.O. Hansson (eds), *Handbook of Bereavement: Theory, Research and Intervention*. Cambridge: Cambridge University Press. pp. 397–410.

Sugarman, L. (2001) *Life-Span Development: Frameworks, Accounts and Strategies*. Hove: Psychology Press.

Tagore, R. (1923) *Poems*. London: Macmillan.

Thompson, R. (2006) *Dear Charlie – Letters to a Lost Daughter*. London: John Murray.

Thompson, R.A. (2000) 'Early Attachment and Later Development', in J. Cassidy and R.R. Shaver (eds), *Handbook of Attachment*. New York: Guilford Press. pp. 265–86.

Thompson, S. (2002) 'Older People', in N. Thompson (ed.) *Loss and Grief*. Basingstoke: Palgrave. pp. 162–73.

Tompkins, P., Sullivan, W. and Lawley, J. (2005) 'Tangled Spaghetti in My Head: Making Use of Metaphor', *Therapy Today*, 16 (8): 32–6.

Trevane, J. (2005) *Invisible Women: True Stories of Courage and Survival*. London: Hodder and Stoughton.

Umberson, D. and Terling, T. (1997) 'The Symbolic Meanings of Relationships: Implications for Psychological Distress Following Relationship Loss', *Journal of Social and Personal Relationships*, 14 (6): 723–44.

Vachon, M.L.S. and Styllianos, K.L. (1988) 'The Role of Social Support in Bereavement', *Journal of Social Issues*, 44: 175–90.

Van Gennep, A. (1909) *The Rites of Passage*. London: Routledge and Kegan Paul.

Varley, S. (1992) *Badger's Parting Gift*. London: Picture Lions.

Walter, T. (1996) 'A New Model of Grief: Bereavement and Biography', *Mortality*, 1 (1): 7–25.

Walter, T. (1999) *On Bereavement: The Culture of Grief*. Buckingham: Open University Press.

Walter, T. (2005–06) 'What is Complicated Grief? A Social Constructionist Perspective', *Omega*, 52 (1): 71–9.

Weiss, R.S. (1988) 'Loss and Recovery', *Journal of Social Issues*, 44: 37–52.

Whitaker, A. (ed.) (1984) *All in the End is Harvest*. London: Darton, Longman and Todd.

White, M. and Epston, D. (1990) *Narrative Means to Therapeutic Ends*. New York: Norton.

Worden, W. (2003) *Grief Counselling and Grief Therapy*. London: Tavistock/Routledge.

Wortman, C.B. and Silver, R.C. (1989) 'The Myth of Coping with Loss', *Journal of Consulting and Clinical Psychology*, 57: 349–57.

Wortman, C.B. and Silver, R.C. (2001) 'The Myths of Coping with Loss Revisited', in M.S. Stroebe, R.O. Hansson, W. Stroebe, and H. Schut (eds), *Handbook of Bereavement Research*. Washington: American Psychological Association. pp. 405–29.

Zaider, T. and Kissane, D. (2007) 'Resilient Families', in B. Monroe and D. Oliviere (eds), *Resilience in Palliative Care*. Oxford: Oxford University Press. pp. 67–81.

Zigmond, A.S. and Snaith, R.P. (1983) 'The Hospital Anxiety and Depression Scale', *Acta Psychiatr Scand*, 67: 361–70.

Index

This index is in word by word order. Page numbers in *italics* indicate tables and diagrams.

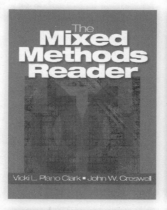

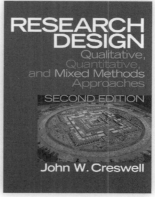

The Qualitative Research Kit

Edited by Uwe Flick

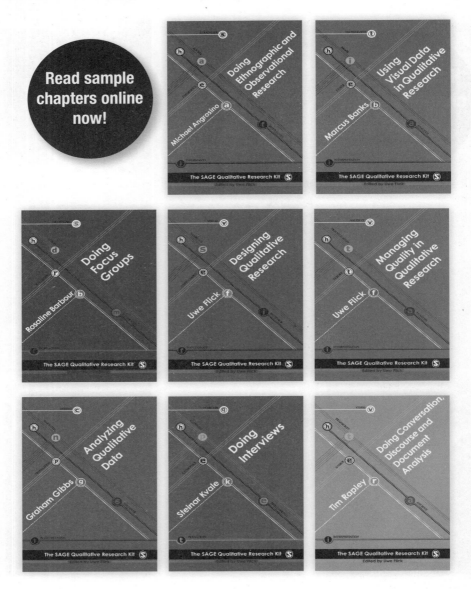

Read sample chapters online now!

Doing Ethnographic and Observational Research — Michael Angrosino — The SAGE Qualitative Research Kit

Using Visual Data in Qualitative Research — Marcus Banks — The SAGE Qualitative Research Kit

Doing Focus Groups — Rosaline Barbour — The SAGE Qualitative Research Kit

Designing Qualitative Research — Uwe Flick — The SAGE Qualitative Research Kit

Managing Quality in Qualitative Research — Uwe Flick — The SAGE Qualitative Research Kit

Analyzing Qualitative Data — Graham Gibbs — The SAGE Qualitative Research Kit

Doing Interviews — Steinar Kvale — The SAGE Qualitative Research Kit

Doing Conversation, Discourse and Document Analysis — Tim Rapley — The SAGE Qualitative Research Kit

www.sagepub.co.uk